W9-CSB-080

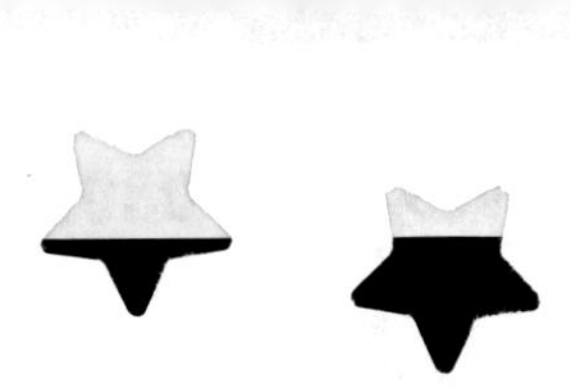

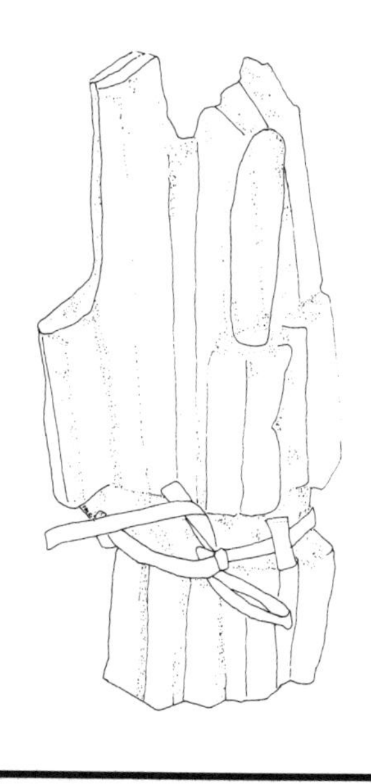

A Guide to the Best Whitewater in the State of California

Second Edition
1988

A Guide to the Best Whitewater in the State of California

Chuck Stanley and Lars Holbek

Don Banducci

PUBLISHED BY FRIENDS OF THE RIVER BOOKS

Dedicated to James G. Smith and Clarke Stanley who introduced the authors to kayaking. Were it not for their past and patient teachings, this guide could never have been written.

Friends of the River, founded in 1975, is a membership organization dedicated to the preservation of California's remaining free-flowing streams. For information about programs and membership, please contact Friends of the River, Building C, Ft. Mason Center, San Francisco, CA 94123.

A GUIDE TO THE BEST WHITEWATER IN THE STATE OF CALIFORNIA is a limited edition Friends of the River Books publication. Additional copies may be obtained directly from the publisher, prepaid, for $12.95 + $0.75 handling and postage. Order from: *Friends of the River Books, 2297 Harvard St., Palo Alto, CA 94306.*

ISBN 0-9611524-0-0

 PUBLISHED BY FRIENDS OF THE RIVER BOOKS

ACKNOWLEDGEMENTS

Thanks are most gratefully extended to the many friends and relatives who gave generously of their time and energy in bringing this book to pass.

Proofreading and Editing

Don Ahlert, John Armstrong, Cheryl Bly, John Cassidy, Nancy Cassidy, Cody Cassidy, Julie Fife, Kiki Foote, Christina Gardner, Mimi Holbek, Suren Holbek, Katherine McNeil, Eric Magneson, Ed Maloney, Roxanne Maloney, Karen Masters, Richard Montgomery, Katie Rutherford, Joan Schlax, Marian Spotswood, Clarke Stanley, Leslie Stanley.

River Descriptions

John Cassidy, Louis Debret, Reg Lake, Eric Magneson, John Magneson, Bob Porter, Michael Schlax, Barry Wasserman, Charlie Albright.

Photography

John Armstrong, Don Banducci, Ed Barry, Rick Fernald, Kiki Foote, Walt Garms, Reg Lake, Eric Magneson.

Cover Photo

John Armstrong

Art

Robin Center

Photo Consulting and Lab Work

John Armstrong

River Flow Information

Bill Helms of the California State Department of Water Resources.

Logistics

Special thanks to Ken Horwitz and Hydra for their support; and to Yvon Chouinard and Patagonia.

Spiritual Support

The Sierra Nevada

Miscellaneous

Steve ("Eddie") Everett.

PREFACE

BOMBING DOWN STEEP, BOULDER-CONGESTED MOUNTAIN RIVERS IN POINTY little plastic boats differs from its adrenal-sport counterparts (hang-gliding, skiing and rock-climbing) in one important social respect: there is no geographical center where the practitioners can congregate and push their sport in view of each other. There is no Yosemite, Owens Valley, or Jackson Hole.

Most new or difficult rivers are done by small groups on weekends or concentrated outings. Afterwards, no camp or dingy bar exists where the protagonists can return to tell the usual inebriated lies about the ". . . steepest, most continuously difficult section of technical class XV whitewater I've ever seen. I mean, we are talking ONE HUNDRED AND FIFTY FEET PER MILE!!!"

Most of the stories and the accompanying information (generally diluted, distended, or exaggerated) about new runs or techniques are passed on by rumor and word-of-mouth. As yet, there isn't even a magazine devoted to difficult whitewater. Guidebooks have helped this situation only slightly. In the past, only two describing California whitewater have been published. And while both are quite useful, they provide more a picture of the past of the sport, rather than any idea of what the kayaking scene is like today, ten years later.

The need for an update has been amply filled by the volume you hold in your hand. Many of the runs described in this book were considered unrunnable by the earlier authors. But the advent of plastic boats, new techniques and a simultaneous group loss of mental capacity, have put a number of them well within the reach of the strong intermediate paddler. Burnt Ranch Gorge on the Trinity and Giant Gap on the North Fork of the American are cases in point.

Among the handful of boaters who have pushed kayaking out to its new limits, Chuck Stanley and Lars Holbek, the authors of this guide, have been outstanding. The time and energy spent by Lars and Chuck, separately and then as a team, on searching out new sections of rivers to run, and investigating stories of the unrunnability of old ones, would truly amaze anyone uninitiated to the obscure rites of this sport. Both of them have been seen to shake with excitement after finding on some map, some hidden little stretch of some obscure river or creek.

Not that they were alone, but I must admit that some of their proposed exploratories were inspired (although hare-brained at the time). I can clearly recall shaking my head and planning my "I-told-you-so," after having been talked into some Holbekian fantasy of an absurd trip like the Lovers Leap stretch on the South Fork of the American. Admittedly, some of them didn't turn out (fortunately, I had the curse of employment to blame for missing out on the Bear River portage classic), but fiascoes like these were part of what was supposed to provide the adventure or excitement that our less maladjusted contemporaries got out of Safeway Bingo.

The descriptions of the runs in this book barely scratch the surface of what might have been written. Stories about the epics and mishaps that occurred on so many of the runs aren't told. Even if the effort were made, though, what would probably be missed would be the substance of it all— sitting in the rain, waiting for the shuttle, consuming overdoses of cookies and milk in vain attempts to bring blood sugar levels back up to something life sustaining. Feeling the van slide backwards in the mud on the way out of the canyon. Trying to sleep at the put-in while the roar of the water feeds all the uncertainties in your mind. Driving away in a golden haze of fatigue and blurred recollections of miles of steep, unending staircases of rocks and water and concentration and tight moves. Feeling the throbbing stillness and heat at the top of some Sierran canyon in the early morning before the hike in. Feeling the apprehension as the next rapid appears as a line of boulders with no far side. Experiencing the exhilaration of looking back and seeing the last three rapids stacked on top of one another, steeper than you could believe.

And afterwards, arguing with some local in a bar about whether or not you really did run whatever it was that he almost got killed on in an inner tube last summer. Arguing that it is *too* a lot easier than Cherry Creek, or that it's probably runnable, or wondering how close you came to ending on in there, and where did that dachshund go now?

Michael Schlax
Santa Rosa, California 1984

This book provides a true service to the paddling community. I'm glad to know that when I'm old and gray and these guys have moved on to lawn bowling or running lava flows on the second moon of Jupiter in asbestos boats, I'll be able to turn to this book and still find my way to the put-ins for some of the runs I did with the bro's.

Richard Montgomery
Berkeley, California 1984

CONTENTS

COAST RANGE RIVERS - West Slope

COAST RANGE RIVERS - East Slope

SIERRA NEVADA RIVERS - West Slope

SIERRA NEVADA RIVERS - East Slope

ADDITIONAL RUNS

APPENDICES

INTRODUCTION

IN CALIFORNIA, AS WELL AS THE REST OF THE WORLD, THE PAST DECADE OF whitewater boating has seen a dramatic rise in standards, due in part to the advent of the plastic kayak, but mainly the result of a new generation of boaters realizing, and pushing, the limits of the sport. Rivers that ten years ago were described as "unrunnable" or "impossible" are today frequently run by an ever-increasing number of boaters.

Unavoidably, the guidebooks that were yesterday's bibles are today somewhat out of date. The only two worthy of praise, *Sierra Whitewater* (by Charlie Martin), and *West Coast River Touring* (by Dick Schwind) are excellent guides, but the rising standard of the sport has created the need for updating, a need which we have tried to fill with this volume. We have tried to make this a guide to the best and highest quality whitewater in the state, and consequently much of the information is for the experienced boater, one who is already familiar with the standard runs and seeks the more obscure classics (chapters on basic strokes, how to get started, types of boats, etc., are not included). At the same time, though, many good, moderate runs that we feel will appeal to intermediate level boaters are also included.

One third of the runs in this book were first done in the past 6 years, and are described in book form here for the first time. Several of those remaining have been described in other guides; we include them here because they are such classics that any guidebook would be incomplete without them. In choosing which runs to include and which to exclude we eventually came to the realization that the final criteria would have to be subjective, reflecting our own biases and personal weirdnesses.

Plastic Kayaks and New Techniques

Fiberglass kayaks first began appearing on the West Coast in the early 60's, and in the hands of Bryce Whitmore, Noel Debord, Carl Trost, Gunter Hemmersbach, Dick Sunderland, Walt Harvest and other pioneers in extreme boating, new runs were established up and down the state. The Camp 9-to-Parrott's Ferry stretch on the Stanislaus, for example, was first done without carries in 1961; the Lumsden-to-Wards Ferry stretch on the Tuolumne, in 1965.

The early 70's saw the next generation of kayak technology, the plastic River Chaser by Hollowform. Subsequently, Perception and, most recently, Hydra, have taken the lead in making roto-molded boats whose construction has made severe kayak abuse practically a family activity.

Using rocks, either to launch from (a portage shortener), or in the river to skitter off (hazard avoidance), is now almost standard plastic boat practice. Also, in the event of a long portage, dragging a plastic boat is a degenerate innovation recently embraced by many.

One of the greatest dangers in kayaking, vertical entrapment, is an experience worth avoiding. "Ski jumping" is another plastic boat technique whose employment can go a long way towards reducing this particular hazard. The idea is to fly over suspicious vertical drops by means of a high-speed approach. If you lay far back on the deck as you take off, you can hold your nose up and frequently clear any rocks or nasty backwash. Alternatively, you can cut hard across the lip and "belly flop" into the eddy. The idea in both cases is to avoid plunging into shallow rocks or recycling backwash.

When Do The Rivers Flow?

Deciding when a river has sufficient water is a tricky art, mainly a function of experience and current knowledge of precipitation factors.

Generally, the Sierra offers the best boating from April through July, though in heavy snowfall years, such as 1980, '82, and '83, some rivers ran high into September. Relatively warm winter storms, of tropical origin, usually produce the highest annual flows on all the Sierra rivers.

The coast ranges can generally be divided into two parts as far as boating season and geography go. The drainages north of the Bay Area, encompassing all of the Russian, Eel, Van Duzen, and Mad Rivers and the East Slope as far north as Red Bluff, are fed largely by rain. These rivers are runnable only during the rainy season—with a few dam-controlled exceptions—typically extending from November through April.

The northern ranges—the Siskiyou Mountains, Marble Mountains, and Trinity Alps, yield a wide range of seasons for whitewater. The best season (in our opinion) for this region is early spring, when the snowmelt is in force and the days are often warm and sunny. These rivers, as with all those in California, run highest in winter. Because these mountains are relatively low (maximum of 9,000 feet elevation) and carry a small snowpack, their rivers are normally too low for boating by July.

Specific information on estimating flow is provided on each description under the "Gauge" heading. Resource telephone numbers are also provided in the appropriate appendix.

Kayak Camping

Multi-day kayak trips have become increasingly popular of late, and outings of 3 to 5 days are possible on several California rivers. Carrying gear for 5 days on a run that is sure to have portages demands that close attention be paid to equipment. One needs to keep the camping gear as light as possible, while still maintaining some vague standard of personal care.

We have found it possible to keep total individual gear weight to 10 pounds for a 5-day trip by omitting all but the absolute essentials. Typically, our summer kayak camping load consists of the following: bivi-sac, 1 lb.; down sleeping bag, 1.5 lb.; throw rope, 8 oz.; first aid kit, 6 oz.; camera and drybox, 1.5 lb.; dehydrated food, spoon, knife and aluminum pot, all totalling 4 to 5 lbs.

One should carefully decide what is really needed. Those extra pounds can be true torment at the end of a quarter-mile carry. On any river that runs far from the road, it is always wise, and often crucial, to carry emergency bivouac gear and matches.

Maps

Detailed maps covering put-ins and take-outs have not been included. It is the authors' experience that reprinted or hand-drawn maps are often confusing and force referral to AAA or USFS maps anyway. General orientation maps of the rivers are included, giving an idea of where the river lies in the state, but are not designed for midnight, dirt road navigation.

Accuracy

Of the 141 runs described in this guide, the authors have personally done all but 7. The exceptions are so noted in the descriptions. We have made every effort to check our facts for accuracy, using AAA, USFS, and USGS topographical maps to reinforce our memories, but, given the tendency of the universe towards disorder, some errors may have crept in. So saying, we'd appreciate any feedback you, the user, might be able to give us in terms of incorrect information, updates on new runs, or new conditions on old runs. Send them to our publisher and we'll try to improve any subsequent printings.

Safety

The sport of kayaking revolves around the use of good judgment, and no information in this book is intended as a substitute for your own. Our assessment of the difficulty of various runs has been pegged against the standards used by the International Canoe Federation (see the section on whitewater classification), but an unavoidable degree of latitude exists in the interpretation of any standard.

Our sincere recommendation is that you use our description of difficulty as a guide, while remembering that the final responsibility for a safe and enjoyable trip remains, as always, yours.

Good boating,

Lars Holbek
Chuck Stanley

Key to the River Descriptions

DIFFICULTY and FLOW

Difficulties of river at various flows, measured by the International Canoe Federation class I-VI system (see the appropriate appendix for the official definitions). Where only one comparison of rating to flow exists, this indicates the authors have not done the run at other flows or do not feel qualified to rate the river at other flows. Remember!! Difficulty ratings are only general guidelines, a reflection of the popularly agreed upon severity as well as our interpretation of the ICF standards. Most of the flow figures are also estimates, again the product of group consensus.

OPTIMUM

The flow that the authors consider the easiest, generally a level that is technically simplest and with minimal hydraulics.

MILES

Distance from the put-in to the take-out via the river. When a run flows into a reservoir or another river, this distance is part of the total. The breakdown (river miles and reservoir miles) is included in the run description.

PORTAGES

In this instance we deviate from the conventions of this guide. Here the number of portages listed does NOT represent the recommended number of portages that the average paddler might make. In this case the stated number is mainly an historical record in that it represents the least number of portages known to have been done on the run by a single person. Rarely are the severe runs done with as few portages as are listed here. Regard this number only as a record—not as an indication of how many carries you might expect to do. Deciding what is safe and within your abilities is, as always, up to you. *ALWAYS APPROACH A RAPID WITH NO REGARD AS TO WHETHER OR NOT IT IS NORMALLY PORTAGED. INSPECT AND DECIDE FOR YOURSELF.*

PUT-IN

Starting point with elevation above sea level at the river.

TAKE-OUT

Finishing point with elevation at river.

SHUTTLE

Mileage from the put-in to the take-out via dirt or paved roads. Walk-ins are always noted in the descriptions. When the roads are even worse than normal, some note is generally made. Distances are generally accurate, but should not be thought of as exact.

RAFTS

"YES" indicates the authors consider the river raftable and would not hesitate to raft it. "NO" indicates that the authors, both of whom are maniacal at the controls of a raft, want to take no responsibility in calling the river raftable, whether or not it is.

AVERAGE GRADIENT

This number is the total drop of the run divided by the distance from the put-in to the take-out. It gives an overall idea of the steepness of the run, expressed in feet per mile (fpm).

Occasionally the average gradient is followed by the gradient of each mile or notes about specific steep miles. When the gradient is relatively even or fairly low, the mile-by-mile gradient is not given. Unless otherwise noted, all mile-by-mile gradients start at the put-in. If the mile-by-mile listing abates before the finish of the run, this indicates the gradient has fallen to a negligible point.

BOATING SEASON

The calendar season when the run is normally boatable. All rivers in this book are usually runnable much of the winter, though many are not listed as such because of the misery factor and the authors' biases.

WATER SOURCE

This heading has been divided into three categories: Natural, Spill and Power.

"Natural" indicates the river runs as a result of runoff from rain or melting snow with no interference from dams or diversions.

"Spill" indicates water that is spilling from a full reservoir. On coast range rivers this usually happens in late winter, and in the Sierra rivers, in late spring.

"Power" means that water is released to the river for hydro-electric or irrigation purposes. No distinction is made as to what type of release it is; it simply means that one can boat on the out-flow of some industry.

GAUGE

Where to get river flow information. A collection of the little tidbits and helpful hints we've picked up over the years that enable us to make some kind of guess as to what's happening on a particular river.

For most of the runs in this guide, a great deal of information can be gleaned from the State Department of Water Resources "Flow Phone," a pre-recorded telephone recording updated 3 times a week. The recording provides flow information, in cubic feet per second, at selected gauging stations on most of the major river systems in the state. The number is in Sacramento, 916/322-3327. Appendix VI describes all the rivers given on the recording.

When the flow phone has pertinent information for a particular run, the gauging station to listen for will be in italics.

Use the information in this section as a guide, not a cookbook. Take a look at the map if the gauging point is some distance from the stretch you're interested in and see if there are any major tributaries that intervene. If there are diversions that we know about, we'll include them in the description. Most of all, consider the time of year, weather and snowpack conditions. Then flip a coin and get going.

USFS or AAA and TOPOS

Any run covered adequately by a USFS map will have the correct map listed. Failing that, the appropriate AAA map is listed.

USGS topographic maps covering the run are listed, ideally by the corresponding 7.5 minute series. If the area is not covered by 7.5 minute, the appropriate 15 minute topo is listed. (See appendix for map availability.)

AAA refers to the American Automobile Association. USFS refers to the United States Forest Service. USGS refers to the United States Geological Survey (both the Forest Service and Geological Survey are branches of the U.S. Department of the Interior).

Coast Range Rivers
West Slope

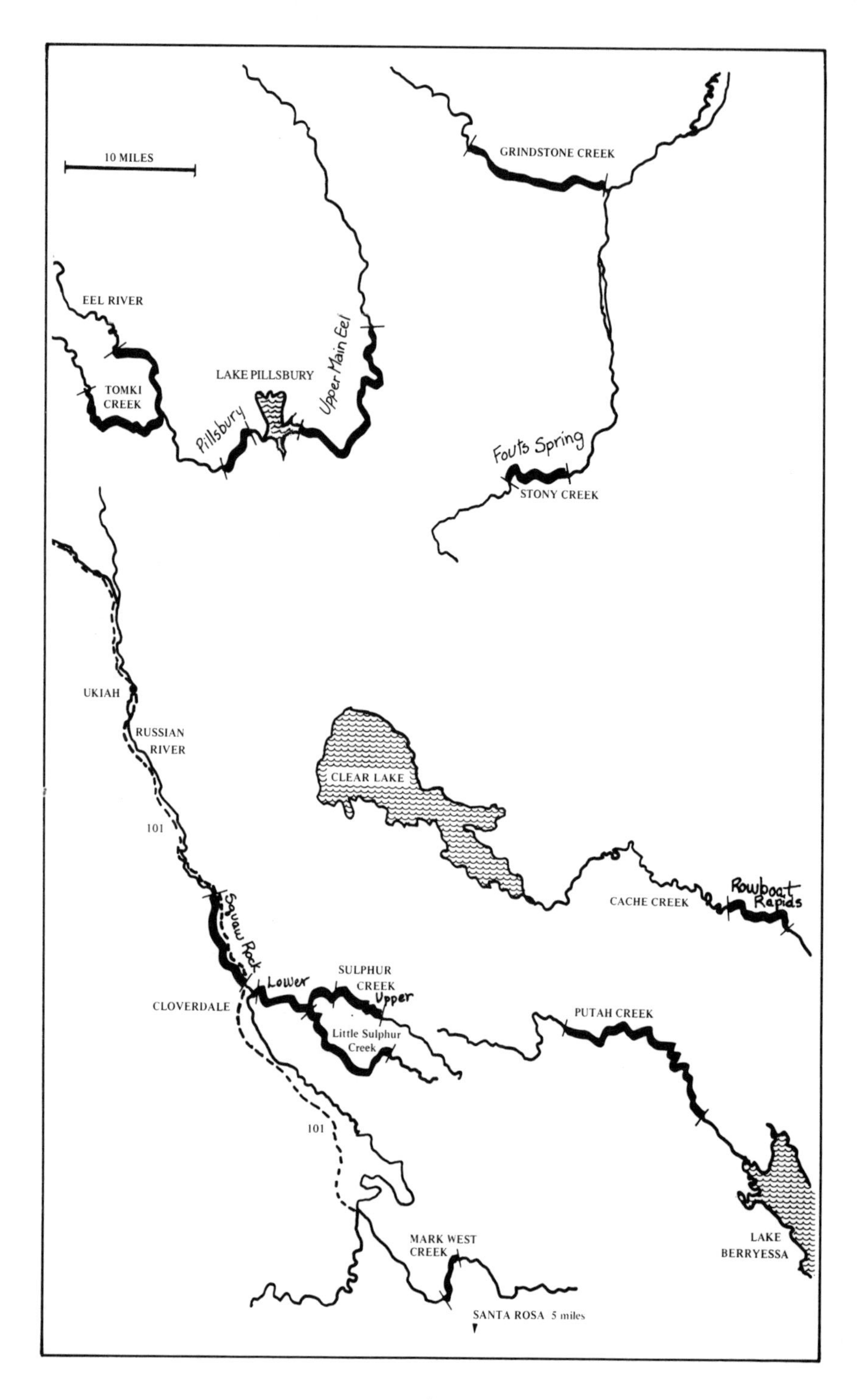

10 MILES
GRINDSTONE CREEK
EEL RIVER
TOMKI CREEK
LAKE PILLSBURY
Upper Main Eel
Pillsbury
Fouts Spring
STONY CREEK
UKIAH
RUSSIAN RIVER
101
CLEAR LAKE
CACHE CREEK
Rowboat Rapids
Squaw Rock
SULPHUR CREEK
Lower
Upper
CLOVERDALE
Little Sulphur Creek
PUTAH CREEK
101
MARK WEST CREEK
LAKE BERRYESSA
SANTA ROSA 5 miles

SAN LORENZO RIVER

DIFFICULTY	FLOW	OPTIMUM	MILES	PORTAGES
III	500-1000	1000	6	0
III+	1000-1500			
IV	>1500			

PUT IN:	**Henry Cowell State Park Bridge (220 ft.)**
TAKE OUT:	**Boardwalk Amusement Park (sea level)**
SHUTTLE:	**9 miles**
RAFTS:	**YES (watch out for logs)**
AVERAGE GRADIENT:	**37 fpm; one mile of 80 fpm**
GAUGE:	**None, but runnable after a recent storm.**
BOATING SEASON:	**Winter**
WATER SOURCE:	**Natural**
AAA and *TOPO MAPS*:	**Santa Cruz; *Santa Cruz, Felton* (7.5 series)**

The San Lorenzo is a great run if you live in Santa Cruz, a good run if you live in San Jose, a fair run if you live in Berkeley, and a waste of time if you live in Sacramento. The scenery is nice, but nothing breathtaking. The whitewater is good, but inconsistent.

This is one of the more reactionary streams around; the flow can vary from 200 to 20,000 in the winter months. The river runs when it rains hard. I've done the river only once; the flow was a paltry 700 cfs. A couple of weeks before my excursion, the San Lorenzo went hog wild and overflowed its banks. We saw several logs resting comfortably on a living room couch—while still in the living room.

In addition to furniture and whatnot, there can be severe logjam hazards at high water. On our run we encountered a river wide redwood which, due to the low flow, was easily portaged. At 5,000 cfs the same obstruction could be disastrous to even the most wary expert paddler—please be cautious.

To get to the put-in, drive from Santa Cruz on Hwy. 9 towards Felton until you reach Henry Cowell State Park. After turning right into the park entrance, you'll see the bridge. Park along the road and put in below the bridge. To get to the take-out, return to Santa Cruz on Hwy. 9 and follow the signs to the Boardwalk Amusement Park. There is a parking area about a hundred yards from the river.

—*CS*

MARK WEST CREEK

DIFFICULTY	FLOW	OPTIMUM	MILES	PORTAGES
III-IV	400-1000	1000	4	0
IV-V	1000-2000			

PUT IN:	**Mark West Lodge (420 ft.)**
TAKE OUT:	**Mark West Road (180 ft.)**
SHUTTLE:	**4 miles**
RAFTS:	**NO**
AVERAGE GRADIENT:	**60 fpm; .5 mile of 160 fpm in mile 3**
GAUGE:	**Runnable after a recent storm and when *Russian at Hopland* is greater than 5,000 cfs (flow phone).**
BOATING SEASON:	**Winter**
WATER SOURCE:	**Natural**
AAA and *TOPO MAPS*:	**North Bay Counties; *Mark West Springs* (7.5 series)**

This surprisingly good run is only 10 minutes north of Santa Rosa. During high school, I ran this on unofficially extended lunch breaks. After a rainstorm of only a few inches this creek is usually runnable, but due to the small drainage area, usually only for a few days.

The first 2 miles flow through beautiful redwood forests. After a few class III rapids the river makes a 90 degree left turn, marking the start of a mile of continuous action. The biggest rapid comes near the end of this mile, a long bouldery "S" turn that should be scouted.

Always beware of logs on this run. During every flood old logjams wash out and new ones form. Luckily, most of the logs tend to collect below the third mile in a chronic logjam zone. Beyond here the gradient drops off and brush is the major obstacle.

When Mark West Road comes into view, it's best to stay on the creek while it parallels the road and take out at a grassy strip just before the creek swings away from the road. This take-out is private; keeping a low profile has saved us from conflicts with the landowner.

To reach Mark West Creek, take the River Road-Calistoga exit 5 miles north of Santa Rosa on U.S. 101. Turn right and drive up Mark West Road a mile or so to a broad bend in the creek. This is the take-out. The put-in is 4 miles further, where the road crosses the creek.

—LH

LITTLE SULPHUR CREEK

DIFFICULTY	FLOW	OPTIMUM	MILES	PORTAGES
IV-V	200-500 (put-in)	400	10.9	7

PUT IN: Healdsburg-Geyserville Road (1860 ft.)
TAKE OUT: Big Sulphur Creek (640 ft.)
SHUTTLE: 14 miles
RAFTS: NO
AVERAGE GRADIENT: 111 fpm; mi/mi: 70, 200, 190, 140, 80, 150, 95, 150, 60, 45, 40
GAUGE: Runnable after a recent storm and when *Russian at Hopland* is between 3,000 and 10,000 cfs (flow phone).
BOATING SEASON: Winter
WATER SOURCE: Natural
AAA and *TOPO MAPS*: North Bay Counties; *The Geysers, Jimtown, Asti* (7.5 series)

I had wanted to do this run for some years, but frankly, when these guys beat me to it, my enthusiasm nose-dived—how could anyone top their epic? Louis Debret supplied the following description.

On January 30 and 31, 1981, John and Eric Magneson and I put in on the 15-foot-wide stream at 11:30 a.m. Lots of brush and fallen trees made for slow going, not to mention the 190 fpm gradient that we had neglected to fully appreciate on our pre-run topo map check.

After a bit, the river mercifully opened up, and there were some enjoyable, tight class III-IV drops between a few unrunnable sections. The countryside is very beautiful, with constantly changing scenery and incredible rock formations.

In one of the easier sections, about 3-4 miles down, the river charged over an abrupt 4-foot drop and disappeared around a rock outcropping on the left. As we plunged over the drop, and rounded the corner one by one, we came upon the alarming sight of the proverbial "river nightmare"—a tiny funnel-like slot between huge slabs of rock, obviously a deathtrap. Luck was with us, for there was a small eddy behind the rock outcropping just big enough for the 3 of us.

Clinging to each other, we awkwardly balanced out of our boats onto the safety of a sloping slab. Needless to say, after this incident we paid more attention to the river, and less to the scenery.

As we paddled on, an awareness developed among us that the run seemed to be much longer than it had appeared on the map. Someone made allusions to the twilight zone, that we were destined to stay on the river for eternity. As the light began to fade, the joke suddenly became serious. We desperately pushed on into the growing dusk, running drops that should have been scouted, until it became too dark to continue.

We stopped where a high rocky ridge jutted out from the left shore, causing the river to make a noisy horseshoe bend—a characteristic place for big drops. We had a short pow-wow and decided that since the river was still very steep, we could not hope to paddle in the dark; we voted to hike out. After 2 attempts, one with boats, one without, we realized that we were boxed in by nearly vertical walls in a starlit gorge.

The reality of our unpreparedness hit hard: no food (we'd eaten our p.b.&j. sandwiches at the put-in), wet matches, and John without even a wetsuit. We made a nest of moss and twigs atop the rocky ridge, thinking it might retain some heat—no such luck! As we lay cuddled together in our big robin's nest, with a breeze further cooling our wet bodies, John, in a most untimely fashion, confided that he had seen snow on the peaks surrounding The Geysers while doing the bicycle shuttle that morning. Hypothermia was on our minds throughout that cold, sleepless night, and only sardine-style heat conservation measures saved us from a frozen fate.

At the first hint of light we slowly, very slowly, stretched our numbed bodies and chipped the ice from our paddles. As we lined our boats to the river, we glanced at the rapid we'd almost run in the dark. It had a class IV lead-in to a narrow slot in solid rock that dropped 8 feet into a pool below; runnable, but not in our condition. We ran the last steep mile without mishap and paddled the remaining few miles to Big Sulphur Creek.

The challenging and continuous nature of the high-caliber rapids, the beautiful scenery and stunning geologic formations, along with the remoteness of the canyon, make Little Sulphur Creek a very rewarding, enjoyable and adventurous run. Future parties should consider the demands of the run and avoid the casual approach (11:30 put-in) that caused us to bivouac.

To reach this run, refer to the directions in the lower Sulphur Creek description. From the take-out of the lower run, drive towards The Geysers and the iron bridge put-in. Little Sulphur Creek enters Big Sulphur Creek just above the long flat stretch that ends at the rancher's house. I assume the take-out here is on the rancher's land, so trespass at risk or continue down Sulphur Creek. Continue driving past the iron bridge until almost to the put-in for the upper run. The Healdsburg-Geyserville Road takes off to the right, and crosses Little Sulphur Creek at its put-in in about 5-6 miles.

— LH

The authors about to execute a "Polish Pirouette" at the Trinity River Rodeo, 1984.
Pinky Collamer

SULPHUR CREEK (Upper Run)

DIFFICULTY	FLOW	OPTIMUM	MILES	PORTAGES
III-IV+	300-700	1000	4.6	2
IV-V	700-1500			

PUT IN:	**Near The Geysers (1,360 ft.)**
TAKE OUT:	**Iron Bridge (850 ft.)**
SHUTTLE:	**4.6 miles**
RAFTS:	**NO**
AVERAGE GRADIENT:	**111 fpm; mi/mi: 180, 140, 100, 60, 30**
GAUGE:	**Runnable after a recent storm and when *Russian at Hopland* is between 3,000 and 10,000 cfs (flow phone).**
BOATING SEASON:	**Winter**
WATER SOURCE:	**Natural**
AAA and *TOPO MAPS*:	**North Bay Counties; *The Geysers, Asti* (7.5 series)**

In January 1979, Michael Schlax and I ventured up to Sulphur Creek to check out an old horror story. Several years earlier Gunter Hemmersbach and Bert Welti had put in at high water and gone only a short distance before abandoning their attempt. The stories grew, and during my formative years on the Russian River, Sulphur Creek was held in mystical esteem. We went there once when the creek was flooding and threw a 55-gallon drum in the huge rapid that can be seen from the road, to see if anything could make it through the maelstrom. Of course it did, but we were very naive back then. Our kayaking mentor, Jim Smith, went so far as to say that he would physically restrain anyone who tried to run the river—for their own good.

Much later, and disregarding Jim's advice, Mike did have the misfortune of experiencing a 30-second vertical entrapment in a drop on the lower run, but overall we have since found the river to be relatively reasonable.

The mile that begins .3 mile below the put-in drops 210-220 feet and has been run without portages. Generally, though, two or more are done in this section. Lots of scouting and tight maneuvering are necessary throughout the run. Drops 6-8 feet wide and 4-6 feet high are not uncommon at low water.

To find the put-in: One mile north of Cloverdale, just past the Russian River Bridge, turn right on The Geysers Road. Continue 15 miles to The Geysers. On our first several runs we put in at the bridge right at The Geysers, but now, due to "security reasons," one must put in a few tenths of a mile downstream.

When the guarded gate is reached, at the old hot springs resort, turn around and go a short distance to a dirt road that leads down to the right. The little field here seems to be a safe place to leave a vehicle, though boaters have been ripped off in this area. The creek is just below.

The take-out is the iron bridge that crosses the creek.

—LH

Larry, Curly and Moe go kayaking. ***Rick Fernald***

SULPHUR CREEK (Lower Run)

DIFFICULTY	FLOW	OPTIMUM	MILES	PORTAGES
IV+	400-1000	1500	9	2
IV-V	1000-3000			

PUT IN: Iron Bridge (850 ft.)
TAKE OUT: Washed out crossing (320 ft.)
SHUTTLE: 9.5 miles
RAFTS: NO
AVERAGE GRADIENT: 59 fpm
GAUGE: Runnable after a recent storm and when ***Russian at Hopland*** is between 3,000 and 10,000 cfs (flow phone).
BOATING SEASON: Winter
WATER SOURCE: Natural
AAA and *TOPO MAPS*: North Bay Counties; ***Asti, Cloverdale*** (7.5 series)

A day after running the upper stretch of this creek, Mike Schlax and I were joined by Richard Montgomery for a memorable run of the lower section. Directly below the put-in at the iron bridge is a steep, long rapid that changes annually. Below this rapid the river mellows gradually, and at the confluence with Little Sulphur Creek it becomes very flat and shallow. After 2 miles of flatwater, a ranch house is passed on the right. Please don't put in or take out here. I've talked with the rancher, and he is adamant about trespassing.

Below the ranch house the rapids start up again, and a broken dam creates part of the first rapid. The next involved rapid, called "Shinbone," deserves a scout from the left bank. Shortly below this is "Mike's Monastery," the site of a vertical entrapment on the first run. Beware of the central drop at the top of the rapid! Farther on is a double falls, two 10-foot drops in close succession. This area has changed radically in past years from mud slides, and the whole mess is best portaged on the right.

One mile below here is the big rapid that can be seen on the drive to the put-in. Take out just above this rapid and scramble up to the road, or portage the top of the rapid on the left and run the bottom. To do this, execute a scary rock launch just above the final 5-foot drop. One-half mile below here is the washed out crossing. To find this, turn right onto the first paved road after turning onto The Geysers Road from U.S. 101.

—LH

RUSSIAN RIVER (Squaw Rock Run)

DIFFICULTY	FLOW	OPTIMUM	MILES	PORTAGES
II-III	400-1000	1500	8.4	0
III-IV	1000-8000			
IV-V	>8000			

PUT IN:	**Pieta Creek (440 ft.)**
TAKE OUT:	**101 Bridge (310 ft.)**
SHUTTLE:	**8.4 miles**
RAFTS:	**YES (2 low bridges)**
AVERAGE GRADIENT:	**16 fpm**
GAUGE:	***Russian at Hopland* is 5 miles above put-in (flow phone).**
BOATING SEASON:	**Winter / Spring / Summer / Fall**
WATER SOURCE:	**Ntrl./Spill / Ntrl./Spill / Power / Power**
AAA and *TOPO MAPS*:	**North Bay Counties; *Hopland, Cloverdale* (7.5 series)**

This is the only stretch of the Russian River with rapids of class III and better. Its proximity to the North Bay attracts an array of river travelers, from inner tubers (in summer) to rafters and kayakers.

The put-in at Pieta Creek allows one to warm up before negotiating a narrow drop, "the Slot," and the ensuing "Graveyard." These rapids, located directly below the towering Squaw Rock, are the most difficult on the run. One can put in directly below the Slot, running only the Graveyard, or start at a beach a half mile downstream to avoid the whole section.

Below here, a few brushy class II rapids lead to a low bridge made of railroad flatcars. At low flows, passage underneath is easy in kayaks. Use increasing caution as clearance disappears! At 30,000 cfs this bridge creates a great surfing wave. Soon after is a series of rapids near Commisky Station Road. The first is called "The Room." At lower flows, one must run a slot on river right that appears to be blocked by a large boulder. Closer inspection reveals that clearance exists for at least a medium-sized raft. Below this are 3 evenly spaced rapids.

A few class II rapids lead to the last major rapid on the run, "C Turn." This rapid sweeps to the left and holds a large hole near the bottom in high water. Below "C Turn" is a long stretch of flat water, followed by a swift gravel-bar riffle which leads into another low bridge. Watch out! Easy water remains in the last miles to take-out at the U.S. 101 bridge.

This run is reached by driving to Cloverdale, 1.5 hours north of San Francisco on U.S. 101. From Cloverdale continue a few miles to the Russian River. This is the take-out. The put-in is 8 miles farther.

—LH

EEL RIVER (Upper Main Eel)

DIFFICULTY	FLOW	OPTIMUM	MILES	PORTAGES
IV-V	500-1500	1000	18	4

PUT IN:	Horse Creek (2,640 ft.)
TAKE OUT:	Lake Pillsbury (1,830 ft.)
SHUTTLE:	13 miles (dirt)
RAFTS:	NO
AVERAGE GRADIENT:	62 fpm: miles 6 & 7; 140, 110
GAUGE:	None, but runnable after a recent storm.
BOATING SEASON:	Winter Spring
WATER SOURCE:	Natural Natural
USFS and *TOPO MAPS*:	Mendocino NF; *Kneecap Ridge, Crockett Peak, Lake Pillsbury* (7.5 series)

This is a surprisingly good run, in a wild setting with many challenging rapids. I first did this run alone in the winter of '78 and found it frightening. By returning the next year with other boaters, I got a chance to reckon with my fear.

After 4-5 miles of moderate boating, including a portage, Cold Creek enters on the left. Here the river makes a 130-degree turn and charges into a cataract. On river right are high rock walls, so portage on the left, through muck and over boulders. After a bit, the gradient tapers off, and one can get back in the river. The next 4-5 miles are filled with action. Occasional easy stretches are passed, giving the impression that it's all over, but don't be fooled.

Shortly before running into the lake, the river flows through wide, shallow gravel bars. The tranquil 5-mile paddle across Lake Pillsbury in sharp winter air can be relaxing after the perils of the river above. Sunset Campground, on the northeast corner of the lake, provides a convenient take-out point.

The logistical crux of this run is timing. One must catch it after the shuttle road is free of snow, but before the river is too low to boat, usually in February or March. Often, it can be run in early winter, before heavy accumulations of snow occur.

To reach the put-in, proceed past the Pillsbury Run (see following run description) to Lake Pillsbury. Drive around the north side of the lake past Sunset Campground, the take-out. From here the road climbs up and over into the Black Butte River drainage. Along the 13 miles to Horse Creek there are a few views of the river below.

—LH

Chuck Stanley in Misnomer Falls on the Eel. *John Armstrong*

EEL RIVER (Pillsbury Run)

DIFFICULTY	FLOW	OPTIMUM	MILES	PORTAGES
II-III	300-800	1500	5	0
III-IV	800-2000			
IV-V	2000-6000			

PUT IN:	Below Lake Pillsbury (1,650 ft.)
TAKE OUT:	Bucknell Creek (1,520 ft.)
SHUTTLE:	5 miles
RAFTS:	YES (above 1,000)
AVERAGE GRADIENT:	26 fpm
GAUGE:	*Inflow to Van Arsdale* is 3 miles below take-out, (flow phone).

BOATING SEASON:	Winter	Spring	Summer	Fall
WATER SOURCE:	Spill/Pwr.	Spill/Pwr.	Power	Power

USFS and *TOPO MAPS*: Mendocino NF; *Lake Pillsbury, Potter Valley* (15 series)

This run is a great introduction to the geology of the Eel and Russian drainages. Most of the rapids are created by slides, and one will see plenty of gooey, grey mud on this run. There are many bouldery rapids of moderate drop, and the river seems steeper than it is.

At low flows (there are 300-400 cfs all summer and fall), the run is technical. There are many tight, narrow spots amongst big boulders. These turn into fearsome holes in winter floods.

To reach the river, turn onto Route 20 from U.S. 101, 5 miles north of Ukiah. In 5 miles turn left onto Potter Valley Road and follow for 6 miles to Eel River Road. Turn right and go over the divide to Van Arsdale Reservoir. The road on the south side of the river is best for shuttling. The take-out is 3 miles up, at Bucknell Creek. The put-in is 5 miles farther, where the road comes back down to the river.

—LH

MAIN EEL RIVER (Dos Rios to Alderpoint)

DIFFICULTY	FLOW	OPTIMUM	MILES	PORTAGES
II-III+	1000-3000	5000	46.6	0
III-IV	3000-10000			

PUT IN: Dos Rios (860 ft.)
TAKE OUT: Alderpoint (270 ft.)
SHUTTLE: 85 miles
RAFTS: YES
AVERAGE GRADIENT: 13 fpm
GAUGE: *Eel at Fort Seward* is 8 miles below take-out (flow phone).
BOATING SEASON: Winter / Spring
WATER SOURCE: Natural/Spill / Natural/Spill
AAA and *TOPO MAPS*: NW California; *Dos Rios, Iron Peak, Updegraff Ridge, Lake Mtn., Jewett Rock, Alderpoint* (7.5 series)

Though not as remote as the Middle Fork of the Eel, this run still gives one a feeling of being in a semi-wilderness. Aside from the occasional cabin up on a hillside and the Northwestern Pacific Railroad (NWPRR) paralleling the river, little else in the scenery is likely to remind one of the twentieth century.

Up to Spy Rock (on the right at mile 13) the river is fairly easy, mostly class

II with a few class III's. At mile 22.5, the North Eel comes in on the right. From here rapids become more frequent and culminate with Island Mountain Falls, the largest rapid on the run. From the approach to this rapid, one will see evidence of a NWPRR work camp on the left. Scout on this side. At high water (10K) a big hole extends halfway across the left side of the river ('79), though this may have changed in recent major floods. One-half mile below here the railroad enters a one-mile tunnel, cutting straight through the mountain, while the river makes a 4-mile horseshoe bend to reach the same point. About halfway through this bend is a large drop, probably the second largest rapid on the run. At mile 36.5 Kekawaka Creek comes in on the right. After this the river is generally easier; long flat stretches separate easy rapids. A selection of topos covering this run is nice for picking out major landmarks.

The put-in for this run is the take-out for the Middle Eel, or one can put in further upstream near the Outlet Creek confluence.

To reach the take-out from Dos Rios, cross the bridge over the Eel and continue west for 13 miles to Laytonville. Turn north on U.S. 101 and proceed 49 miles to Garberville. From Garberville follow Alderpoint Road east for 20 miles to the take-out.

—LH

TOMKI CREEK

DIFFICULTY	FLOW	OPTIMUM	MILES	PORTAGES
III+	200-600 (put-in)	400	17.5	0

PUT IN: Hearst Rd. at Rocktree Creek (1,660 ft.)

TAKE OUT: Hearst (1,290 ft.)

SHUTTLE: 5 miles

RAFTS: NO (too small)

AVERAGE GRADIENT: 25 fpm on Tomki, 16 fpm on Main Eel

GAUGE: Runnable after a recent storm and when *Release from Van Arsdale* is greater than 3,000 cfs (flow phone).

BOATING SEASON: Winter

WATER SOURCE: Natural

AAA and *TOPO MAPS*: North Bay Counties; *Potter Valley* (15 series)

Anybody out there like to do long kayak runs with shuttles so short that you can send a dachshund off to fetch the car?

Tomki Creek runs south and east for 9.3 miles to the Eel River, which then flows north and west. The result is a drainage that runs almost in a circle, with only a low divide separating the start from the finish.

At the put-in Tomki Creek will look miserably low and brushy, which it is for the first few miles. Soon, though, after the creek has swung to the east, the canyon begins to deepen and occasional enjoyable rapids occur. The flow increases rapidly as side creeks enter; by the time one reaches the Eel, the flow may have doubled. The runout on the Eel ought to be fast, for there should be a sizable flow when Tomki is runnable. There are a few class II-III rapids on the main Eel before the bridge at Hearst.

To reach the put-in, turn east off U.S. 101 at the center of Willits. Go 2.7 miles to a "T" intersection at East Side Road. Turn left here and go to the next "T." Turn right here and climb out of the valley through Berry Canyon. In approximately 3.5 miles there is another "T" intersection. Turn left here, crossing Tomki Creek shortly, and drive 1.7 miles to yet another "T." To your left is a ford across Tomki Creek, just above the confluence with Rocktree Creek. Put in here.

Turn right and go 5 miles to reach Hearst. The bridge just upstream of Hearst serves as the take-out.

—LH

MIDDLE FORK EEL RIVER

DIFFICULTY	FLOW	OPTIMUM	MILES	PORTAGES
II-IV	800-2000	2000	32	0
II-V	2000-5000			

PUT IN: Black Butte River confluence (1,460 ft.)

TAKE OUT: Dos Rios (860 ft.)

SHUTTLE: 30 miles

RAFTS: YES

AVERAGE GRADIENT: 19 fpm

GAUGE: Runnable when *Eel at Fort Seward* is between 3,000 and 10,000 cfs (flow phone).

BOATING SEASON: Winter Spring

WATER SOURCE: Natural Natural

AAA and *TOPO MAPS*: NW California; *Newhouse Ridge, Covelo East, Jamison Ridge, Thatcher Ridge, Dos Rios* (7.5 series)

This big, silty river courses out of the western flank of the Yolla Bolly Wilderness and carves its way for over 60 miles to the Main Eel River. Few other rivers in the state give the same feeling of remoteness; floating along the Middle Fork of the Eel, one can dream of British Columbian outback.

Nothing very serious occurs in the first 26 miles; however, there are good play spots in the many class II rapids. The river is generally quite broad; nonetheless, one should be aware of logs broached on boulders and other obstacles. Good camping is available at 15.5 miles where Thatcher Creek comes in on the left. At mile 17, Elk Creek enters on the left, the largest creek on the run.

At mile 26 is the first big rapid, "Skinny Chutes." It is "skinny" only at the lowest flows; at more reasonable flows, it's a good class III-IV rapid with big drops and waves. Shortly below here, at mile 27, a long class III rapid leads to near the start of the biggest rapid on the run.

In the past several years this rapid, Coal Mine Falls, has proved easiest to run on the left, so one should pull out here to scout. This powerful, precipitous rapid seems to hold above average potential for underwater entrapment; it should be carefully scouted if run. Portaging is possible, but looks difficult on either side.

In the next 3 miles, the river cuts through a beautiful, deep canyon with several class II rapids. The canyon opens up and the shuttle road can be seen on the right. A 150-foot-high outcrop called Swallow Rock looms ahead. A respectable class III rapid lies below this promontory and contains a reversal that many will want to scout. The next mile to the Main Eel holds several moderate rapids and the canyon continues to open up. Take out at either the confluence, or a few hundred feet down the Main Eel under the Dos Rios bridge.

To reach the take-out, go north from Willits 13 miles and turn right onto Route 162, the Covelo Road. Follow this along Outlet Creek and then the Main Eel, until crossing the Middle Eel in about 15 miles. Just after the Middle Eel bridge, a road cuts back left to Dos Rios and a bridge across the Main Eel. The best take-out is here, under the Main Eel bridge.

To find the put-in, continue on the Covelo Road another 13 miles to Covelo and go 1.5 miles past town. Turn right on Mendocino Pass Road, go 14 miles, and cross the Middle Eel at the Black Butte Guard Station. The campground here provides a good organizational site, and launching spots abound on the beaches surrounding the campground.

— LH

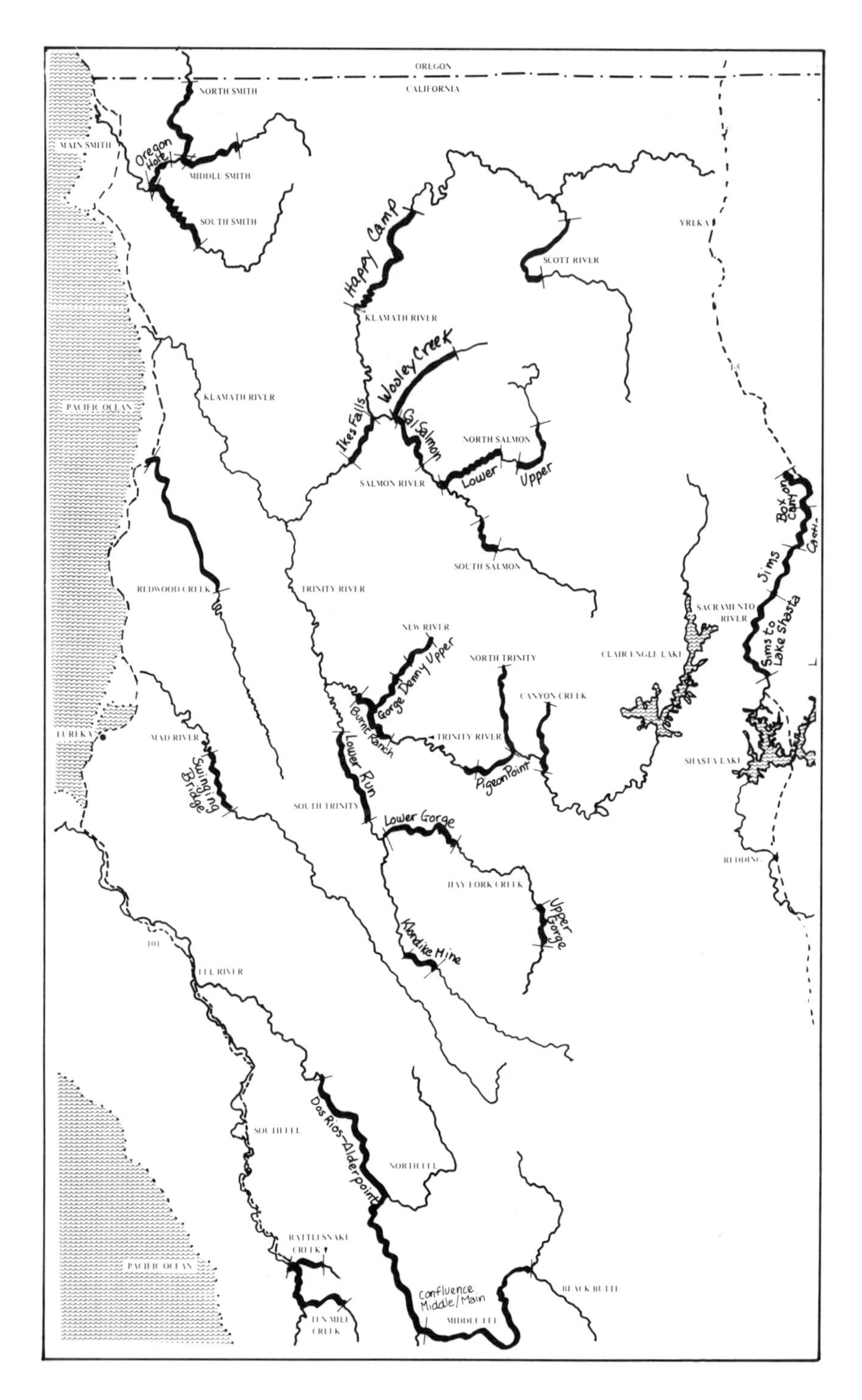
OREGON
CALIFORNIA
NORTH SMITH
MAIN SMITH
Oregon Hole
MIDDLE SMITH
SOUTH SMITH
Happy Camp
KLAMATH RIVER
SCOTT RIVER
YREKA
Wooley Creek
Ikes Falls
Cal Salmon
NORTH SALMON
Lower
Upper
SALMON RIVER
KLAMATH RIVER
PACIFIC OCEAN
I-5
Box Canyon
Sims
Sims to Lake Shasta
SOUTH SALMON
REDWOOD CREEK
TRINITY RIVER
SACRAMENTO RIVER
NEW RIVER
Gorge Denny Upper
NORTH TRINITY
CLAIR ENGLE LAKE
CANYON CREEK
Burnt Ranch
TRINITY RIVER
Pigeon Point
EUREKA
MAD RIVER
Swinging Bridge
Lower Run
SOUTH TRINITY
SHASTA LAKE
Lower Gorge
REDDING
HAY FORK CREEK
Upper Gorge
Klondike Mine
101
EEL RIVER
SOUTH EEL
Dos Rios-Alderpoint
NORTH EEL
RATTLESNAKE CREEK
PACIFIC OCEAN
Confluence Middle/Main
BLACK BUTTE
MIDDLE EEL
TEN MILE CREEK

SOUTH FORK EEL RIVER
(Ten Mile Creek)

DIFFICULTY	FLOW	OPTIMUM	MILES	PORTAGES
IV	1500-3000	2500	15.8	0
IV+	3000-8000			
V−	>8000			

PUT IN:	**Ten Mile Creek at gauge station (1,460 ft.)**
TAKE OUT:	**Big Bend (810 ft.)**
SHUTTLE:	**12 miles**
RAFTS:	**YES**
AVERAGE GRADIENT:	**43 fpm; last mile of Ten Mile drops 100 fpm**
GAUGE:	***South Eel at Leggett* is 5 miles below take-out (flow phone).**
BOATING SEASON:	**Winter**
WATER SOURCE:	**Natural**
AAA and *TOPO MAPS*:	**NW California; *Leggett, Tan Oak Park* (7.5 series)**

This is the standard class IV winter run on the Eel drainage, and it's very good in terms of both whitewater and scenery. There are many fun class III and IV rapids that are evenly dispersed along the length of the section. The scenery is tops; one paddles through an unspoiled roadless area, with many vertical rock cliffs. Bald eagles have been known to soar down the canyon.

There are two ways to run this section of the Eel. The one I recommend is to start at Ten Mile Creek and paddle 6.3 miles to the confluence with the South Fork. An alternative is to put in on the South Fork itself. This put-in is approached from Laytonville on Branscomb Road. Drive past Branscomb a few miles and find a place to put in. Watch out for private property. This option greatly increases the shuttle length.

The South Fork of the Eel River is entirely dependent on rainfall for its flow. It isn't unusual for the stream to fluctuate from 500 to 10,000 cfs overnight and be back to 500 after several days. You'll want to catch this one just after a winter storm. In general, the flow of Ten Mile Creek and the South Fork are equal. Ten Mile Creek comes up faster when it rains, but also drops off quicker. Thus, if you catch the river on the rise, Ten Mile will have about 60% of the flow; on the wane, the South Fork will carry about 60%.

Paddling through a wonderful wilderness area in January has its problems. Remember, the road is a very long hike away, the weather is cold

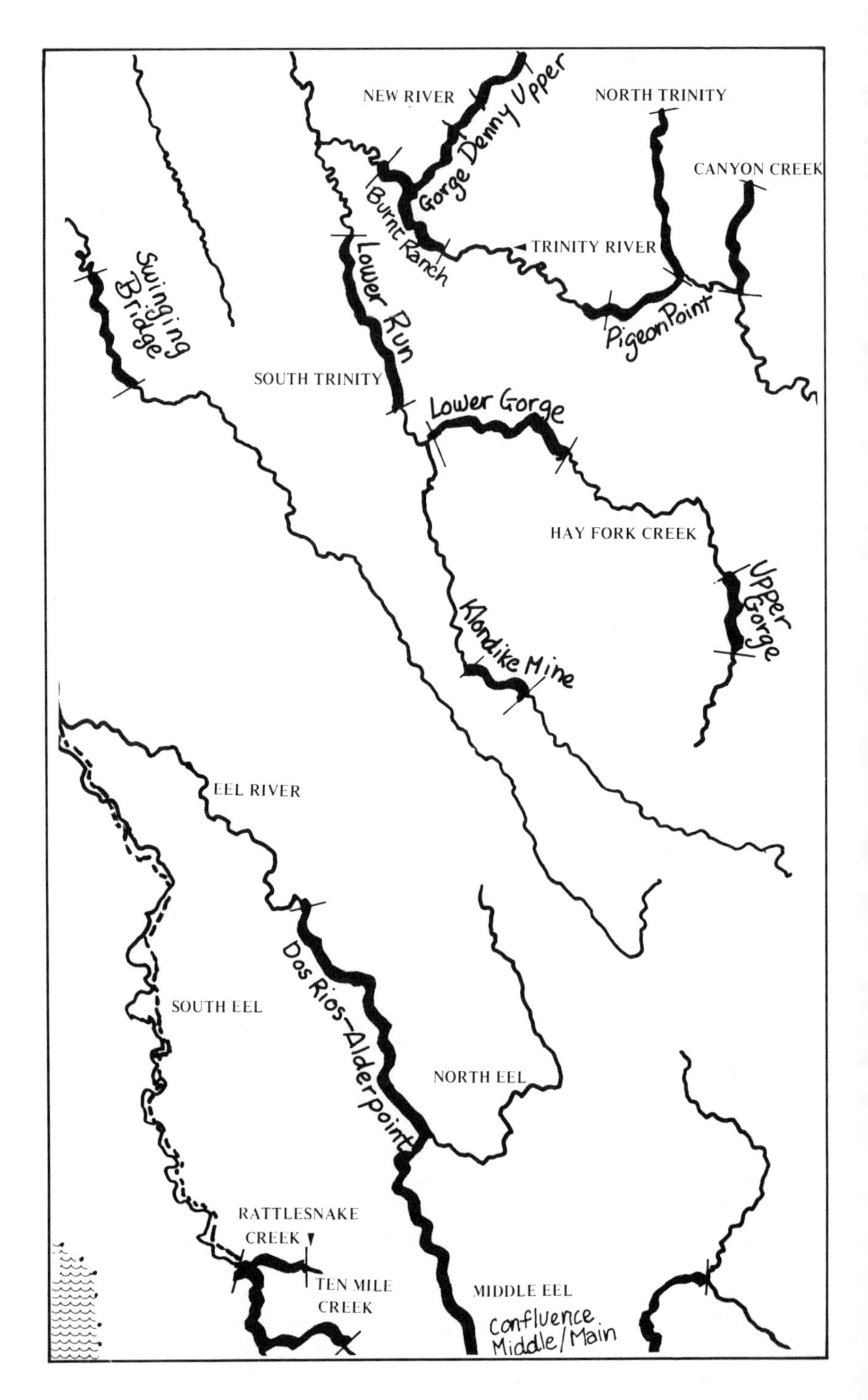
NEW RIVER
Gorge
Denny
Upper
NORTH TRINITY
CANYON CREEK
Burnt Ranch
TRINITY RIVER
Swinging Bridge
Lower Run
Pigeon Point
SOUTH TRINITY
Lower Gorge
HAY FORK CREEK
Upper Gorge
Klondike Mine
EEL RIVER
Dos Rios—Alderpoint
SOUTH EEL
NORTH EEL
RATTLESNAKE CREEK
TEN MILE CREEK
MIDDLE EEL
Confluence Middle/Main

(especially at 3 a.m.), and darkness falls earlier than hoped. Once you're about halfway, the only exit is via the river, either up or downstream. Hiking along the bank is very tough. The beautiful rock cliffs become mammoth obstacles—it's either swim or climb. So Uncle Chuck sez, "Get an early start, carry a spare paddle (or an excellent hand roll), carry some bivouac gear (at least waterproof matches and a knife), and have fun."

The traditional take-out for the run used to be the Hermitage. Access to this private property is now denied due to a group of rude rafters having given the caretaker a hard time. Don't take out there. Instead, continue downriver 1.4 miles to Big Bend. Here the landowners are kind enough to allow you to take out for a reasonable fee. Please pay them, as the next potential take-out is 5 miles farther.

To get to Big Bend, drive north from Laytonville on U.S. 101, take the Cummings exit, and turn left. Drive 2.8 miles to Big Bend. The put-in also has its problems; some folks have run into an ungracious rancher who owns the area. The best policy is to suit up at the rest area near Tan Oak on U.S. 101 (halfway between the put-in and take-out) and execute a commando put-in. I've never had any problem with putting in or parking cars, but be forewarned. The put-in is a bit obscure. From Laytonville, drive north on U.S. 101, the road follows Ten Mile Creek. About 6 miles from town, keep your eyes peeled for a gauge on the left: this is the put-in.

—CS

CAMPING ON THE SOUTH FORK OF THE EEL

This is a story about some unhappy campers. These campers began their journey intending to be kayaking. The story begins with Dave, Jerry, Pat and Warren putting in on Ten Mile Creek. The water is high and rising. The weather is bad; it's raining.

Dave, the most experienced of the crew, was confident; the other fellows weren't as sure. The first test arrived with the last part of Ten Mile Creek, about 5 miles into the 15.8 mile run. Here the rapids are continuous stiff class IV. Jerry flipped and had to eject. After a long swim, he was fortunate to emerge undamaged and with his boat. His paddle was a loss. At this point, 5 miles from the road, he began a long, wet, cold walk back to the car. He made it back to civilization by 8 p.m. As it turned out, his was the easiest lot.

One mile below Jerry's swim, Ten Mile Creek joins the South Fork of the Eel. Here the addition of the two streams doubles the flow. The next couple of miles are continuous class IV rapids. That day the river was running 8,000 cfs. In this section, the scenery is beautiful: rugged mountainsides, heavily forested. There's no evidence of civilization anywhere, just steep side canyons and precipitous outcroppings. On this particular day, it's raining and the river is rising.

After sending Jerry on his way,

the remaining three continued down the creek to the confluence. Ten Mile Creek's last mile, continuous demanding class IV water, severely tested the group. It was with a sigh of relief that they reached the pool at the confluence. Unfortunately, their respite was short-lived.

The section below the confluence isn't as steep as the roughest sections of Ten Mile Creek, but the flow is doubled. The trio battled pummeling waves and big water hydraulics in the freezing weather, holding their own in a situation suddenly grown quite serious.

Then, suddenly, Pat and Warren were over and out of their boats. Under the circumstances, there was no time to worry about equipment. With Dave's help, the swimmers managed to make it to shore. Warren even held on to his boat, but Pat's was gone.

Once on the shore, the trio faced a major decision. It was a rainy winter day and they were in the middle of nowhere. Without a boat, at least one of them would have to walk out of the river canyon. The group elected to stick together and start hiking for The Hermitage, some 5 miles downstream.

The kayaks didn't make it 200 yards before Dave and Pat abandoned the effort and cached them. The thick underbrush made the going extremely tough. The first side stream was a formidable obstacle, overflowing as it was from the rain. The men were forced to struggle upstream until the creek was small enough to cross with the assistance of a throw rope belay. This process was repeated at each of the many creeks. When darkness fell they had traveled only 2 miles downstream.

Darkness found the three badly unprepared — no tarps, sleeping bags, flashlight, or fire. They hadn't even stopped before dark to prepare a sleeping site. In total blackness they attempted to cut branches to prepare a small shelter. Dave couldn't see a thing as he groped in the dark for boughs. The night passed very slowly as the three huddled together for warmth.

At daybreak it was more of the same: hike downstream along the steep river canyon until a creek forced them inland to find a place to ford. Once across, it was back to the main river and down to the next one.

It was early afternoon when they reached Rattlesnake Creek, which was flowing 5,000 cfs. Crossing the tree-strewn creek was impossible. Their exhausted state ruled out swimming the main river, which was running by this time 20,000 cfs.

After half an hour of yelling, the caretaker at The Hermitage noticed their plight. He promptly called the sheriff to the scene, who made an effort to throw a rope across the swollen stream. The three quickly indicated they wanted nothing to do with such a scheme.

Eventually, a California Highway Patrol helicopter was called to the scene and transported the men to the other side where they were presented with a bill for $4,000.

That's the kind of weekend it had been.

Several weeks later, Dave and a friend returned with a lower priced helicopter to recover the two left-behind kayaks. They were even able to locate all the missing paddling gear.

—CS

RATTLESNAKE CREEK (U.S. 101 to Big Bar)

DIFFICULTY	FLOW	OPTIMUM	MILES	PORTAGES
IV+	400-700	700	5	3
V	>700			

PUT IN:	**Bridge on U.S. 101 (1,350 ft.)**
TAKE OUT:	**Big Bend (fee) (810 ft.)**
SHUTTLE:	**5 miles**
RAFTS:	**NO**
AVERAGE GRADIENT:	**108 fpm**
GAUGE:	**Runnable when *South Eel at Leggett* is between 3,000 and 6,000 cfs (flow phone).**
BOATING SEASON:	**Winter**
WATER SOURCE:	**Natural**
AAA and *TOPO MAPS*:	**NW California; *Tan Oak Park, Leggett* (15 series)**

Let's not mince words here, the "Snake" is a little rocky creek. If you're out to tame some rompin', stompin', white horses, this isn't your cup of tea. But if you're after an enjoyable rock dodging run, through very pleasant wooded scenery, look no further. A 50-foot tunnel, blasted by our friends at Cal Trans, is an interesting added feature. When Richard, Lars, and I ran it, there was only a small drop at the bottom. Just downstream of the tunnel is a portage. All of the portages are easy and at river level.

The flow at the beginning of the run is tiny, but the creek quickly picks up water as it travels downhill. Since there is no access to The Hermitage, judging the flow at the confluence with the South Fork of the Eel isn't possible. I recommend viewing the lower section of the run from U.S. 101 to get a feeling for the true flow.

To get to the put-in, drive from Laytonville on U.S. 101 until you reach the first bridge over the creek. There is a 4-foot weir at the bottom of the bridge, so watch out. The take-out is found by continuing north on U.S. 101 to the Cummings exit. Take the exit and turn left. Drive about 3 miles to Big Bend. Be prepared to pay a fee to take out.

—CS

MAD RIVER (Swinging Bridge Run)

DIFFICULTY	FLOW	OPTIMUM	MILES	PORTAGES
III-IV+	700-2000	1500	10	1
IV-V	>2000			

PUT IN: Suspension Bridge at Jackshaw Road (690 ft.)

TAKE OUT: Maple Creek Road (320 ft.)

SHUTTLE: 21 miles

RAFTS: NO (difficult portage)

AVERAGE GRADIENT: 37 fpm

GAUGE: ***Mad River at Arcata*** **is 20 miles below the take-out (call the Eureka recording, 707/ 443-9305).**

BOATING SEASON: Fall Winter

WATER SOURCE: Natural Natural

AAA and *TOPO MAPS*: **NW California; *Mad River Buttes, Iaqua Buttes, Maple Creek, Korbel* (7.5 series)**

Like much of the Eel, Russian, and Van Duzen rivers, the Mad displays classic examples of rampant erosion. The same thick, gray, gooey muck is found here; jumbled rapids caused by bank erosion are the rule. Despite all this, the run is still quite enjoyable. According to Mike Schlax (my consultant in these matters), the geology is very interesting. There are prime examples of pillow basalt and blueschists.

The river is fairly easy in the first few miles; there are warm-up boulder slaloms in swift current. A major rapid occurs and is quickly followed by a jumble of giant boulders. With flows as high as 2,000 cfs, we've had to portage this. Shortly below here is the biggest rapid on the run, a long, complicated class IV-V.

Below here the river eases considerably, though good current and class II rapids continue for some distance. In this lower section are the pillow basalts which fascinate the kayaker/geologist.

The put-in is reached by turning east on Myrtle Road at the north end of Eureka. After 5 miles, Old Arcata Road comes in on the left. Here I believe the name changes to Kneeland Road. In any event, follow signs toward Kneeland. About 14 miles from U.S. 101, Maple Creek Road enters on the left (north). (This is called Butler Valley Road on most maps.) The take-out is 6 or 7 miles down this road.

Continue on the Kneeland Road. Approximately 4 miles past Maple Creek Road, take a left on Mountain View Road, following signs toward the Kneeland airport. After 8 miles on this road, turn left on Jackshaw Road (so labeled on AAA maps) and go 2 miles to a dead-end at the swinging bridge. A trail leads to the river on the downstream, near side.

— LH

C. Stanley doing his Doc Watson impression. ***John Armstrong***

LARS HOLBEK: GREAT BALLS OF FIRE

Lars Holbek is renowned for his direct manner of obtaining goals. When he portages, it's from Point A to Point B with no detours around anything if it can be climbed over, under, up, or down. Overall this style makes Lars the fastest portager west of the Mississippi; occasionally it gets him into trouble.

The first time I saw Lars falter was on the classic Bear River portage-fest (Hwy. 49 to Camp Far West Reservoir). After portaging at river level halfway down a class VI canyon, we were forced to climb up the right canyon wall 500 feet to complete the carry. Richard and I wisely chose to pull our kayaks up a gully with ropes, although this was slightly longer than climbing directly up the 50 degree rock face. As always, Lars went straight up the cliff.

Lars was making good time climbing with his boat on his shoulder; he was 200 feet above the river on the steep rock cliff when he slipped. Richard and I looked on in horror as he slid towards the water. Only a desperate one-handed grab, after 10 feet of falling, stopped his descent. His paddle luckily fell only 20 feet farther to a ledge and stopped. Very exciting.

We continued to portage until nightfall caught us. We bivouacked high on the hill next to a cheery fire.

Another time, on the Swinging Bridge run on the Mad River, Lars, Terry Allen, and Mike Schlax approached the river from the north (instead of the normal south-side put-in) by hiking one mile from Maple Creek Road. The walk went easily until the river's edge where a brushy 100-foot cliff blocked the path to the river. Terry and Mike started down a steep gully to the right, Lars thought a gully to the left looked better. By the time Mike and Terry yelled that their route was clear, Lars was irreversibly halfway down the cliff.

The further Lars went, the steeper the poison-oak-covered cliff became. Lars (who instinctively avoids the stuff because of nasty childhood bouts with the plant) knew the situation was desperate when he was forced to cling to the vile plants for handholds. At one point, he was stuck on a small ledge. His only escape was a dirt hummock 5 feet to one side.

Lars' plan was to lower his boat as far as possible on his 50-foot rope, and then drop it. Free of the boat, he would use his paddle as a bridge to get to the hummock. As he gingerly tested his weight on the paddle, a blade cracked, and the broken paddle tumbled. His only remaining option was to jump to a fir tree some 10 feet away from the cliff and scramble down this to safety. After 20 minutes of deliberation, for it was a long jump, he vaulted into the tree and landed with a death grip. He quickly climbed down the tree and raced to the river, where he desperately tried to wash off the poison oak.

The trio sprinted down the river, paced by Lars, who was frantic to get some soap!

He arrived at the take-out a half hour ahead of his mates (Mike had loaned him his paddle and used the broken one) and charged into the task of hoofing the shuttle. After a sweaty 10-mile trot, he retrieved the vehicle and sped to the nearest creek. In the car he found no soap; he knew it was too little, too late. In desperation, he grabbed a can of gasoline and doused all of his body, painfully burning any tender skin.

It was all to no avail, for within 8 hours, Lars came down with a super wicked case of that fiery hot itch.

—CS

REDWOOD CREEK (Lacks Creek to Orick)

DIFFICULTY	FLOW	OPTIMUM	MILES	PORTAGES
III (one IV)	500-1500	1200	25	0
III+	>1500			

PUT IN: Lacks Creek (480 ft.)
TAKE OUT: Orick (26 ft.)
SHUTTLE: 48 miles
RAFTS: YES
AVERAGE GRADIENT: 18 fpm
GAUGE: *Redwood Creek at Orick* is the take-out (call the Eureka recording, 707/443-9305).
BOATING SEASON: Winter Spring
WATER SOURCE: Natural Natural
AAA and *TOPO MAPS*: NW California; *Orick*, *Rodgers Peak*, (15 series); *Coyote Peak* (7.5 series)

Ten minutes after I started paddling down Redwood Creek, I doubted the wisdom of this winter run. My fingers, despite being encased in wetsuit gloves, were in agony. The rapids were class II; the scenery was Early American Redwood clear-cut. After 10 miles of this treatment, I was ready to join James Watt on the first helicopter back to civilization. However, my dissatisfaction melted away upon entering the Emerald Mile—paddling through a virgin redwood forest is an unforgettable experience. The lovely scenery on the lower section of the river makes the trip worth the suffering.

If you're looking for an adrenalized whitewater trip, don't waste your time here. In general, the river is class II with a few class III rapids. There is one hard IV/easy V that can be portaged with moderate effort. Our trip lined the rafts through with moderate success. I've heard various disaster stories associated with this drop, so please be forewarned. From the Emerald Mile down, the river flows through virgin redwood forest. Fortunately one's view of the scenery is undisturbed — there are no rapids harder than class I.

On my raft-supported trip, we camped across the river from the Tall Trees Grove; these are the tallest trees in the world that haven't been cut down yet. Our camp scene was short of delightful as it was raining — a common occurrence in the area. If you plan to camp, be prepared for the worst.

To get to the put-in, drive east from the Eureka area on Hwy. 299 until you reach Bair Road. Go north on Bair Road to the river, where you turn left on Stover Road. Follow Stover Road, which follows the river, to the end of the line. Be sure to ask permission from the nearby house, as this is private property. There are also other potential put-in's farther upstream from the end of the road.

The take-out is reached by driving back towards U.S. 101 on Hwy. 299. Head north on U.S. 101 until you get to Orick. Continue one mile past Orick to Bald Hills Road, where you turn right. Go on the river right opposite the lumber mill.

—*CS*

TRINITY RIVER (Pigeon Point Run)

DIFFICULTY	FLOW	OPTIMUM	MILES	PORTAGES
II-III	500-1000	1500	5.7	0
III-IV	1000-4000			

PUT IN: Pigeon Point Campground (1,360 ft.)
TAKE OUT: Big Flat (1,225 ft.)
SHUTTLE: 5.7 miles
RAFTS: YES
AVERAGE GRADIENT: 24 fpm
GAUGE: ***Release from Lewiston*** **is 37 miles above the put-in. Add to that your estimate of the combined flows of Canyon and Weaver Creeks, plus the North Fork of the Trinity. Use the flow phone for the release from Lewiston; use a map and some common sense for the tributaries.**

	Winter	Spring	Summer	Fall
BOATING SEASON:				
WATER SOURCE:	Ntrl./Power	Ntrl./Power	Power	Power

USFS and *TOPO MAPS*: Trinity NF; ***Helena, Hayfork*** **(15 series)**

This is surely the most popular intermediate run on the main Trinity. It's a favorite playing run for Arcata area boaters as well as many rafting groups. At flows much above 5,000 cfs, it tends to wash out, leaving little of interest to the hotdogger.

Pigeon Point Campground, just downstream of the North Fork of the Trinity, is a good camping and launching area. The campground has no fee system, and is relatively uncrowded in spring.

About 2.5 miles from the put-in is a drop known locally as "Z" drop. Instant nosestands are possible here at the summertime flows. Less than a mile farther comes "Dynamite," which usually has a good-sized hole on river left.

Between here and the take-out are a few more class III rapids, the last of which is in view of the take-out, which is on the right near "downtown" Big Flat.

The put-in at Pigeon Point Campground, just off Route 299, is 80 miles east of Arcata and U.S. 101, 65 miles west of Redding and I-5.

—LH

TRINITY RIVER (Burnt Ranch Gorge)

DIFFICULTY	FLOW	OPTIMUM	MILES	PORTAGES
IV-V	500–5000	1500	8.5	0
V+	>5000			

PUT IN: Bridge near Cedar Flat (980 ft.)
TAKE OUT: Bridge near Hawkins Bar (590 ft.)
SHUTTLE: 9 miles
RAFTS: Possible, but wild.
AVERAGE GRADIENT: 46 fpm; 110 fpm at mile 3.5
GAUGE: ***Trinity at Hoopa*** **is 25 miles below take-out. This stretch ought to be okay when the reading is between 1,000 and 5,000 cfs (flow phone).**
BOATING SEASON: Spring Summer
WATER SOURCE: Natural/Power Power
USFS and *TOPO MAPS*: Shasta-Trinity NF; ***Iron Side Mtn., Willow Creek*** **(15 series)**

Burnt Ranch Gorge is a classic. When driving above the run, the canyon appears very deep and the river is far, far away. Paddlers are always drawn to canyons that can be seen from the road—they present such an obvious challenge.

The river is generous and starts slowly. The first mile of class II and III provides an excellent warm-up for what lies below. The rapids pick up upon entering the gorge. The first drop is class IV. This is closely followed by a vicious class IV, named "Auto End-on." I know of three cases of severe end-ons here; all the victims had to be carried out of the canyon, one with a broken ankle. The problem is a rock in the middle of the 6-foot drop which is unseen from above. The rock is safely covered at flows above 1,000 cfs. Be sure to personally scout this one—don't follow anyone down it without looking! From here the rapids are pool and drop down to Burnt Ranch Falls.

Rick Fernald in Burnt Ranch Gorge. ***Lars Holbek***

The frequency and severity of the rapids reach a crescendo in the Burnt Ranch Falls section. Here there is a series of 3 class V rapids; the first is named "Fountain Head." All of these can be portaged at river level without undue effort. Below the falls area is the confluence of the New River. The river is class IV down to Gray's Falls.

Gray's Falls looks awful but actually isn't all that bad. Here the river drops over a 6-foot ledge, and just downstream is a headwall which forms a massive cushion. At higher flows, 1,500-2,500 cfs, the cushion is monstrous. All you need to do is hit the right side and wash out—please don't go to the left and get trapped in the wicked eddy. Gray's Falls marks the end of the action. One can hike up the hard-to-spot trail to Gray's Falls campground (which I don't recommend) or continue on to Hawkins Bar bridge.

Burnt Ranch has been run as low as 400 cfs and as high as 5,000 cfs (by Lars and Richard Montgomery). At higher water, the action is much faster and less forgiving. I recommend sticking to flows in the 800-2,500 cfs range.

Burnt Ranch can be approached on Hwy. 299 from either Eureka or Redding. In either case, the put-in is found by driving 2.5 miles east from Burnt Ranch on Hwy. 299 to Cedar Flat. Park at the roadside rest on the east side of the bridge. The take-out is found by driving 8.5 miles from Cedar Flat to Hawkins Bar. Turn right onto Denny Rd. and drive a short distance to the bridge over the river.

—CS

CANYON CREEK

DIFFICULTY	FLOW	OPTIMUM	MILES	PORTAGES
III-IV	400-1000	1000	8.5	0
III-IV+	1000-2000			

PUT IN:	**Bridge 8.5 miles upriver from Junction City (2,120 ft.)**
TAKE OUT:	**Junction City (1,450 ft.)**
SHUTTLE:	**8.5 miles**
RAFTS:	**NO (too narrow)**
AVERAGE GRADIENT:	**79 fpm**
GAUGE:	**Runnable when *Trinity at Hoopa* is greater than 3,000 cfs (flow phone).**
BOATING SEASON:	**Winter Spring**
WATER SOURCE:	**Natural Natural**
USFS and *TOPO MAPS*:	**Trinity NF; *Hayfork*, *Helena* (15 series)**

This entertaining little run is a good one to do when on a tour of the area, but not worth driving to from the Bay Area for a weekend's diversion. If one is exploring the more difficult tributaries of the Trinity, Canyon Creek could serve as a sort of rest day.

Much of the stream can be seen along the road to the put-in. Three-and-a-half miles upstream from Rte. 299 is a narrow rock gorge, by far the most difficult rapid on the run. One can put in 8.5 miles up from Rte. 299 at the first bridge that crosses Canyon Creek. The river looks runnable farther up-stream and the road follows it for a few miles, though I know of no one who has run this section.

Most of the first 5 miles of this run is swift water flowing over gravel beds, broken up by many spots where the creek runs directly into small cliffs. In these areas one must make precise 90-degree turns to avoid "encliffment."

Junction City lies about 9 miles west of Weaverville on Route 299 and is easily located on a state map. Canyon Creek Road takes off to the north from the center of this two-horse town.

—LH

NORTH FORK TRINITY RIVER

DIFFICULTY	FLOW	OPTIMUM	MILES	PORTAGES
IV-V	500-1000	800	14	2

PUT IN:	Hobo Gulch (2,840 ft.)
TAKE OUT:	Bridge on Hobo Gulch Road (1,390 ft.)
SHUTTLE:	15 miles (dirt)
RAFTS:	NO
AVERAGE GRADIENT:	104 fpm; mi/mi: 190, 130, 100, 110, 100, 110, 90, 100, 70, 70, 90, 120, 80, 90
GAUGE:	Runnable when *Trinity at Hoopa* is between 3,000 and 5,000 cfs; also, when the old gauge 0.25 miles below the take-out reads between 8 and 9 (flow phone).
BOATING SEASON:	Spring
WATER SOURCE:	Natural
USFS and *TOPO MAPS*:	Trinity NF; *Helena* (15 series)

This is probably the steepest and most difficult run in the north coast mountains. The North Trinity River lies in a remote canyon, and maintains a serious atmosphere all the way to the take-out.

I first ran this river in the spring of '78 with Gunther Hemmersbach. We made 15-20 portages on this exploratory and took 9 hours to complete the run. On subsequent trips the number of portages has been minimized, but even with small, fast teams, the run still takes at least 8 hours. The possibility of a bivouac ought to be considered.

Just below the put-in is the first portage. This is the longest carry on the run, though others require more effort. After 6 or 7 miles, the river eases up temporarily and flows through a small valley. There is an occupied cabin on the left in this valley that could be used as an emergency take-out. The shuttle road is about 4 miles uphill by trail at this point.

To attempt to describe this run in detail is not necessary. If you're thinking of making this descent, you don't need a rapid-by-rapid description, just an early start and expertise in a kayak.

One-fourth mile below the take-out bridge, near a house trailer, is an old flow gauge. We've done the run at 8 and 9 on the scale. I don't know what the cubic-feet-per-second (cfs) conversion is, but 8 (600–800 cfs) is a good level. Below 8 is quite rocky.

The put-in is reached by turning off Route 299, 8 miles east of Big Bar, onto the road that goes up the North Trinity at Old Helena. About one mile up this road the river is crossed. This is the take-out. Continue 2.5 miles up this road along the East Branch of the North Trinity to a dirt road on the left. This is Hobo Gulch Road. It may not be marked (the sign seems to routinely disappear) but this is the major dirt road in this area and is relatively easy to find. A few dirt driveways go up the hill in this area, but they are smaller than Hobo Gulch Road.

—LH

Mike Schlax below the steepest cataract on the North Trinity, 1979. ***Lars Holbek***

NEW RIVER (Upper Run)

DIFFICULTY	FLOW	OPTIMUM	MILES	PORTAGES
III-IV	300-800	1000	4.5	1
IV-V–	800-2000			

PUT IN: East Fork confluence (1,650 ft.)
TAKE OUT: Denny (1,350 ft.)
SHUTTLE: 4.5 miles
RAFTS: NO
AVERAGE GRADIENT: 67 fpm
GAUGE: Runnable when *Trinity at Hoopa* is between 3,000 and 5,000 cfs (flow phone).
BOATING SEASON: Winter Spring
WATER SOURCE: Natural Natural
USFS and *TOPO MAPS*: Six Rivers NF; ***Ironside Mtn.*** (15 series)

This excellent, short run contains several small gorges with respectable rapids. One gorge in particular has overhanging walls on one side.

Several rapids require scouting, since they drop into vertical walled gorges and are often blind. The first rapid that forces a scout has a large boulder blocking most of the river just below the initial turbulent drop. Depending on the water level, a 2-to-4-ft.-wide drop exists on either side of this boulder. The crux is getting to one of these drops straight enough to avoid broaching. The most difficult stretch is more or less the middle 2 miles of the run.

Directions to the New River area are in the Lower Gorge description.

Put in at the bridge 3 miles upstream from Denny, or a mile farther at the East Fork confluence. At low flows, it's pretty scratchy this far upstream, so the bridge is a good alternative.

In the last mile or so the river opens up and becomes easier to the rickety log bridge at Denny. To get to this take-out, turn off at the school just north of Denny. Follow the dirt road around to the back until it becomes too steep for vehicles. It is a short carry to the bridge from here.

—LH

NEW RIVER (Denny Run)

DIFFICULTY	FLOW	OPTIMUM	MILES	PORTAGES
II-III	500-800	1000	4.1	0
III-IV	800-2000			

PUT IN:	Denny (1,350 ft.)
TAKE OUT:	Panther Creek (1,110 ft.)
SHUTTLE:	4.1 miles
RAFTS:	YES (above 1,000 cfs)
AVERAGE GRADIENT:	59 fpm
GAUGE:	Runnable when *Trinity at Hoopa* is between 3,000 and 5,000 cfs (flow phone).
BOATING SEASON:	Winter Spring
WATER SOURCE:	Natural Natural
USFS and *TOPO MAPS*:	Six Rivers NF; *Ironside Mtn.* (15 series)

This relatively easy run is a great introduction to the New River, and it is distinctly different from the runs above and below. It is mostly class II with some class III in a beautiful canyon. The exception is a series of class III rapids in the last mile that stack up to earn a class IV rating. An intermediate can make the run with perhaps a portage or two in this last mile. The water in this river is crystalline at lower flows, much like the North Trinity and the Smith rivers.

Directions to the New River area are in the Lower Gorge description. The put-in is the rickety log bridge described in the preceding run.

The take-out is the site that was once Panther Creek Campground, but is now privately owned. The present owners are amiable and we've had no trouble taking out here. Please be respectful when taking out on their land. The turnoff is unmarked, but is fairly easy to find. Approximately 4 miles before reaching Denny, a dirt road cuts back right from the main road and leads down a few hundred feet to the remains of the campground. A trot down the trail to river level will help one recognize the take-out "beach" at Panther Creek.

—LH

Mark Allen "no paddle" paddling on Cherry Creek. *Chuck Stanley*

NEW RIVER (Gorge Run)

DIFFICULTY	FLOW	OPTIMUM	MILES	PORTAGES
IV-V	400-800	700	11.2	1

PUT IN:	Panther Creek (1,110 ft.)
TAKE OUT:	Hawkins Bar Bridge (New River at Trinity River: 650 ft.)
SHUTTLE:	14 miles
RAFTS:	NO
AVERAGE GRADIENT:	(on New River only) 63 fpm; 220 ft. in first 6 miles; 250 ft. in last 1.5 miles
GAUGE:	Runnable when *Trinity at Hoopa* is between 3,000 and 5,000 cfs (flow phone).
BOATING SEASON:	Winter Spring
WATER SOURCE:	Natural Natural
USFS and *TOPO MAPS*:	Six Rivers NF; *Ironside Mtn.* (15 series)

In the spring of 1979, after doing enjoyable runs on the New River upstream of Panther Creek, Mike Schlax, Richard Montgomery, and I kayaked the lower New River which comes out into Burnt Ranch Gorge.

The first 5 or 6 miles are relatively easy; the last 1.5 miles is where the "good" stuff is. In places, the box canyon is intimidating and, in one spot, an unrunnable rapid first appears unportageable. Luckily, a mountain-goat route exists high up on the left wall. There are 3 possible portages above here. The final half-mile runout to the Trinity is all runnable (visible from a turnout high up on Rte. 299), though most of the rapids are technical and require scouting.

To get to the New River from Arcata, drive east on Route 299 and take the Denny turnoff at Hawkins Bar, 4.5 miles east of Salyer. Drive 14 miles to the old Panther Creek Campground (see previous run). A USFS map is quite helpful for making the correct turns.

From the confluence it is 2.2 miles on the Trinity to Gray Falls, where one can effect a strenuous take-out. The more logical take-out is another 1.5 miles downstream at the Hawkins Bar bridge.

—LH

HAYFORK CREEK (Upper Gorge)

DIFFICULTY	FLOW	OPTIMUM	MILES	PORTAGES
III-IV+	500-1000	700	5.7	3
IV-V	800-1200			

PUT IN: Gemmill Gulch Picnic Ground (3,190 ft.)
TAKE OUT: East Fork Hayfork Creek (2,660 ft.)
SHUTTLE: 6 miles
RAFTS: NO
AVERAGE GRADIENT: 93 fpm
GAUGE: Runnable when *Trinity at Hoopa* is between 3,000 and 10,000 cfs (flow phone).
BOATING SEASON: Winter Spring
WATER SOURCE: Natural Natural
USFS and *TOPO MAPS*: Trinity NF; *Dubakella Mtn.* (15 series)

This run encompasses the wildest section of upper Hayfork Creek. Between Route 36 and the put-in, Hayfork Creek is easy and swift, with few rapids of interest. Below the put-in, the creek maintains a moderate gradient, though it is narrow and logs may be a problem. Shortly below a log bridge is a narrow drop in which the current pushes into a slightly overhanging boulder on the right, "Roxy's Rock." This is immediately followed by "Ed's Eddy." Below here, the creek is steeper; class III-IV drops are frequent until a narrow gorge. The main drop in this short gorge appears only marginally runnable, and portaging is the norm.

Just above the first rapid in this gorge is a small eddy on the left with a shallow gully leading up and right. We portaged here, climbing up 80 feet, then traversed a short distance before descending to the creek via broken, brushy slabs. Immediately below lies a sharp drop, which we ran safely on the far right.

Class III and IV rapids continue for a few miles to another portage; this one is easy. Several more good rapids lead to a fishladder. For reference, note a flume on the left bank shortly before this last portage. The road is quite close here if one wishes to quit. Alternatively, portage around the gorge in which the fishladder lies and boat one mile to the East Fork confluence of Hayfork Creek. There is a beach just upstream from this junction and a dirt road leads down to it from Wildwood Road.

From Red Bluff go 54 miles west on Route 36 to the Trinity County line. Just past here, turn right onto Wildwood Road and go 4 miles to Gemmill Gulch Picnic Ground. The take-out is 6 miles farther, where the road comes back to river level.

Above Route 36 is a 3-to-4-mile-long class III+ run. The creek is typically 20 feet wide, and drops 90 fpm.

—LH

HAYFORK CREEK (Lower Gorge)

DIFFICULTY	FLOW	OPTIMUM	MILES	PORTAGES
IV-V	700-2000	1000	15.5	1

PUT IN:	**Hyampom Road (2,045 ft.)**
TAKE OUT:	**Hyampom (1,260 ft.)**
SHUTTLE:	**15 miles**
RAFTS:	**NO**
AVERAGE GRADIENT:	**51 fpm: miles 7-10: 95, 65, 85, 85; mile 12: 105**
GAUGE:	**Runnable when *Trinity at Hoopa* is between 3,000 and 10,000 cfs (flow phone).**
BOATING SEASON:	**Winter Spring**
WATER SOURCE:	**Natural Natural**
USFS and *TOPO MAPS*:	**Trinity NF; *Hyampom* (15 series)**

Rick Fernald in Gray's Falls, Burnt Ranch Gorge, 1980. ***Lars Holbek***

This superb section of Hayfork Creek flows through two distinct gorges on its last push to join the South Fork of the Trinity River. Carl Trost made the first run, solo, at low water in 1982. On our run, there were 2,000 to 3,000 cfs, which was rather pushy. At the put-in, 8 miles below the town of Hayfork, the "creek" is actually a river.

There are a few class III+ drops in the first 6 miles below the put-in; the gradient runs between 40 and 60 fpm in this stretch. At mile 7, Miners Creek enters on the right, marking the start of 4 serious miles in a narrow canyon. A trail opposite from Miners Creek presumably leads to the shuttle road. This is a possible take-out. Many big rapids churn through the canyon below. A few are class V, and several would be difficult to portage. At mile 10.5, Corral Creek enters on the right; it is the largest side creek on the run. This marks the end of the first steep section.

From here 3 miles of class II-III bring one to the final gorge. In this section, a dirt road and several old buildings are close to the river on the left, a possible emergency take-out.

The river drops 80 feet in the next two-thirds mile. Following a few big ledge drops is the last "rapid" on the run, a class VI mess called "Griz Falls." It is named for a member of our trio who unfortunately swam above the falls and was unable to reach shore in time! Much to the relief of our adrenaline-wracked bodies, he survived the initial 10-foot drop onto rocks and made it to shore before being swept down the 100 yards of class IV below. Amazingly (aside from the fact that he lived), he held onto his paddle.

After we were assured that he was only mildly battered, we chased his boat and found it snagged 0.5 mile downstream. Soon we were floating on the remaining easy water to Hyampom, and were again forced to marvel at the river's forgiving nature. A rousing "second chance" celebration graced the drive back to Hayfork.

To reach the put-in, go to Hayfork on Route 3, 23 miles west of Douglas City and Route 299, or 10 miles downriver from the take-out of the upper Hayfork Creek run. On the western edge of Hayfork, take the road for Hyampom. This road crosses from river right to left in 8 miles. Put in several hundred feet upriver of the bridge. The take-out in Hyampom is 15 miles farther. The bridge just upstream of the South Trinity serves for disembarkation.

—LH

SOUTH FORK TRINITY RIVER (Klondike Mine Run)

DIFFICULTY	FLOW	OPTIMUM	MILES	PORTAGES
IV-V−	500-1500	1000	4.5	2

PUT IN: Route 36 Bridge (2,250 ft.)
TAKE OUT: Klondike Mine (1,920 ft.)
SHUTTLE: 5 miles
RAFTS: NO
AVERAGE GRADIENT: 73 fpm; mi/mi: 30, 70, 70, 110, 50
GAUGE: Runnable when *Trinity at Hoopa* is between 3,000 and 10,000 cfs (flow phone).
BOATING SEASON: Winter Spring
WATER SOURCE: Natural Natural
USFS and *TOPO MAPS*: Six Rivers NF; *Pickett Peak* (15 series)

The river looks peaceful below the put-in bridge, but it soon picks up speed. In the first section of rapids is a difficult drop that we dubbed "Elbow Hit"; the body-width chute near the top caused some of us considerable pain. Below here is one of the portages, a steep chute with a large boulder clogging the outlet. Splendid rapids ensue to the last big one, a jolly race-horse that we called "Nicknards Delight."

The put-in on Route 36 at Forest Glen is 65 miles east of Alton, at U.S. 101, and 77 miles west of Red Bluff at I-5.

To reach the take-out, go a few miles west from Forest Glen, and turn right onto Klondike Mine Road. This road stops short of the river, and a trail leads to the water. It is a good idea to inspect the take-out before embarking, so as not to miss it.

— *LH*

SOUTH FORK TRINITY RIVER (Lower Run)

DIFFICULTY	FLOW	OPTIMUM	MILES	PORTAGES
III-IV+	700-1200	1500	17	2
IV-V	1200-2000			

PUT IN: Big Slide Campground (1,200 ft.)
TAKE OUT: Low Water Bridge (570 ft.)
SHUTTLE: 50 miles (dirt)
RAFTS: NO
AVERAGE GRADIENT: 37 fpm
GAUGE: Runnable when *Trinity at Hoopa* is between 3,000 and 10,000 cfs, (flow phone).
BOATING SEASON: Winter Spring
WATER SOURCE: Natural Natural
USFS and *TOPO MAPS*: Six Rivers NF; *Sims Mtn., Hennesy Peak* (7.5 series)

This beautiful and challenging run is probably the best on the South Fork of the Trinity, though the shuttle is long and complex.

The first 4.5 miles to the footbridge near Underwood Creek drops 255 feet. In this stretch are several hard rapids and a portage or two. Below this section, the gradient eases, but there are still some big rapids to come. One of note is identified by a large undercut boulder blocking the main chute in the bottom half of the rapid. Richard tried to run this on the left, but barely made it. After hitting a rock head on, and bending the nose of his boat, he got stuck in a hole just above the menacing undercut; his sprayskirt popped, filling the boat with water. Several tense seconds ensued, but he finally submarined out of the hole and barely made the slot next to the deadly boulder. Mike and I happily portaged after watching this near mishap.

To reach the put-in, find your way to Hyampom. Approach via Underwood Mountain Road, which comes from Burnt Ranch, Corral Bottom Road, from Big Bar, or via Hayfork (see directions in lower Hayfork Creek description). From Hyampom, cross the South Trinity and drive downstream 5 miles to Big Slide Campground.

To be perfectly honest, our take-out was a minor fiasco. The low water bridge seemed hard to find, though confusion was prevalent that day. Using a USFS map and common sense, others should have better luck than we did. It may well be easiest to just paddle the remaining 8 miles to Route 299, greatly simplifying the shuttle.

—LH

Chuck Stanley on the Cherry Creek run of the Tuolumne River.
John Armstrong

SOUTH FORK SALMON RIVER

DIFFICULTY	FLOW	OPTIMUM	MILES	PORTAGES
IV-V	300-1000	800	6	0

PUT IN:	**Near Limestone Bluffs (2,160 ft.)**
TAKE OUT:	**Matthews Creek Campground (1,710 ft.)**
SHUTTLE:	**6 miles**
RAFTS:	**NO**
AVERAGE GRADIENT:	**75 fpm: 165 fpm for 0.6 mile near mile 4**
GAUGE:	**You'll have approximately half of the *Flow at Somes Bar*, (26 miles below the take-out), (flow phone).**
BOATING SEASON:	**Winter Spring**
WATER SOURCE:	**Natural Natural**
USFS and *TOPO MAPS*:	**Klamath NF; *Cecilville* (7.5 series)**

Driving along the south fork, above Forks of Salmon, the first view of this run, just beyond Matthews Creek, is rather foreboding. The sight of the final falls coming out of the gorge is enough to catch anyone's eye.

Six miles upstream, the road drops down to river level; there are several good put-ins in the next half mile. The first major rapid reached (in the vicinity of the limestone bluffs) should be scouted. If run, it's advised to sprint it on river left, cutting hard left towards the eddy. I mention this because I've seen several boats hit end-on when running this drop straight.

Below this point, the river sports some incredible rapids. A few are often portaged. The last 2 rapids in the final gorge visible from the road should be carefully scouted. The upper rapid looks deceivingly easy. On river right, the current runs into a small peninsula of rock. The cut left, to avoid this, must be precisely executed. Don Banducci and I have experienced desperate wraps on separate occasions on this projection of rock. My boat was folded nearly in half, directly under the seat. I managed to get free by reaching into the fastest current with my paddle blade and pulling hard until I slid off. The plastic boat suffered a 7-inch crack under the seat. The falls below can be run on the left or portaged on the right. Don't make the mistake of running the falls on the right—it's been done and it took hours to free the boat after it got wedged, its occupant having been forced to climb out. A few more rapids lead around the corner to the take-out.

From the Klamath River Highway (Hwy. 96), turn onto the Salmon River Road, just south of Somes Bar. It's 17 miles to Forks of Salmon. Go roughly 9 miles up the south fork to the take-out.

—LH

NORTH FORK SALMON RIVER (Upper Run)

DIFFICULTY	FLOW	OPTIMUM	MILES	PORTAGES
III-IV	800-1500	1200	7.9	1

PUT IN: Idlewild Campground (2,800 ft.)
TAKE OUT: Sawyers Bar (2,160 ft.)
SHUTTLE: 8 miles
RAFTS: NO (narrow)
AVERAGE GRADIENT: 81 fpm
GAUGE: Runnable when *Klamath at Orleans* is between 5,000 and 10,000 cfs (flow phone).
BOATING SEASON: Winter Spring
WATER SOURCE: Natural Natural
USFS and *TOPO MAPS*: Klamath NF; *Tanners Peak, Sawyers Bar* (7.5 series)

This run is actually quite good, but my memory of it is foul. It seems every time I've kayaked this stretch, I froze my *patuchi* off and arrived at the take-out so discombobulated that removing the sprayskirt was a major task.

The 2 miles of river to the main road run through a small gorge and there are some exciting drops. In this section is a defunct wood bridge hanging in the water. Be sure to get out well in advance; portaging is possible on either side.

Below the main road, the river runs through an area of gravel beds, and soon enters a pleasant gorge in which lie many class III+ rapids. Much of this section can be seen from the road a few hundred feet above. The river eases somewhat before the old mining town of Sawyers Bar, and below is class II+ until the start of the following run at Little North Fork.

To reach this run from Somes Bar (located on Route 96), drive 17 miles along the Salmon River to Forks of Salmon. Drive 14 miles up the North Salmon to Sawyers Bar, the take-out. From here it's 8 miles to Idlewild Campground; the last 2 miles are on a dirt road that leaves the main road where it crosses the river.

Put in at the footbridge over the North Salmon. This is the start of a trail into the Marble Mountain Wilderness Area.

—LH

Lars Holbek, the last rapid on the Grand Canyon of the Tuolumne, 1983. *Chuck Stanley*

NORTH FORK SALMON RIVER (Lower Run)

DIFFICULTY	FLOW	OPTIMUM	MILES	PORTAGES
III-IV	600-1000	1500	11.3	0
IV-V	1000-3000			

PUT IN:	Little North Fork (1,980 ft.)
TAKE OUT:	Forks of Salmon (1,190 ft.)
SHUTTLE:	11.3 miles
RAFTS:	NO
AVERAGE GRADIENT:	70 fpm: 100 fpm in places
GAUGE:	Runnable when *Klamath at Orleans* is between 5,000 and 10,000 cfs (flow phone).
BOATING SEASON:	Winter Spring
WATER SOURCE:	Natural Natural
USFS and *TOPO MAPS*:	Klamath NF; *Forks of Salmon*, *Sawyers Bar* (7.5 series)

Most of this delightful run is visible from the shuttle road. There are many possible put-ins and take-outs. The campground at Little North Fork, a trailhead for the Marble Mountains, offers a convenient put-in.

The first rapid below here is long and devious. There are many beautiful, long boulder gardens on this run, and many steep, exhilarating drops.

Towards the end of the run is a section where the riverbed changes from an open one with granite boulders to a debris-choked gorge. Here the river takes on a villainous appearance. All of the rapids in this section have been run, but careful inspection is urged. In particular, there is a devious route down the right side of the second (?) rapid in this set, the largest and most difficult of the entire run. Below this are many beaches where local hipsters partake in nude sunning. Be careful not to drift into obstacles in this area.

The put-in is 11 miles upriver from Forks of Salmon; the take-out is at the bridge in town. Forks of Salmon is 17 miles from Route 96 and Somes Bar.

—LH

SALMON RIVER (Cal Salmon Run)

DIFFICULTY	FLOW	OPTIMUM	MILES	PORTAGES
III-IV+	500-2000	1500	10.2	0
IV-V	2000-5000			

PUT IN:	**Nordheimer Creek (1,040 ft.)**
TAKE OUT:	**Wooley Creek (560 ft.)**
SHUTTLE:	**10.2 miles**
RAFTS:	**YES (commercial run)**
AVERAGE GRADIENT:	**47 fpm**
GAUGE:	***Flow at Somes Bar*, 5 miles below the take-out, is what you'll have, (flow phone).**
BOATING SEASON:	**Winter Spring**
WATER SOURCE:	**Natural Natural**
USFS and *TOPO MAPS*:	**Klamath NF; *Forks of Salmon, Orleans Mtn.* (7.5 series)**

Until the summer of '83, the wicked "Entrance Falls," or "Bloomers Falls," was the largest and most dangerous drop on the river. In the summer of '83, the Department of Fish and Game dynamited the falls, reducing it to a class II+ chute. Despite this loss, the river still has plenty of action.

In the first half of the run are many class III to IV+ rapids; the largest is "Grant's Bluff" at mile 5.5. This rapid is visible from the road, as is "Big Joe," the rapid just above it. At certain water levels, the reversal at the bottom of

"Big Joe" has been known to suck adrenaline from kayakers for up to two minutes. The threat of wiping out in this hole, and swimming the precipitous Grant's Bluff just around the corner, prompts some to portage.

One mile below here is Butler Flat. A long, innocuous rapid ends in a river-wide ledge hole. The remaining 3.5 miles to Wooley Creek contain several good rapids. One of note is a long class IV that ends in yet another river-wide hole.

Nordheimer Creek, 10 curvy miles from the take-out, provides a good put-in and allows a short warm-up before the action begins.

The take-out is on river right at the bridge just upstream of Wooley Creek, 4.5 miles up the Salmon River Road from Somes Bar on Route 96.

—LH

KLAMATH RIVER (Ikes Falls Run)

DIFFICULTY	FLOW	OPTIMUM	MILES	PORTAGES
III-IV	1000-4000	3000	7	0
III-V–	4000-10000			

PUT IN: Ishi Pishi bridge (450 ft.)
TAKE OUT: Orleans (390 ft.)
SHUTTLE: 7 miles
RAFTS: YES
AVERAGE GRADIENT: 8.5 fpm
GAUGE: ***Klamath at Orleans*** **is the take out (flow phone).**

BOATING SEASON:	Winter	Spring	Summer	Fall
WATER SOURCE:	Ntrl./Power	Ntrl./Power	Power	Power

USFS and *TOPO MAPS*: Klamath NF; ***Orleans, Forks of Salmon*** **(15 series)**

There are many good class II-III runs on the Klamath above and below the Ikes run, but they are beyond the focus of this guide, and have been described in great detail in Dick Schwind's *West Coast River Touring*.

The majority of the action on this run happens in the first 2 miles. Ikes Falls is the major rapid in this section. At the water levels in which I've seen this run, there are a few good drops, one with a substantial reversal.

I've never been along when big water nuts run this in excess of 15,000 cfs, but I've heard stories. Bob Porter once did 7-8 successive back-enders in a big roller in Ikes Falls.

To reach this run from Arcata, drive east on Route 299 to Willow Creek. Turn north here and drive 47 miles to Somes Bar.

The easiest put-in is at the Ishi Pishi bridge, below Somes Bar. Ishi Pishi Falls, upstream around the bend, is worth looking at, either from the turnout at Somes Bar or at river level.

The take-out is at Orleans, downriver 7 miles on Route 96 from Somes Bar.

—LH

For 2 additional Klamath River runs, see pages 243 and 245.

SCOTT RIVER

DIFFICULTY	FLOW	OPTIMUM	MILES	PORTAGES
III-V–	500-2000	1500	13.8	0
IV-V	2000-4000			

PUT IN:	**Indian Scotty Campground (2,460 ft.)**
TAKE OUT:	**Scott Bar (1,660 ft.)**
SHUTTLE:	**14 miles**
RAFTS:	**YES (below Kelsey Creek)**
AVERAGE GRADIENT:	**58 fpm**
GAUGE:	**Runnable when *Klamath at Orleans* is between 5,000 and 10,000 cfs (flow phone).**
BOATING SEASON:	**Winter Spring**
WATER SOURCE:	**Natural Natural**
USFS and *TOPO MAPS*:	**Klamath NF; *Scott Bar* (7.5 series)**

The Scott River is interesting in that, although it originates on the northeastern flank of the Trinity Mountains, it also drains much of the northern Marble Mountains. After meandering through the Scott Valley, the river cuts generally northwest and descends sharply to the Klamath River. It is in this area, along the northeastern fringe of the Marble Mountains, that the Scott exhibits some great whitewater.

By starting near Indian Scotty, one can run the mile of class IV-V rapids above Kelsey Creek. This steepest section of the Scott is class V at high water and at some levels requires a portage. Most of this stretch can be seen from the road.

Below Kelsey Creek the canyon deepens, and the next 10 miles contain many exhilarating rapids. Some of these should be scouted, and verge on class V at higher flows.

From Yreka, 30 miles south of the Oregon border on I-5, go 17 miles southwest on Route 3 to Fort Jones. Just south of town, turn right on Scott River Road and drive 14 miles to Indian Scotty Campground. The take-out is 14 miles farther along, at the bridge in the town of Scott Bar.

—LH

MIDDLE FORK SMITH RIVER

DIFFICULTY	FLOW	OPTIMUM	MILES	PORTAGES
III+	500-1000	1500	8.4	0
III-IV	1000-2500			

PUT IN:	Patrick Creek (800 ft.)
TAKE OUT:	Gasquet (325 ft.)
SHUTTLE:	8.5 miles
RAFTS:	YES (above 1,000)
AVERAGE GRADIENT:	57 fpm
GAUGE:	Divide the flow at *Smith at Jedediah Smith State Park* by 3 for a rough estimate (flow phone).
BOATING SEASON:	Winter Spring
WATER SOURCE:	Natural Natural
USFS and *TOPO MAPS*:	Six Rivers NF; *Gasquet* (15 series)

This river is the most ravaged of the three forks of the Smith. Erosion from road cuts and bridge construction, along with debris from bridges downed in major floods, has greatly altered the natural state of this river. Reinforcing steel from this wreckage poses a hazard. In many places, the banks are plastered with cement to retard further erosion.

There are many good rapids on this run, and, if one can tolerate the devastation, it can be quite enjoyable. Practically the whole run can be seen from the road, so I won't go to lengths describing what can be seen at a glance. The biggest rapid on the run is just below the first bridge, about 2.5 miles below Patrick Creek.

Less than a mile upstream from the put-in is a gorge that can be partially scouted from the road. Mike Schlax and Lynn Myers ran this in 1981 and reported it to be easy class V.

To reach the put-in, go 4 miles north on U.S. 101 from Crescent City to Route 199. From here it is 15 miles to Gasquet, the first several miles of which go through Jedediah Smith State Park. Continue up Route 199 to Patrick Creek.

—*LH*

NORTH FORK SMITH RIVER

DIFFICULTY	FLOW	OPTIMUM	MILES	PORTAGES
III-IV	800-2000	1500	13.3	0
IV-V–	2000-4000			

PUT IN:	Low Divide Road (875 ft.)
TAKE OUT:	Gasquet (325 ft.)
SHUTTLE:	42 miles (dirt)
RAFTS:	YES (above 1,500)
AVERAGE GRADIENT:	41 fpm
GAUGE:	Divide the flow at *Smith at Jedediah Smith State Park* by 3 for a rough estimate (flow phone).
BOATING SEASON:	Winter Spring
WATER SOURCE:	Natural Natural
USFS and *TOPO MAPS*:	Six Rivers NF; *Gasquet, Crescent City* (15 series)

At times on the North Smith River, the water is so transparent and free of telltale ripples that the boater has the feeling of flying in a kayak a few feet above a dry gravel bed.

This fantastic river flows through beautiful scenery. Rapids alternate between narrow gorges and wide-open boulderfields. The drive to the put-in is long, although the run is well worth the effort.

To reach the put-in, go west on Rte. 199 from Gasquet, and turn north on 197 in 11 miles. Follow this 2.5 miles to Low Divide Road. Turn right here and go about 8 miles to a "T" intersection, the junction with Rowdy Creek Road. Turn right here and go up past Wimer Springs, over the divide, and down to the bridge across the North Smith.

The best take-out is on the left at the confluence of the North and Middle Smith rivers in Gasquet.

—LH

SMITH RIVER (Oregon Hole Gorge)

DIFFICULTY	FLOW	OPTIMUM	MILES	PORTAGES
III-IV+	800-4000	2500	5.2	0

PUT IN: Route 199 Bridge (260 ft.)
TAKE OUT: South Fork Road (110 ft.)
SHUTTLE: 5.2 miles
RAFTS: YES (Scout the gorge!)
AVERAGE GRADIENT: 29 fpm
GAUGE: Two-thirds of the flow reported at *Smith at Jedediah Smith State Park* is a rough estimate (flow phone).
BOATING SEASON: Winter Spring Fall
WATER SOURCE: Natural Natural Natural
USFS and *TOPO MAPS*: Six Rivers NF; *Hiouchi* (7.5 series)

The Smith River cuts through a final gorge before joining the South Smith and meandering to the Pacific Ocean. The flush through the Oregon Hole Gorge is a classic stretch that has surely caught the eye of all but the most mesmerized motorist careening down Route 199.

The 4-plus miles below the put-in contain several class III rapids—plenty of warm-up material for the gorge below. This half-mile-long gorge contains several constricted rapids, ranging from class III+ to IV+, depending on the water level. One can also put in 2.5 miles above the stated put-in bridge, at the North Smith confluence in Gasquet. There are a few good playspots in this section.

This short, attractive run is reached by driving some 16 miles east on Route 199 from Crescent City to the second crossing of the Main Smith River.

The take-out is shortly below the gorge at the bridge that crosses over to the South Fork. A steep trail leads up to the road on the right.

—*LH*

SOUTH FORK SMITH RIVER

DIFFICULTY	FLOW	OPTIMUM	MILES	PORTAGES
III-IV	800-1200	1000	13.7	0

PUT IN:	**Fourth Bridge (545 ft.)**
TAKE OUT:	**First Bridge (100 ft.)**
SHUTTLE:	**13.7 miles**
RAFTS:	**YES (above gorge)**
AVERAGE GRADIENT:	**32 fpm**
GAUGE:	**Divide the flow at *Smith at Jedediah Smith State Park* by 3 for a rough estimate (flow phone).**
BOATING SEASON:	**Winter Spring**
WATER SOURCE:	**Natural Natural**
USFS and *TOPO MAPS*:	**Six Rivers NF; *Ship Mtn., Gasquet* (15 series); *Hiouchi* (7.5 series)**

The water in this stream, like the North Smith, is incredibly clear in spring and summer. The rapids are mostly short and of moderate drop, none of them particularly prominent.

The last mile of this run is through a class IV gorge with vertical rock walls. Upriver 1.5 miles from the take-out is a weigh station on the left. A trail leads down to the river here, just above the gorge. Look at this alternate take-out if you aren't planning to run the gorge.

Embarkation and disembarkation sites are possible along most of this run. Just upstream of the fourth bridge across the Smith River, a short road leads to the river. This is a good starting point.

The take-out below the gorge is on the right, below the bridge, and just above the confluence with the Main Smith River.

The South Smith is approached in the same manner as is the Middle Smith, except one goes only 8 miles from U.S. 101 instead of all the way to Gasquet. There are signs pointing the way to South Fork Road. Cross the Main Smith and then the South Fork in a few hundred yards.

— LH

Coast Range Rivers
East Slope

GRINDSTONE CREEK

DIFFICULTY	FLOW	OPTIMUM	MILES	PORTAGES
III+	500-1000	1500	12	1
III-IV	1000-2500			

PUT IN:	Grindstone Road (1,190 ft.)
TAKE OUT:	Road 306 (650 ft.)
SHUTTLE:	18 miles (6 miles dirt)
RAFTS:	NO (brush, portage)
AVERAGE GRADIENT:	45 fpm; 75 fpm in miles 1-4
GAUGE:	No gauge, recent storm, logical deduction, blind luck.
BOATING SEASON:	Winter
WATER SOURCE:	Natural
USFS and *TOPO MAPS*:	Mendocino NF; *Elk Creek* (15 series)

Grindstone Creek, east of the divide between the Middle Eel and Black Butte rivers, offers a good introduction to the drier east slope of the coast range. Here, precipitation supports much less vegetation; manzanita, buck brush and digger pine are the chief photosynthesizers. Nonetheless, Grindstone and the rivers around it have good whitewater and are usually boatable after sizeable storms.

After perhaps 4 miles of wonderful class III water, one comes to a portage. In another 4 miles, the canyon opens up and the river is flat and swift to the bridge. Just upstream of this take-out bridge is a small dam, usually runnable after inspection.

To reach the put-in from I-5, take the Willows exit and go west 21 miles on Route 162 to Road 306. Turn right and go 3.5 miles to Alder Springs Road. Turn left and go just over 11 miles to where the road makes a sharp swing to the left (SW). In this vicinity, the Grindstone Road takes off to the right, following Long Point Ridge to the north, down into the canyon. This dirt road switchbacks to the river in 6 miles, descending over 2,000 feet. On my run, the road was blocked by slides 0.5 mile before the river, obliging me to walk this distance.

The take-out is 1 mile north of the Alder Springs turnoff, on Road 306.

—LH

STONY CREEK (Fouts Springs to Dam)

DIFFICULTY	FLOW	OPTIMUM	MILES	PORTAGES
IV	500-1500	1200	5	0
IV+	>1500			

PUT IN: Fouts Springs (1,620 ft.)
TAKE OUT: Diversion Dam (1,300 ft.)
SHUTTLE: 5.6 miles
RAFTS: YES (note dam at take-out)
AVERAGE GRADIENT: 65 fpm
GAUGE: No gauge, recent storm. If *Cache Creek at Rumsey* is booming, you can bet this will be too (flow phone).
BOATING SEASON: Winter
WATER SOURCE: Natural
USFS and *TOPO MAPS*: Mendocino NF; *Fouts Springs, Gilmore Peak, St. John Mtn., Stonyford* (7.5 series)

This run is really a big creek. There are some good class IV rapids and some brushy class II shoals. Overall, I'd say it's worth doing a couple of times for a change of pace. The scenery is pleasant, with few man-made intrusions. The dam at the take-out has moving water right to the lip; at high water this could be particularly dangerous. Be sure to scout the take-out before embarking.

To reach Stony Creek, go west on Sites-Lodoga Road from Maxwell at I-5. Drive 23 miles to Lodoga, turn right on Lodoga-Stonyford Road, and go 8 miles to Stonyford. It is possible to approach via Bear Creek Valley (from Hwy. 20), but this road is rough. To reach the take-out, drive west from the thriving metropolis of Stonyford on Fouts Springs Road. After 3.2 miles, you'll reach a public campground. The take-out is just down the hill. Be sure to scout the approach to the dam before putting in. To get to the put-in, continue west on Fouts Springs Road until you reach the bridge across Mill Creek. You can put in here, or continue downstream to any of the other potential put-ins.

—*CS*

CACHE CREEK (Rowboat Rapid Run)

DIFFICULTY	FLOW	OPTIMUM	MILES	PORTAGES
II+	500-1000	2000	6	1
III	1000-3000			
IV	>5000			

PUT IN: Bear Creek (630 ft.)
TAKE OUT: Boy Scout Camp (460 ft.)
SHUTTLE: 6 miles
RAFTS: YES (popular with tubers in summer)
AVERAGE GRADIENT: 28 fpm
GAUGE: ***Cache Creek at Rumsey*** **is 2 miles below the take-out (flow phone).**

BOATING SEASON:	**Winter**	**Spring**	**Summer**
WATER SOURCE:	**Spill**	**Irrigation/Spill**	**Irrigation**

AAA and *TOPO MAPS*: **North Bay Counties; *Rumsey*, *Glascock Mountain* (7.5 series)**

Cache Creek is a classic winter run. The combination of low elevation, reliable flows, and close proximity to the San Francisco and Sacramento areas draws multitudes of paddlers to the creek on winter weekends. The overall good access to the road from the river (in case of an ever-lurking wipeout) and the easy shuttle further enhance the run. During the rainy season, the flow can vary from 1,000 cfs to ten grand—*yahoo!*

The nature of Cache Creek changes radically with the flow. During the summer months, the water is low (500 cfs) and lukewarm. I've done the run once in these conditions and barely recognized the place. At this level, the run is class II overall and Rowboat (the rapids just below the bridge) is a class III. A fair number of beginners paddle the river under these conditions. There is also a raft rental concession which disgorges a large number of unguided *kamikaze* rafts. Personally, I've sworn never to return during the summer months, and I haven't been back when the air temperature exceeded 70 degrees F. I prefer to shoot the shoals the day after a big storm when the river is flowing high (4,000 to 8,000 cfs). At this level, I'd call the run class IV. At moderate flows, 1,500 to 3,000, it's a strong III; Rowboat is an easy IV. At all but the highest flows, one must keep one's eyes peeled for the low water bridge; it's 2.9 miles below the put-in. At moderate flows a vicious river-wide hydraulic forms. Although foolish daredevils (myself included) shoot the bridge hole, there is an easy portage on the right.

At my favorite flow, around 5,000 cfs, the rapids are fairly continuous affairs with big bouncy waves. There are a few good riding holes and, for those so inclined, some excellent surfing waves. At this level, the trees are just entering the water, but they aren't a major concern. At high flows, 8,000 to 10,000, the trees effectively guard the shoreline against swimming paddlers. Please don't swim.

To get to the take-out, drive 2.1 miles west of the tiny little "town" of Rumsey until you see an old abandoned stone house on the right. There is ample parking and good access to the river. I've been told that this was/is an old Boy Scout Camp (Camp Haswell). To get to the put-in, drive upstream on Hwy. 16, 6 miles to the confluence of Bear Creek and Cache Creek. There is adequate parking here on the left side of the road. This is private property—I've had no problems, but please be forewarned. You have missed the put-in if the road leaves the main creek (i.e., Cache) and follows the much smaller Bear Creek.

—*CS*

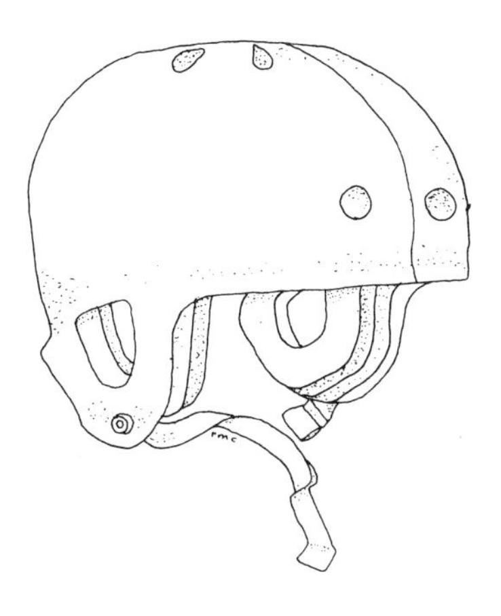

PUTAH CREEK (Hwy. 29 to Lake Berryessa)

DIFFICULTY	FLOW	OPTIMUM	MILES	PORTAGES
IV	1000-2000	3000	16	0
IV+	2000-6000			
V−	>6000			

PUT IN: Hwy. 29 bridge (960 ft.)
TAKE OUT: Lake Berryessa (460 ft.)
SHUTTLE: 15 miles
RAFTS: NO (too brushy except at high flows)
AVERAGE GRADIENT: 32 fpm
GAUGE: No gauge, recent storm. If *Cache Creek at Rumsey* is booming, go for it (flow phone).
BOATING SEASON: Winter
WATER SOURCE: Natural
AAA and *TOPO MAPS*: North Bay Counties; *Lower Lake*, *Morgan Valley* (15 series)

Don't be fooled by the low average gradient. This creek has some awesome rapids! I've only shot the run at high flow (about 10,000 cfs) and it was great, but it bordered on class V. There are some giant drops. There are also some long stretches of class I water, hence the low average gradient. At lower flows, 500 to 1,500 cfs, some of the rapids are a maze of willows. Many good stories have been generated by the Putah's infamous class IV willow rapids; be careful when entering a willow jungle.

The scenery is pleasant low rolling hills that are sparsely wooded; an occasional black rock outcropping can be seen. The impact of man is minimal, and most of the run is unblemished. Bald eagles are often observed on the lower half of the river.

The put-in is the Hwy. 29 bridge over the river. It's 4 miles north of Middletown. There is good parking on the river left. The take-out is found by driving 3 miles back towards Middletown, to Butts Canyon Road. Turn left here and drive 10.5 miles. Turn left on Snell Valley Road, and go 1.5 miles to the river/reservoir. Please respect the private property at the take-out.

—*CS*

Sierra Nevada Rivers
West Slope

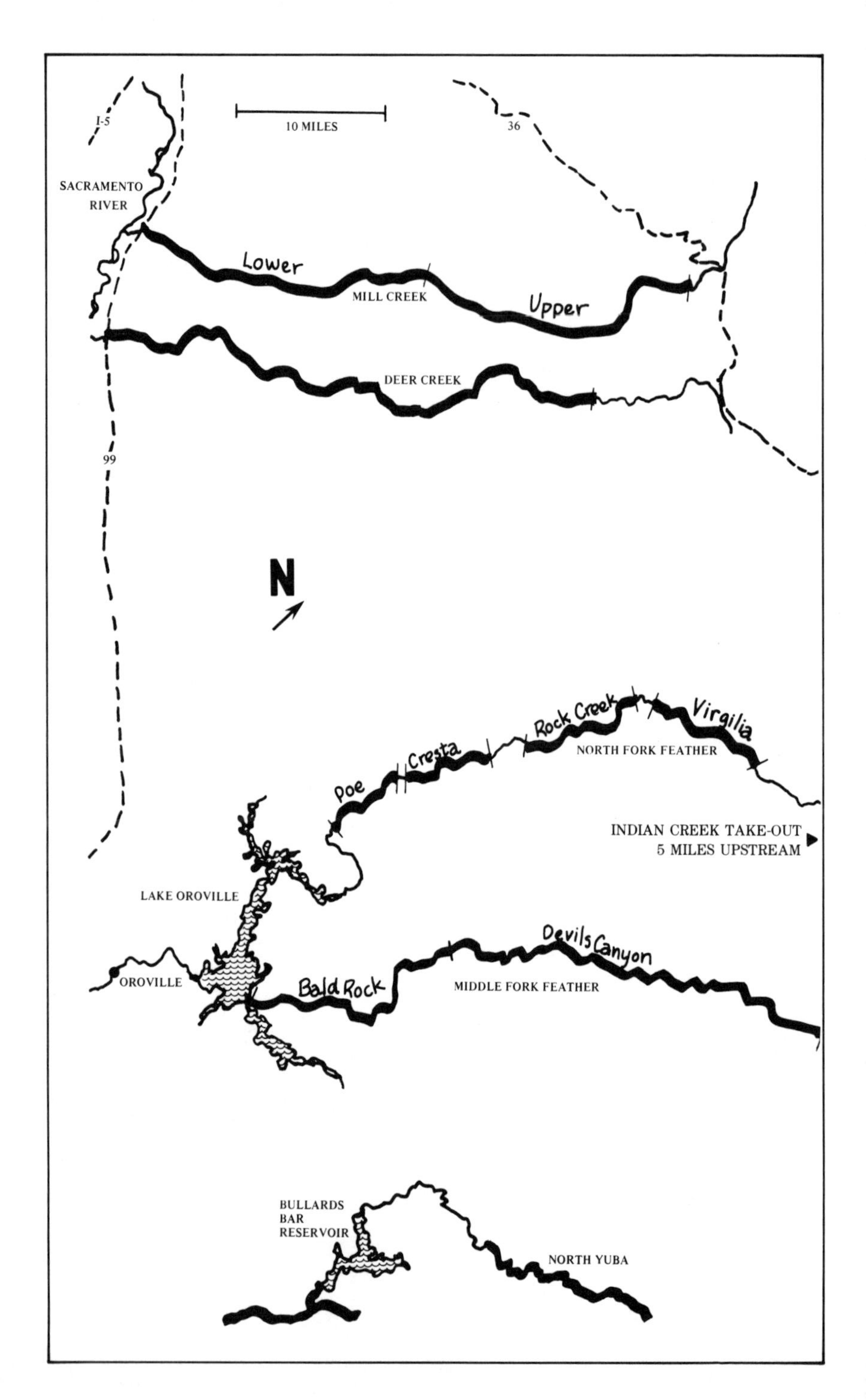

I-5
10 MILES
36
SACRAMENTO
RIVER
Lower
MILL CREEK
Upper
DEER CREEK
99
N
Rock Creek
Virgilia
Cresta
NORTH FORK FEATHER
Poe
INDIAN CREEK TAKE-OUT
5 MILES UPSTREAM
LAKE OROVILLE
Devils Canyon
OROVILLE
Bald Rock
MIDDLE FORK FEATHER
BULLARDS
BAR
RESERVOIR
NORTH YUBA

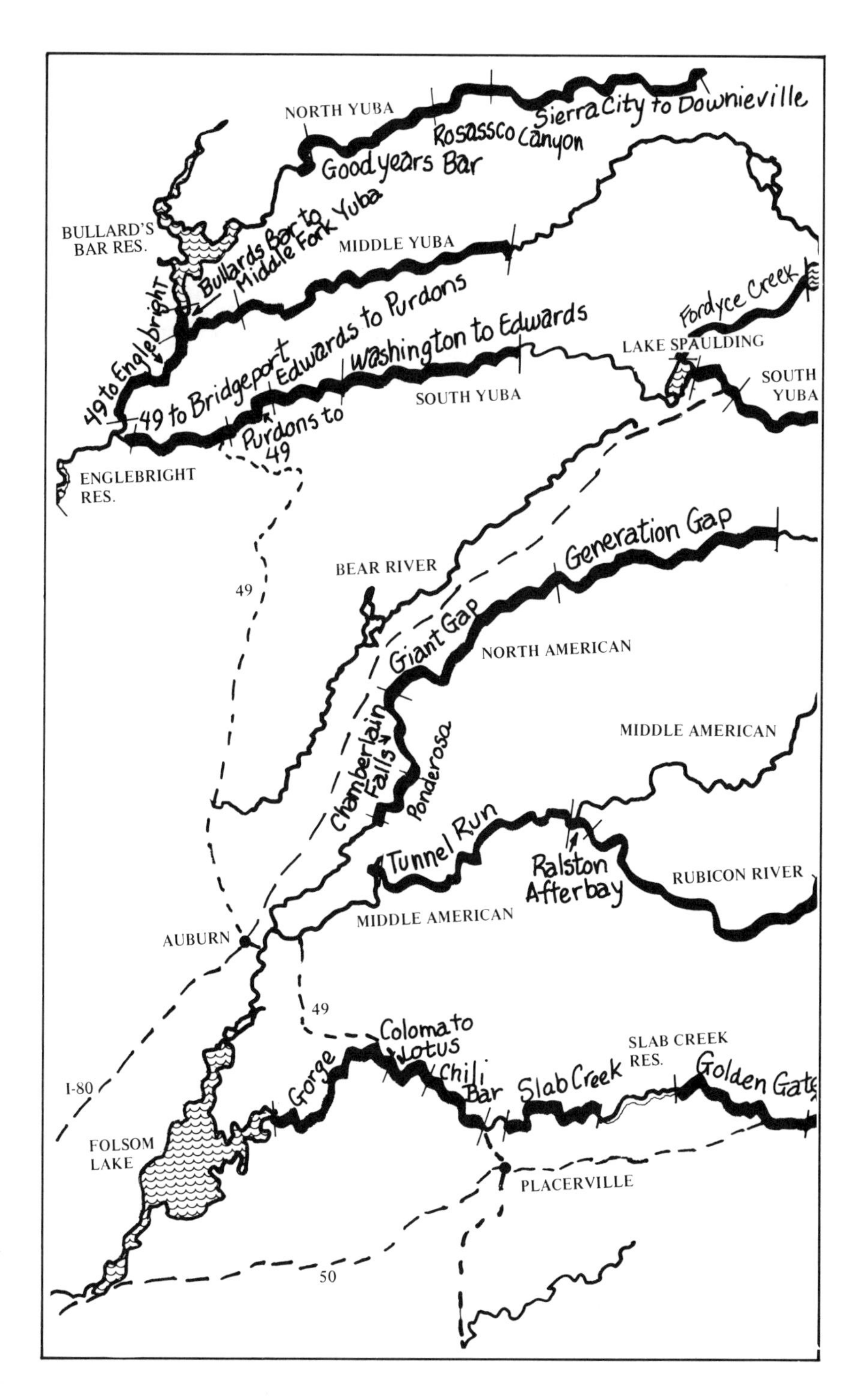
NORTH YUBA
Sierra City to Downieville
Rosassco Canyon
Good years Bar
BULLARD'S BAR RES.
Bullards Bar to Middle Fork Yuba
MIDDLE YUBA
49 to Englebright
Edwards to Purdons
Washington to Edwards
Fordyce Creek
LAKE SPAULDING
SOUTH YUBA
49 to Bridgeport
SOUTH YUBA
Purdons to 49
ENGLEBRIGHT RES.
Generation Gap
BEAR RIVER
49
Giant Gap
NORTH AMERICAN
MIDDLE AMERICAN
Chamberlain Falls
Ponderosa
Tunnel Run
Ralston Afterbay
RUBICON RIVER
MIDDLE AMERICAN
AUBURN
49
Coloma to Lotus
SLAB CREEK RES.
Gorge
Chili Bar
Slab Creek
Golden Gate
I-80
FOLSOM LAKE
PLACERVILLE
50

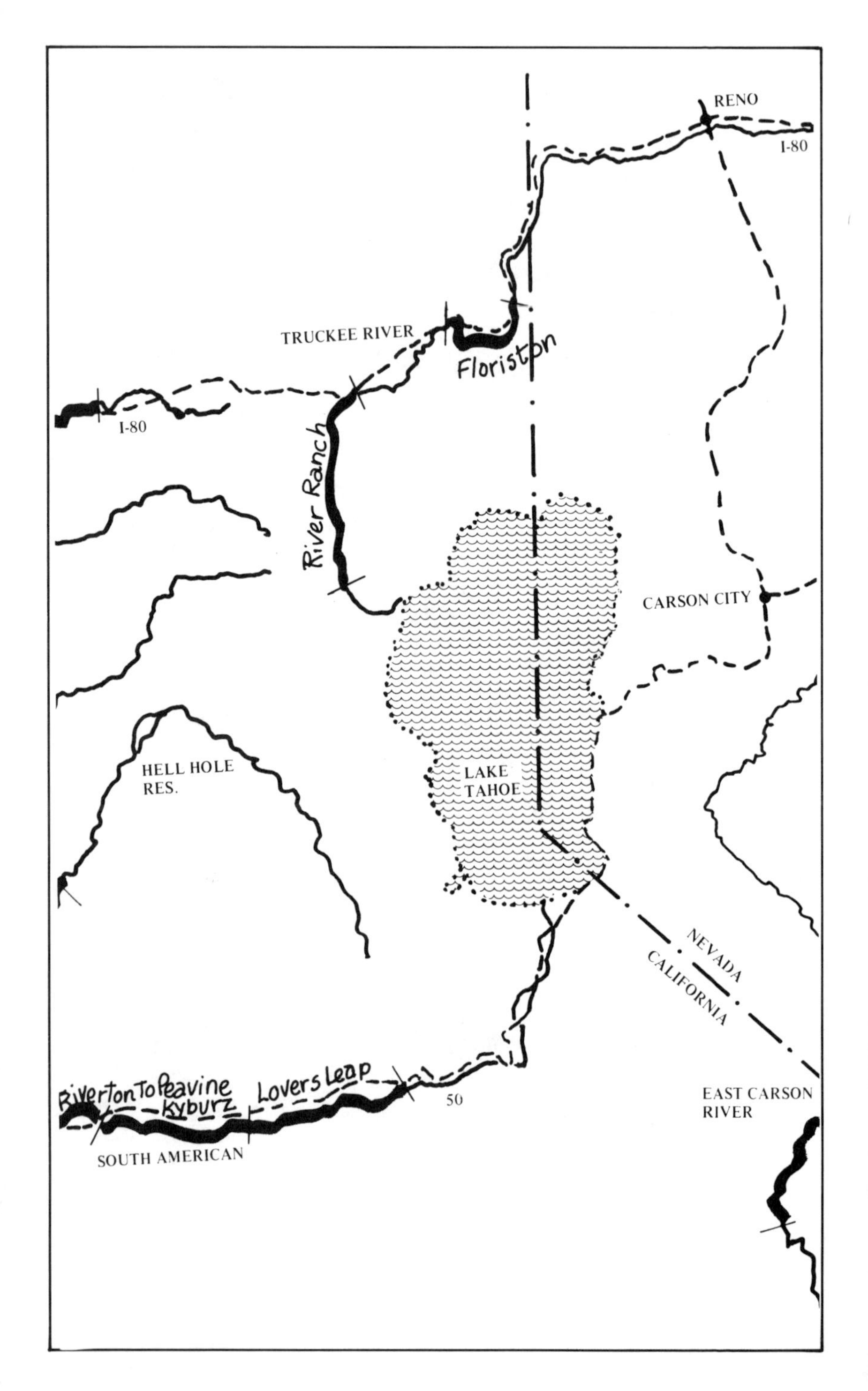
RENO
I-80
TRUCKEE RIVER
Floriston
I-80
River Ranch
CARSON CITY
HELL HOLE
RES.
LAKE
TAHOE
NEVADA
CALIFORNIA
Riverton To Peavine
Kyburz
Lovers Leap
50
EAST CARSON
RIVER
SOUTH AMERICAN

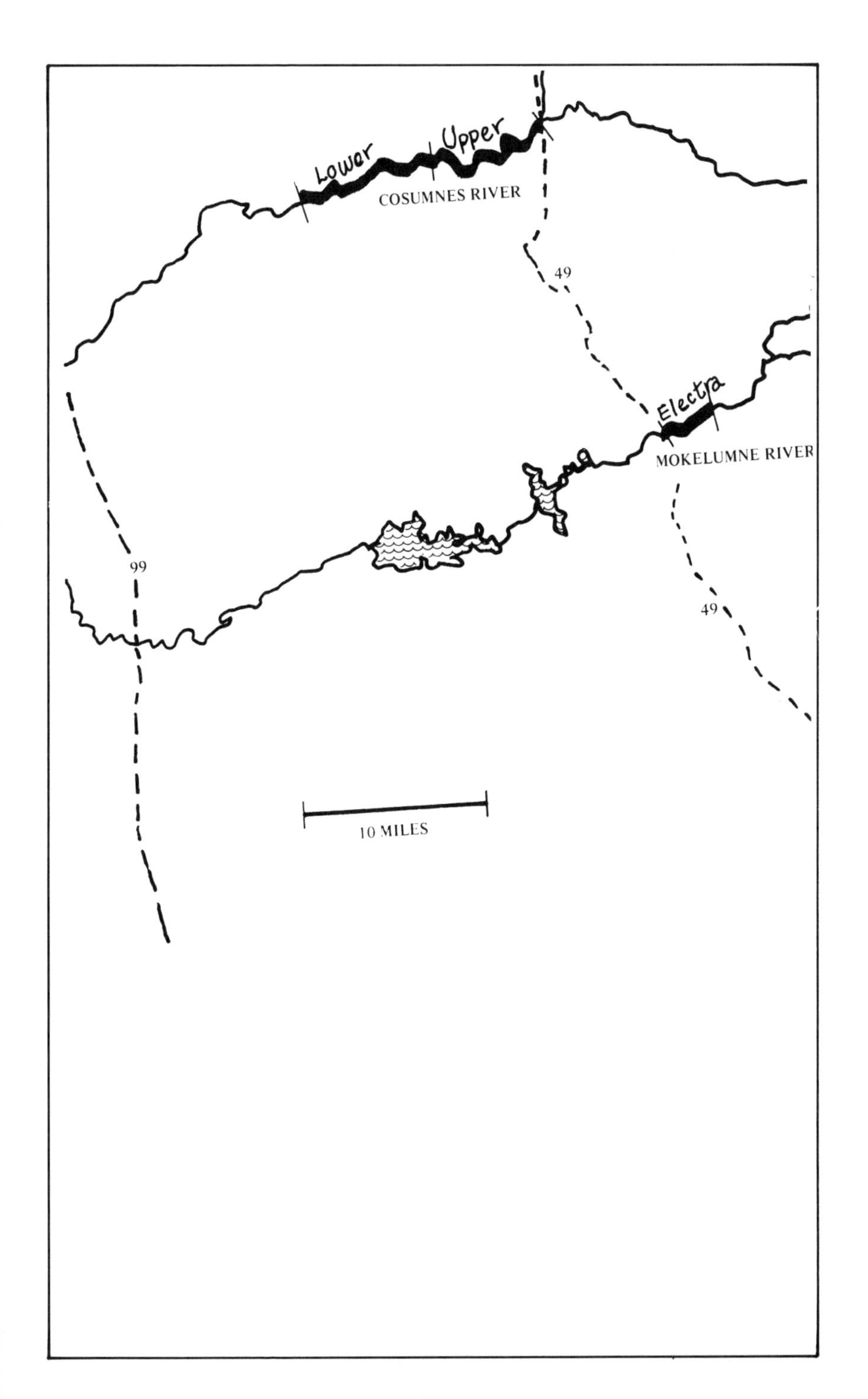
Lower
Upper
COSUMNES RIVER
49
Electra
MOKELUMNE RIVER
99
49
10 MILES

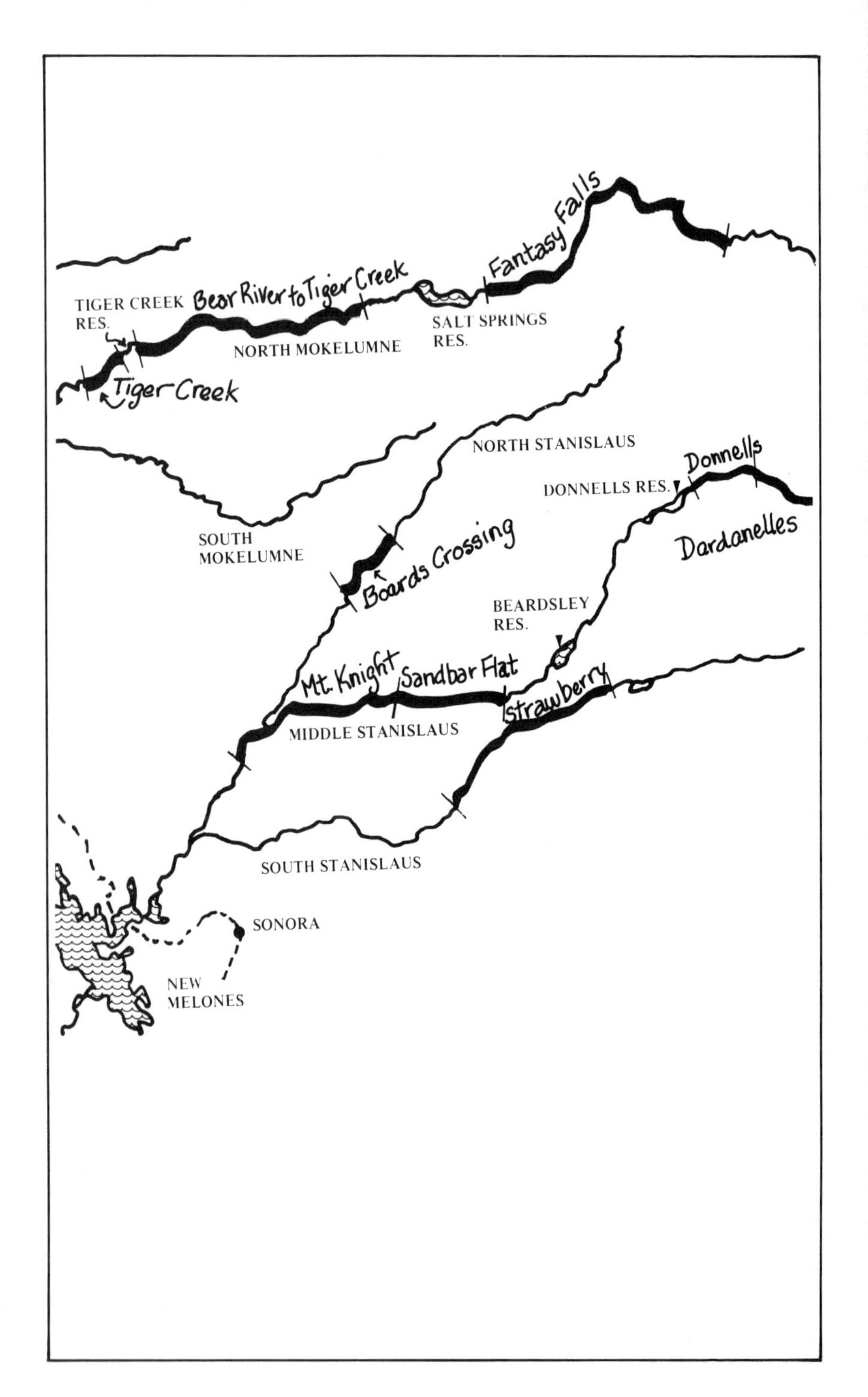
Fantasy Falls
Bear River to Tiger Creek
TIGER CREEK
RES.
SALT SPRINGS
RES.
NORTH MOKELUMNE
Tiger Creek
NORTH STANISLAUS
Donnells
DONNELLS RES.
SOUTH
MOKELUMNE
Boards Crossing
Dardanelles
BEARDSLEY
RES.
Mt. Knight
Sandbar Flat
Strawberry
MIDDLE STANISLAUS
SOUTH STANISLAUS
SONORA
NEW
MELONES

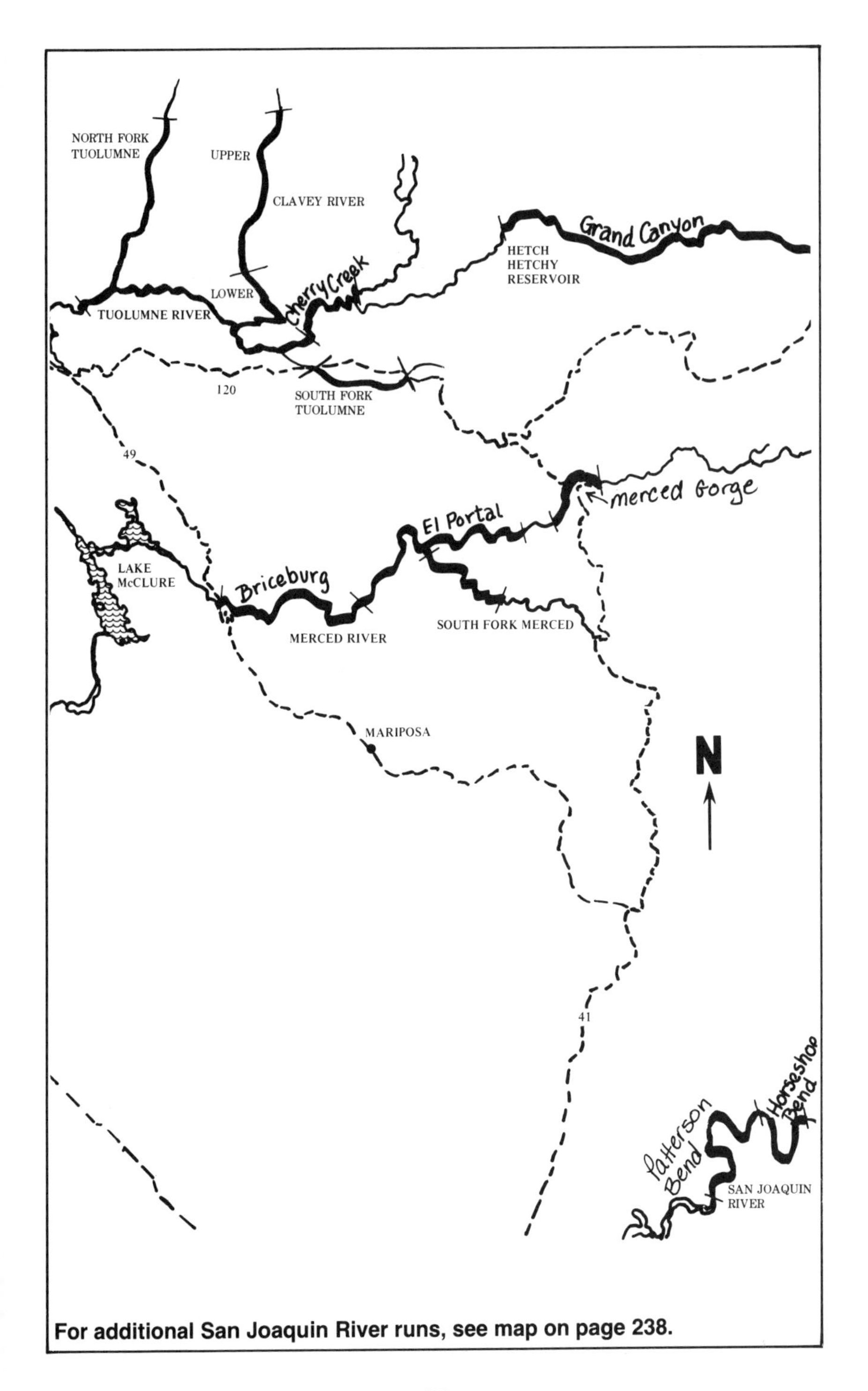

For additional San Joaquin River runs, see map on page 238.

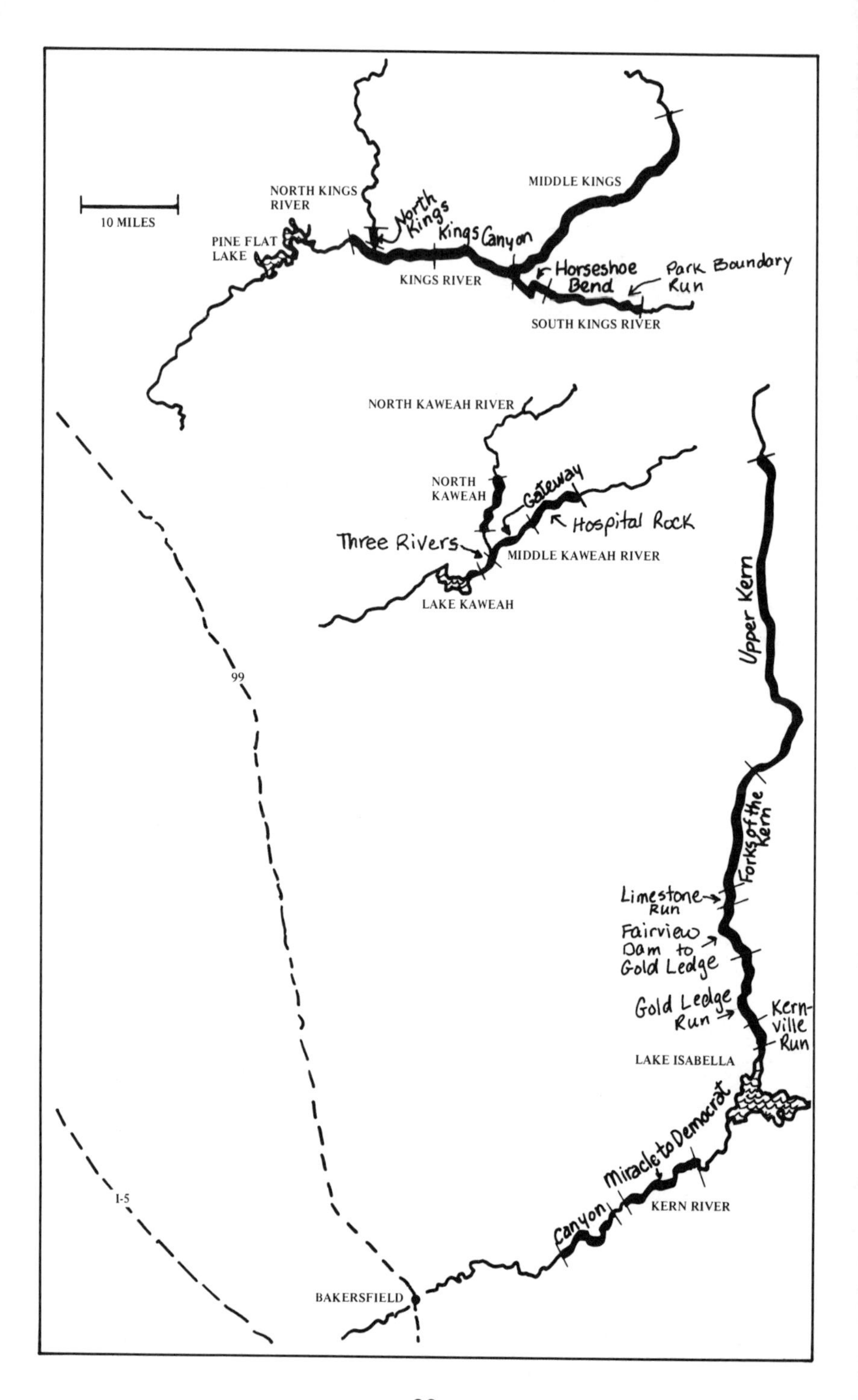
10 MILES
NORTH KINGS RIVER
PINE FLAT LAKE
North Kings
Kings Canyon
MIDDLE KINGS
KINGS RIVER
Horseshoe Bend
Park Boundary Run
SOUTH KINGS RIVER
NORTH KAWEAH RIVER
NORTH KAWEAH
Gateway
Hospital Rock
Three Rivers
MIDDLE KAWEAH RIVER
LAKE KAWEAH
99
Upper Kern
Forks of the Kern
Limestone Run
Fairview Dam to Gold Ledge
Gold Ledge Run
Kern-ville Run
LAKE ISABELLA
Miracle to Democrat
Canyon
KERN RIVER
I-5
BAKERSFIELD

SACRAMENTO RIVER (Box Canyon)

DIFFICULTY	FLOW	OPTIMUM	MILES	PORTAGES
IV−	400-1000	800	7.5	0
IV	1000-1500			
IV+	>1500			

PUT IN: Box Canyon Dam (3,020 ft.)
TAKE OUT: Dunsmuir (2,320 ft.)
SHUTTLE: 7 miles
RAFTS: YES (note put-in)
AVERAGE GRADIENT: 93 fpm
GAUGE: The *Release from Lake Siskiyou* is just above the put-in (flow phone).
BOATING SEASON: Spring
WATER SOURCE: Spill
AAA and *TOPO MAPS*: NE and NW California; *Dunsmuir*, *Weed* (15 series)

Box Canyon is a wonderful class IV run through a vertical-walled gorge. The walls tower several hundred feet over the river for the first couple of miles; within these confines, the river drops over many class IV rapids. Due to steep walls, the water level has a great effect on the difficulty; above 1,000 cfs, the river gets very exciting. Below the gorge, the river drops continuously over class II and III rapids and the scenery is very pleasant. No one will soon forget paddling behind Mossbrae Falls, a beautiful fern-covered spring that showers into the river.

To get to the put-in, drive north on I-5 from Dunsmuir, and take the Central Mt. Shasta exit. Turn left and go over the freeway to Old Stage Road. Turn left here (south) and follow it to where W. A. Barr Road forks off to the right. There are signs here for Lake Siskiyou. Two-tenths of a mile before the dam, turn left on the only dirt road that leads off at ninety degrees from the pavement. At the three-way split, take the middle road. Following this, turn right at the next intersection and drive to a small parking spot in view of a boulder-covered slope (to hinder erosion). Follow the trail down and along the base of this to its end. Then go down a steep trail to an iron ladder that brings one to river level. There are many available take-outs near Dunsmuir. I've taken out below the I-5 bridge on the river right. Use your own good judgment on this one.

—*CS*

SACRAMENTO RIVER (Dunsmuir to Castle Crags)

DIFFICULTY	FLOW	OPTIMUM	MILES	PORTAGES
III	500-1500	1000	5	0
III+	1500-2500			
IV	>2500			

PUT IN: Dunsmuir (2,300 ft.)
TAKE OUT: Castle Crags (2,060 ft.)
SHUTTLE: 5 miles
RAFTS: YES
AVERAGE GRADIENT: 48 fpm
GAUGE: The *Release from Lake Siskiyou* is 8 miles above the put-in. Figure on this plus a bit from seepage, etc. (flow phone).
BOATING SEASON: Spring
WATER SOURCE: Natural/Spill
USFS and *TOPO MAPS*: Shasta NF; *Dunsmuir* (15 series)

This is a nice little run that flows through metropolitan Dunsmuir. In town, there are many small bridges and the shores are formed by rock retaining walls. It reminded me of paddling European rivers. Once out of town, the average scenery is transformed to spectacular by the sight of Mt. Shasta. No one will soon forget seeing the snow-capped peak from river level.

The whitewater is semicontinuous class II with an occasional class III tossed in. The river is a bit brushy in places, but nothing desperate. At high flows (above 1,500 cfs), the brush and low bridges could become hazardous.

To get to the take-out, drive north on I-5 from Lake Shasta until you reach Castle Crags. Get off the freeway and drive to the take-out bridge in Castle Crags. To get to the put-in, continue north on I-5 to Dunsmuir and take the central Dunsmuir exit. Drive north on Dunsmuir Avenue until you cross the put-in bridge.

—*CS*

Richard Montgomery boating without artificial aid. *Lars Holbek*

SACRAMENTO RIVER (Castle Crags to Sims Road)

DIFFICULTY	FLOW	OPTIMUM	MILES	PORTAGES
III (one IV)	500-1500	1000	9	0
IV	>1500			

PUT IN: Castle Crags (2,060 ft.)
TAKE OUT: Sims Flat (1,610 ft.)
SHUTTLE: 10 miles
RAFTS: YES
AVERAGE GRADIENT: 50 fpm
GAUGE: The *Release from Lake Siskiyou* is 15 miles above the put-in. Figure on this plus a bit from seepage, etc. (flow phone).
BOATING SEASON: Spring
WATER SOURCE: Natural/Spill
USFS and *TOPO MAPS*: Shasta NF; *Dunsmuir* (15 series)

This section is a little more challenging than the Dunsmuir run. The main difference is the addition of a couple of "major" rapids of the class IV style. One of the rapids, "Triple Drop," tends towards class V at higher flows (3,000 cfs). There are still some super views of Mt. Shasta to be had from river level.

To get to the put-in, take the Castle Crags exit off I-5 and drive to the bridge. To get to the take-out, drive downstream from Castle Crags to the Sims Road exit. Follow the road to Sims Flat campground.

—*CS*

SACRAMENTO RIVER (Sims Flat to Lake Shasta)

DIFFICULTY	FLOW	OPTIMUM	MILES	PORTAGES
IV	800-3000	1500	13	0

PUT IN: Sims Flat NF Campground (1,610 ft.)
TAKE OUT: Lake Shasta (1,100 ft.)
SHUTTLE: 14 miles
RAFTS: YES
AVERAGE GRADIENT: 40 fpm
GAUGE: The *Release from Lake Siskiyou* is 22 miles above the put-in. Figure on this plus some from seepage and tributaries (flow phone).
BOATING SEASON: Spring
WATER SOURCE: Natural/Spill
USFS and *TOPO MAPS*: Shasta NF; *Dunsmuir, Lamoine* (15 series)

This section is a favorite of class IV cowpokes on their way to and from the big Box Canyon rodeo on the upper reaches of the river. A good idea of what's in store can be had from looking out your window on I-5. Some of the better rapids can't be seen from the road, so mind your "P's" and "Q's."

To get to the take-out at Dog Creek, take the Vollmers exit off I-5. Follow the dirt road down to the bridge across the river. To get to the put-in, continue north on I-5 to the Sims Road exit. Follow the road to the Sims Flat National Forest campground.

—*CS*

Chuck Stanley bronc ridin' at the Trinity River Rodeo, 1984. *Pinky Collamer*

McCLOUD RIVER

DIFFICULTY	FLOW	OPTIMUM	MILES	PORTAGES
III-IV	600-1500	1000	24	2

PUT IN:	**McCloud Reservoir (2,440 ft.)**	
TAKE OUT:	**Lake Shasta (1,020 ft.)**	
SHUTTLE:	**75 miles**	
RAFTS:	**NO**	
AVERAGE GRADIENT:	**59 fpm**	
GAUGE:	**No gauge, but runnable at the peak of the run-off in a normal year.**	
BOATING SEASON:	**Winter**	**Spring**
WATER SOURCE:	**Natural/Spill**	**Spill**
AAA and *TOPO MAPS*:	**NW California; *Shoeinhorse Mtn., Bollibokka Mtn.* (15 series)**	

The McCloud River runs across lava flows in its upper reaches and pours over three spectacular falls not far from the town of McCloud. Below these falls, the river is class II-III until it is impounded by McCloud Reservoir. Below here the river cuts through a beautiful canyon before meeting what used to be the Sacramento River, but is now the McCloud arm of Lake Shasta.

The river is steepest in the first few miles, though the gradient is substantial throughout the run. The problem is finding the river with enough water at the put-in. On our run, only a few hundred cfs were being released from the reservoir, and it was very rocky for several miles. Eventually, side creeks increased the flow, and we had about 800 cfs by the take-out. Both of our portages were in the first few miles, and these would probably be runnable with more water. It would be wiser to make this run after a rainstorm, or when the lake is spilling, for it is a long day at low water.

To find the put-in, go east on Rte. 89 at Mt. Shasta. In 9 miles, at the town of McCloud, turn right at the gas station (south) and go 14 miles to the reservoir. The take-out is reached by turning onto Gilman Road, 38 miles south of Rte. 89 on I-5. It is 14 slow miles to the bridge across the McCloud River, where it is entering Lake Shasta.

—LH

For an additional McCloud River run, see page 247.

MILL CREEK (Upper Run)

DIFFICULTY	FLOW	OPTIMUM	MILES	PORTAGES
V	500-1500	1000	17	1

PUT IN: Town of Mill Creek (4,400 ft.)
TAKE OUT: Ponderosa Way (2,100 ft.)
SHUTTLE: 38 miles (20 miles OK dirt)
RAFTS: NO
AVERAGE GRADIENT: 135 fpm; mi/mi: 100, 100, 150, 90, 50, 90, 220, 180, 190, 220, 210, 170, 140, 90, 100, 110, 110
GAUGE: No gauge, but runnable at the peak of the run-off in a normal year.
BOATING SEASON: Spring
WATER SOURCE: Natural
USFS and *TOPO MAPS*: NE California; *Lassen Peak*, *Butte Meadows* (15 series)

Check out that gradient! This has got to be some of the steepest runnable whitewater in California. The average gradient over the 17 miles is 135 fpm including 5 miles that average 200-plus fpm! When I first looked at this section on the topo maps, I thought, "No way; no how; like never!" I was shocked when I heard that Dennis Johnson and Rob Kirby ran this section in '80 with no portages! I had to check this one out.

After giving up on Deer Creek, because of low water, Walt Garms, Mike Fentress and I decided to investigate the flow on Upper Mill Creek. We arrived at the town of Mill Creek and found only a trickle of water—barely runnable. Having only one car, we searched the nearby campground and found a willing shuttle driver.

Twenty bucks and a few hours of driving found us at the put-in ready to go. Since it was late in the afternoon, we made only about 5 miles before we stopped for the night on a nice little beach.

After a quick breakfast, we were on the water. At our low flow, we were able to boat-scout most of the rapids; occasionally we would get out to look at a steep section. We had a total of 5 portages: 3 were easy, 1 long portage required a hike up the hillside, and the last one, near the take-out, was reasonable.

The final rapid is caused by Black Rock, a monolith around which the river flows. At the base of the rock, the river runs through a steep narrow canyon; a series of ledge holes form the entrance to a bottomless hole at the end of the rapid. The river drops 6 feet into it and recycles for 40! On the first descent, Rob Kirby swam this mess.

After portaging Black Rock Canyon, we were beat; our original goal of Hwy. 99 was a distant 29 miles away and it was 4 o'clock on the second day of our planned 3-day journey. We called it quits. Mike hitched a ride to the car while Walt and I stayed and bummed beers off the local campers.

To get to the put-in, drive east on Hwy. 36 from Red Bluff until you reach Hwy. 172. Take Hwy. 172 to the little town of Mill Creek; this is your last chance to buy life's necessities. After buying your essentials, execute a U-turn and drive about a mile. A substantial dirt road departs to the left (south side of the road), and goes to Hole-in-the- Ground campground. Follow the road a short distance to a fork and take the left-hand turn; the river is a short distance ahead. To get to the take-out, retrace your steps toward Red Bluff. About 10 miles after you turn onto Hwy. 36, you'll come to Ponderosa Way. Turn left and drive a long 20 miles of dirt road to the river.

—CS

MILL CREEK (Ponderosa Way to Hwy. 99)

DIFFICULTY	FLOW	OPTIMUM	MILES	PORTAGES
V	500-1500	1000	30	2 (dams)

PUT IN:	**Ponderosa Way (2,100 ft.)**
TAKE OUT:	**Hwy. 99 (240 ft.)**
SHUTTLE:	**60 miles (20 miles dirt road)**
RAFTS:	**NO**
AVERAGE GRADIENT:	**62 fpm; mi/mi: 60, 100, 110, 60, 90, 90, 90, 100, 90, 80, 90, 80, 60, 50, 70, 70, 60, 50, 40, 40, 50, 60, 50, 70, 15, 15, 40, 40, 35**
GAUGE:	**No gauge, but runnable at the peak of the run-off in a normal year.**
BOATING SEASON:	**Spring**
WATER SOURCE:	**Natural**
USFS and *TOPO MAPS*:	**Lassen NF; *Butte Meadows, Panther Springs, Red Bluff* (15 series)**

The closest I've ever gotten to paddling this section was the shuttle. I had the grand idea of running both the upper and lower sections together in 3 days. By the time we reached Black Rock (Ponderosa Way bridge), take-out for the upper stretch, we were 2 days into our trip and it was painfully obvious that we would never make it down to Hwy. 99 fast enough to return to work on time. We had no desire to repeat Charles Martin's experience of overstaying his welcome on the river, as described in *Sierra Whitewater*. His group planned a 2-day first descent, but required 3. They reported many long portages and many insidious rapids which began easily and ended in boxed-in class VI drops. I figured it would take our group about 2 days to get through it all.

I was surprised when I spoke with Doug Tompkins who ran this section in the spring of '82. He reports no portages, except for 2 around diversion dams in the last 5 miles. I find this hard to believe, in light of Charlie's experience. The combination of plastic kayaks and paddlers not afraid to hit rocks is probably what it took. Their run took 2 days. I imagine that there are many class IV and V drops that will require scouting and perhaps a portage by those possessed by less optimistic judgment or glass boats.

To get to the take-out, drive north from the tiny town of Los Molinos on Hwy. 99. After you cross Mill Creek, turn right on the first road. Take the first right and follow this road a short distance to a bridge on Mill Creek. We left our car here for a weekend and had no problem. This is private property so please be low key. To get to the put-in, drive north on Hwy. 99 to Hwy. 36. Take Hwy. 36 east until you reach Ponderosa Way. Follow this long, dusty dirt road 20 miles to Black Rock Campground.

—*CS*

DEER CREEK

DIFFICULTY	FLOW	OPTIMUM	MILES	PORTAGES
IV-V	600-1200	1000	43	8

PUT IN: Potato Patch Campground (3,400 ft.)
TAKE OUT: Route 99 Bridge (205 ft.)
SHUTTLE: 65 miles
RAFTS: NO
AVERAGE GRADIENT: 74 fpm; 100 fpm for first 17 miles
GAUGE: No gauge, but runnable at the peak of the run-off in a normal year.
BOATING SEASON: Spring
WATER SOURCE: Natural
AAA and *TOPO MAPS*: Feather River and Yuba River Regions; ***Butte Meadows, Panther Spring, Richardson Springs, Corning*** (7.5 series)

The wilderness journey through the Deer Creek Canyon is one of the finest in California. Rarely can one experience a river of such high quality for such a long distance.

During the 16.5 miles to Ponderosa Way, the action is non-stop. In this section, a 30-foot waterfall must be portaged. Ponderosa Way can be reached in one long day, making it possible to get this far without carrying gear. The river continues to plummet, though the gradient gradually tapers off. Much of the canyon scenery is dotted with bizarre lava formations. At certain angles, the weather-beaten pinnacles appear as demons or hunched gargoyles. The experience of descending from 3,400 feet to near sea level is magnificent. Cascading through the forests, snaking through the low foothills, and finally drifting out into the Sacramento Valley makes a memorable trip.

The last 9 miles to Rte. 99 are fairly easy and often shallow. There are a few portages around low dams in this stretch.

To reach the put-in, drive up Route 32 from Chico towards Lassen Park. A few miles beyond Deer Creek is Potato Patch Campground, a bucolic launching place.

The take-out is at the Route 99 bridge, 20 miles north of Chico. It is also possible to take out 3 miles above Route 99 on Leininger Road.

The 9-mile stretch of Deer Creek above Potato Patch is a good class IV, with a portage around a 30-foot waterfall. The gradient is 110 fpm.

—LH

EAST BRANCH NORTH FORK FEATHER RIVER (Virgilia to Belden)

DIFFICULTY	FLOW	OPTIMUM	MILES	PORTAGES
IV–	600-1500	1500	10	0
IV	1500-3000			
IV-V	>3000			

PUT IN: Virgilia (2,680 ft.)
TAKE OUT: Belden (2,280 ft.)
SHUTTLE: 10 miles
RAFTS: YES (note two potential portages)
AVERAGE GRADIENT: 40 fpm
GAUGE: No gauge, but runnable at the peak of the run-off in a big year.
BOATING SEASON: Spring
WATER SOURCE: Natural
USFS and *TOPO MAPS*: Plumas NF; *Almanor* (15 series)

Although I've never actually gotten my backside wet on this section of the Feather, I feel like I'm quite familiar with the river. I've heard plenty of wipe-out stories generated by Five-in-a-Hole and other infamous rapids. My knowledge has been further augmented by a couple of "drinking and driving" scouting trips undertaken when the river was running a fearsome 10,000 cfs. Even with our impaired judgment, we couldn't muster the courage to face Five-in-a-Hole. At high flows, it becomes an unavoidable killer river-wide hole.

It's your good fortune that the road closely follows the entire length of the run; thus, you won't be forced to rely on my beer-augmented memories of the river. The 2 major rapids, which become class V at higher flows, are easily spotted from the highway. At flows in the 500 to 2,500 cfs range, these rapids can be portaged without undue effort on the right. The first of these drops is an irrigated rockpile. The second major rapids, named Five-in-a-Hole (due to five paddlers swimming at once), is a nasty river-wide hole that can be run on the extreme river left. Five-in-a-Hole is about halfway down the run in the steepest part of the canyon. There are a couple of miles of river that break away from the road towards the end of the run. According to my friend, Walt Garms, you'll find some class III rapids.

To get to the take-out, drive east from Oroville on Hwy. 70 until you reach the one-bar town of Belden. The rest area is a good place to take out. To get to the put-in, continue driving 8 more miles on Hwy. 70. Just before Virgilia, there is a picnic table and a 6-foot drop in the river; this is the put-in.

—CS

Ted Anderson ski-jumping Lewis Leap, Cherry Creek. ***Chuck Stanley***

NORTH FORK FEATHER RIVER (Rock Creek Run)

DIFFICULTY	FLOW	OPTIMUM	MILES	PORTAGES
III-IV	800-1500	1500	8	1
IV+	1500-4000			
V	>4000			

PUT IN:	**Rock Creek Dam (2,160 ft.)**
TAKE OUT:	**Rock Creek Powerhouse (1,760 ft.)**
SHUTTLE:	**8 miles**
RAFTS:	**NO**
AVERAGE GRADIENT:	**50 fpm**
GAUGE:	**No gauge, but runnable at the peak of the run-off in a big water year when Rock Creek Dam is spilling (PG&E knows when this happens, if you can get them to tell you).**
BOATING SEASON:	**Spring**
WATER SOURCE:	**Spill**
USFS and *TOPO MAPS*:	**Plumas NF; *Storrie* (7.5 series)**

Rock Creek Dam is the first of a three-dam series on the North Fork. During most of the year, powerhouse diversions render the riverbed between the dams bone dry. It is only during peak run-off that water flows on this section of the river.

With water, this is a wonderful run. There are plenty of fun class IV rapids, all of which are visible from the road. There is a 0.3 mile portage on the road which starts at the silver and black bridges, and ends at a small bridge across the river. The portage is around a big class V+ rapid.

To get to the take-out, drive east from Oroville on Hwy. 70 until you reach Rock Creek Powerhouse. It's at the head of Cresta Dam. The river is very close to the road here.

To get to the put-in, continue east 8 miles on Hwy. 70 to Rock Creek Dam. Park the car just before the left-hand curve; it's a few hundred yards below the dam. From here, follow the developed trail down to the river.

—*CS*

NORTH FORK FEATHER RIVER (Cresta Run)

DIFFICULTY	FLOW	OPTIMUM	MILES	PORTAGES
III-IV	800-1500	1500	6.5	1
IV+	1500-4000		(1.5 on lake)	
V	>4000			

PUT IN: Cresta Dam (1,630 ft.)
TAKE OUT: Poe Dam (1,390 ft.)
SHUTTLE: 6.5 miles
RAFTS: YES (note County Line Hole)
AVERAGE GRADIENT: 48 fpm
GAUGE: Runnable at the peak of the run-off in a big water year when Cresta Dam spills (PG&E knows when this happens, if you can get them to tell you).
BOATING SEASON: Spring
WATER SOURCE: Spill
USFS and *TOPO MAPS*: Plumas NF; *Storrie*, *Soapstone Hill*, *Pulga* (7.5 series)

My only experience with this section of the North Feather is a run at 10,000 cfs. At this level, it's fabulous big water "hair" boating, which consists of crashing waves, pummeling holes and vicious boils. It's big fun.

Fortunately, the road along the river allows a pre-run scout. The major rapids are in the first 2 miles below the Cresta Dam and are visible from the road with one giant exception. There is a killer river-wide hole 1.2 miles downstream of the put-in, which can't be seen from a car on the road. The location of the hole is marked by the county line sign. I strongly recommend scouting County Line Hole from the road. Below here are two more big drops, named Cow Catcher and The Wave. The river is primarily class II and III below the roadside rest area 2.3 miles downstream of the put-in. The only exception is a class IV rapid just above Poe Reservoir.

To get to the take-out, drive east from Oroville on Hwy. 70 until you reach Poe Dam. Take out right next to the dam, on river left, where a dirt road goes to the water.

To get to the put-in, continue east 6.5 miles on Hwy. 70. After crossing Grizzly Creek, drive to the mouth of Elephant Butte Tunnel and park on the left. Walk upstream a short distance to a trail that leads to the river.

—CS

NORTH FORK FEATHER RIVER (Poe Run)

DIFFICULTY	FLOW	OPTIMUM	MILES	PORTAGES
IV+	500-1000	1500	7.5	1
V	>1000			(recommend 2)

PUT IN: Poe Dam (1,360 ft.)
TAKE OUT: Poe Powerhouse (840 ft.)
SHUTTLE: 12 miles (3.5 miles dirt)
RAFTS: NO
AVERAGE GRADIENT: 70 fpm; the two miles below the bridge are 120 fpm.
GAUGE: Runnable at the peak of the run-off in a big water year when Poe Dam spills (PG&E knows when this happens, if you can get them to tell you).
BOATING SEASON: Spring
WATER SOURCE: Spill
USFS and *TOPO MAPS*: Plumas NF; *Pulga, Berry Creek* (7.5 series)

The first and only time I ran this section, we expected a flow of 4,000 cfs. I had visions of giant boat-eating holes, violent suck currents and massive cushions. All previous runs had been made by Bob Porter, et al., at flows in the 3,000-5,000 cfs range. He and I chickened out earlier that spring when we saw 10,000 cfs roaring down the canyon. Our enthusiasm quickly drained when we saw the paltry 1,000 cfs flow — a total dud.

Once on the water, our disappointment turned to amazement as we ran the first big rapid. Even at the low water, it was hard. The drops were steep and rocky, with only brief pools in between. Bob, who had run this rapid at four times the flow, couldn't believe what he saw. We all would have predicted the rapid to be totally unrunnable at the high water Bob had run it.

For the next 2 miles, the surprises continued. Bob would point out his high-water route, usually high on the bank, while we ran some good class V– rapids in the main stream. Approximately 2 miles downstream of the put-in is a giant class VI rapid dubbed "Porter's Portage" by Bob, his stipulation being that the first person to run the drop could re-name it. At 4,000 cfs, the drop is suicide; at 1,000 cfs, it's possible. Gordon Patchin, before whom unrun drops tremble in fear, attacked it with a gleam in his eye. After punching, riding, and fighting several killer holes, Gordon back-ended out of the last with a "*Yahoo!*" We swept aside Porter's Portage and installed Patchin's Passion as the proper name. The drop below Patchin's Passion should be portaged on the left.

After the fireworks of the first few miles, the run peters out to class III. At low flows, this section is a drag; Porter says it's super fun paddling at 4,000 cfs. An added feature at high flows is the wild fluctuation of the flow due to the variable power demand. At a flow of 4,000 cfs, the water can rise or fall 1,000 cfs in a matter of minutes.

To get to the put-in, drive east on Hwy. 70 out of Oroville until you reach Poe Dam. A few hundred yards below the dam, there is an adequate parking area alongside the road. It's a short, but steep hike to the water from here. The take-out is at Poe Powerhouse. Approaching from Oroville, one executes a right turn onto Big Bend Road. About a mile from Hwy. 70, make a left onto the dirt road that leads to Poe Powerhouse; the USFS map is very helpful.

—CS

C. Stanley on the Poe Run. ***Reg Lake***

THE MIDDLE FORK OF THE FEATHER

This is the best multi-day kayaking trip in California. There are 2 runs: The upper is an easy class V and takes 3 days. The lower run is Bald Rock Canyon; it's a hard class V and requires 1 very long day (about 14 hours). The 2 trips can be combined into one super 5-day wilderness trip.

Let me quote from Charlie Martin's *Sierra Whitewater.*

> **I regard the Middle Fork of the Feather River as the most beautiful stream in California . . .. In the 38 miles from Nelson Point to Lake Oroville, the Middle Fork flows through one of the wildest gorges in the United States. Only at one spot, Milsap Bar (six miles above the lake), can ordinary cars be driven down to the river. Several jeep trails can be navigated by four-wheel-drive vehicles, provided their drivers are expert at navigating rough trails pointed straight down a forty-degree slope. Even hiking down these trails is hard, because of the steepness and long distances involved. All roads and trails are badly marked, so check your maps frequently. Despite the difficulty of hiking along the river, it is well worth making at least one trip down to this spectacular canyon. The sculptured rock formations (some overhanging the river), the delicate ledges, and the steep, heavily wooded walls all make this look like the world's prettiest boating run. Alas, there are insurmountable problems, even for the hardy who are willing to carry their boats in and out by steep trails. Below the campground at Milsap Bar, the river cascades over sheets of granite in the famous Bald Rock Canyon. Devils Canyon also has horrendous class VII terrain. Its south rim is a 2,000-foot rock cliff all the way to the river, and even the north bank of the river is a cliff for the first 50 feet. Between these vertical walls, the river drops over 10-foot waterfalls. It would appear that Franklin Canyon may also have unrunnable rapids . . .**

Although the river's rapids have succumbed to plastic kayaks and improved skills, please heed Charlie's comments on the remoteness of the river— hiking out of the canyon would be difficult under the best of circumstances. Please be properly prepared for a wilderness adventure: carry topo and Forestry Service maps, safety equipment, and, most importantly, good judgment.

—*CS*

Curtain Falls, Bald Rock Canyon ***Lars Holbek***

MIDDLE FORK FEATHER RIVER (Devils Canyon)

DIFFICULTY	FLOW	OPTIMUM	MILES	PORTAGES
V−	800–2000	2000	32.5	5
V	>2000			(recommended)

PUT IN: Nelson Point (3,880 ft.)
TAKE OUT: Milsap Bar (1,600 ft.)
SHUTTLE: 125 miles (7 miles OK dirt)
RAFTS: YES (note difficult portages)
AVERAGE GRADIENT: 70 fpm; mi/mi: 30, 30, 40, 60, 50, 50, 40, 70, 110, 100, 100, 40, 40, 60, 80, 80, 70, 80, 80, 110, 90, 60, 70, 70, 85, 45, 50, 90, 65, 70, 45, 60
GAUGE: No gauge, but runnable before or after the peak of the run-off in a normal year.
BOATING SEASON: Spring
WATER SOURCE: Natural
USFS and *TOPO MAPS*: Plumas NF; ***Brush Creek, Cascade, Haskin Valley, Dogwood Peak, Onion Valley, Blue Nose Mountain*** (7.5 series)

This is it! The Middle Fork of the Feather River is the best self-supported wilderness trip in California. The river is deservedly protected by the National Wild and Scenic Rivers Act. The entire length of the run is wilderness: no houses, roads, or people. The scenery is spectacular; the river winds through 3 major canyons, each with its own beauty and character. The first canyon is entered after 8 miles of paddling. It's a steep red rock "V" canyon, with stunted cedar trees climbing the walls that create a surreal beauty. Franklin Canyon follows with its sculpted overhanging walls. Last stands Devils Canyon, an awesome 1,000-foot vertical granite-walled gorge. At the base of the wall is an equally awesome class VI cascade.

In addition to the scenery, there is whitewater "in them thar hills." In general, the river is class III and IV with an occasional class V to spice up the trip. The overall gradient is 70 fpm; the steepest miles are around 110 fpm. There are 3 distinct sections of the river. In the first 10 miles, the rapids are gravel bar affairs which end in 6-foot-high sloping rockpiles. The second section is Franklin Canyon, where the rapids are formed by bedrock and are bordered by rock walls. The third section is Devils Canyon. The rapids are formed by big granite boulders. Overall, the rapids are of the pool and drop type. There are around 10 to 15 (depending on who's counting) easy class V rapids. The portages are evenly spread throughout the trip: one in the first section, two in Franklin Canyon, and two in the Devils Canyon area. All of the portages are short, except the last on the run which is in the heart of Devils Canyon; it's a long (0.3-mile) carry through the bushes around a long, boulder-choked rapid. This last portage is on the right side of the river. A major class V rapid shortly below this portage is another possible portage.

A last note of caution to any thrillseekers out there: Steve Rock discovered that the runnable looking 12-foot waterfall at the beginning of Franklin Canyon isn't recommended. An underwater boulder lurking just downstream of the falls gives the hole added punch.

There are lots of campsites on the run; however, camping life can be very bleak in both Franklin and Devils canyons. I remember spending one desperate night sleeping on a pile of rocks in Devils Canyon.

I've run this section at flows between 500 cfs and 3,000 cfs at the take-out. The lower flow is very rocky, but the rapids are slow; at 2,000 cfs, the river is very nice with fewer rocks, but much faster. Above 3,000 cfs, life would become exciting. The flow at the put-in is much smaller than what you find at the take-out. For the first few miles it is pitiful, but the river picks up water from side creeks. Keep this fact in mind and always check out the flow at the take-out before embarking.

The put-in is found by driving east out of Oroville on Hwy. 70. Just past Quincy is Laporte Road. Turn right and drive 8 miles to a bridge across the river. There is a small campground next to the bridge. The take-out is found by driving east on Hwy. 162 out of Oroville. When you get to Brush Creek, turn right on Bald Rock Road, and about a mile down the road, turn left on Milsap Bar Road. From there, drive 7 miles of dirt road to the river. There is a nice campground across the bridge.

To get to the put-in from the take-out, I recommend driving back to Oroville and taking Hwy. 70. The dirt road short-cut, through Bucks Lake, takes about the same amount of time and will rip guts out of normal cars. I've tried using the dirt road short-cut twice. The first time, the road was covered with snow; the second-time, Walt Garms' Plymouth Duster incurred the wrath of the Road Rock King and suffered removal of its exhaust system and a 5-gallon reduction in gas tank capacity.

—CS

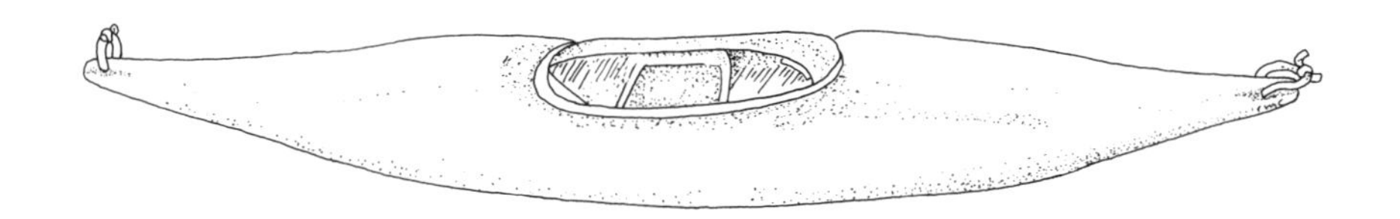

MIDDLE FORK FEATHER RIVER
(Bald Rock Canyon)

DIFFICULTY	FLOW	OPTIMUM	MILES	PORTAGES
V+	600–2500	1400	6.5 (13.3 on lake)	6

PUT IN:	Milsap Bar (1,600 ft.)
TAKE OUT:	Lake Oroville (900 ft.)
SHUTTLE:	26 miles (7 miles OK dirt)
RAFTS:	NO (but it's been done once!)
AVERAGE GRADIENT:	108 fpm; mi/mi: 55, 60, 90, 140, 195, 95, 80
GAUGE:	No gauge, but runnable before or after the peak of the run-off in a normal year. See gauge conversion.
BOATING SEASON:	Spring
WATER SOURCE:	Natural
USFS and *TOPO MAPS*:	Plumas NF; *Brush Creek*, *Forbestown*, *Oroville Dam* (7.5 series)

MILSAP BAR GAUGE CONVERSION

GAUGE	CFS
4.0	0
6.0	850
6.7	1,400
6.8	1,500
6.9	1,550
7.0	1,650
7.8	2,550
10.0	6,850

Bald Rock Canyon is one of the most spectacular canyons in California. Granite walls tower to the sky; awesome rapids dwell in the crotch of the canyon floor. Only real men need apply for passage—quiche eaters will never possess the skills, strength, or sense of purpose to beat Bald Rock Canyon. As of this writing, only a chosen few have accepted the challenge.

Is Bald Rock Canyon worth the trouble? I answer with a resounding, "Yes!" The first 2 miles of the run are pleasant class IV, and Bald Rock Dome provides some fantastic scenery. At the beginning of mile 3, the walls begin to build and rapids grow steeper; a portage or two may be prudent. Mile 4 brings the walls and some mighty rapids which end in Atom Bomb Falls. Below Atom Bomb Falls are several big rapids, followed by Curtain Falls, a river-wide, 30-foot sheer drop. Directly below is the Super Slide, a runnable 10-foot slide into a giant hole. The following mile is very steep, with many class V and VI rapids. The last mile and a half is largely class IV with a couple of easy V's. Believe it or not, you'll probably be glad to see Lake Oroville. The paddle on the lake takes 3 to 4 hours, depending on how tough you are.

When Richard, Lars and I made the first descent of Bald Rock Canyon in April of '80, we portaged 19 times. On our second run, we took 2 days (this was part of a 5-day trip which included the upper section); that time all but 6 of the rapids were run, but each individual made at least 9 portages. All of the rapids, except Atom Bomb Falls, are possible, but not recommended.

First, a word of warning: Do not run Bald Rock Canyon when it reads higher than 6.7 feet on the gauge (1,500 cfs) at Milsap Bar (it's on the river left, a short distance downstream from the bridge). This flow restriction is imposed by a mandatory portage around Atom Bomb Falls, a 40-foot falls formed by apartment house-sized boulders. The portage involves a rappel down a 10-foot waterfall. After getting into the boat, one ferries across the lip of Atom Bomb Falls to continue portaging on the other side. If the flow exceeds 6.7 feet, the rappel and ferry become exceedingly dangerous. Please note that there is no other reasonable option for passage around the falls. Other than Atom Bomb Falls, all the portages are at river level and are relatively safe. Some rapids require expert eddy catching at the lip of class V and VI drops—don't miss the eddy!

To get to the put-in, drive east on Hwy. 162 to the town of Brush Creek. Turn right on Bald Rock Road and go 1 mile to Milsap Bar Road. From there, drive 7 miles of dirt road to the river. There is a nice campground on river left, just across the bridge. The recommended take-out is the campground/boat ramp at Loafer Creek. It's found 1.2 miles west of the Bidwell Bar Bridge (the mini-Golden Gate over the lake) on Hwy. 162. One can also take out at Bidwell Bar Bridge, but the parking is marginal. Be sure to carefully reconnoiter the take-out, as it will probably be dark when you arrive.

—CS

NOTE: The Bald Rock Canyon Run has changed since this writing, particularly Atom Bomb Falls. **See the update on page 91.**

THE FIRST DESCENT OF BALD ROCK CANYON

The day dawned overcast and cool—not ideal weather for a first descent down the most rugged canyon the "hipsters on the move" (Richard Montgomery and the authors) have ever attempted to conquer. True to hip philosophy, we had no shuttle for our planned 1-day, 20-mile run; a 20-mile hitchhike followed by a 7-mile bike ride down the dirt shuttle road waited at the take-out. Richard and Lars remained true to the motto, "Light, lean, and mean"; they carried no overnight gear. I was a bit more realistic and packed a sleeping bag and tarp. At 9:00 a.m., we embarked on the journey.

Just below the put-in, a creek added to the already ample flow, an estimated 1,500 cfs. Much too high for a first descent! The first scout appeared to be an easy rapid with a few punchable holes; much to our dismay, the holes punched us. Our apprehension grew.

Several rapids later, we were at the mouth of the canyon. At this point, we were only 2 miles into the run; this was the last chance to back out. The 3 of us climbed up to survey the rapids that lay ahead. Downstream loomed massive, sheer granite cliffs on both shores, below us lay a class V drop, and overhead dark clouds threatened. We all knew that the next 5 miles would be extremely tough: 2 of the miles dropped 200 feet per mile, the other 3 dropped nearly 100 feet per mile. It was time to make a decision: quit or push on. Fear of the unknown, the high water, and the threatening weather all combined to convince Richard and me to call it quits. We wanted to paddle and carry back to the car and return a better day. Lars declared that he would continue alone. Once again, democracy failed, and we entered the canyon with a tremendous foreboding.

The mood was quickly improved at the humorous sight of Richard windmilling his paddle while doing a vertical nose-stand in the big drop we had just scouted; he looked like a misplaced cartoon character. The rapids grew in frequency and difficulty as we paddled deeper into the canyon. Fortunately, we were able to run or portage, at river level, all of the rapids down to Atom Bomb Falls. This waterfall is bordered by massive, vertical walls, between which, the river plummets 30 feet over megaboulders. The river is solid class V up to the lip of this monster. The portage begins on the right; we carried until we were stopped cold by the walls 40 feet upstream of the lip of the falls. Between the main falls and us lay a 10-foot falls. The only hope of further portage was to get into the

Lars Holbek (on rock), Richard Montgomery and Chuck Stanley doing the rope portage above Atom Bomb Falls on Bald Rock Canyon of the Middle Feather, 1981. *Don Banducci*

pool below the 10-foot falls, and ferry to the opposite shore, on the brink of Atom Bomb Falls. From there, we might be able to continue the portage. From our vantage point, we weren't sure if it would work.

Our first problem was to reach the pool below the 10-foot falls. Next to the right shore, the drop was formed by a large flat boulder; 10 feet from shore lay an exposed round boulder that we could stand on. Our plan was to lower the paddler and then his boat to a small sloping ledge at the base of the large exposed boulder. It was just big enough for a person. From the pool it looked just possible to ferry across the river.

As I lowered myself hand-over-hand down the rope, water cascaded over the falls and onto my head. Once I reached the precarious ledge at the bottom, Lars lowered my boat to me, and I carefully got in without mishap. From there, I began the most frightening ferry of my life. The task was to cross the entire river 10 feet above the lip of the 30-foot falls; to go over was sure death. The river was broken into 3 chutes, separated by boiling eddies behind boulders; each jet went over the falls. At the far shore waited a small eddy whose entrance was guarded by a fence of small rocks. I had to power straight into the eddy.

To cut the suspense—I made it, and discovered the portage on the far shore was good. After me came Richard, using the same technique. While Richard waited in the eddy below, Lars, the rock climber, elected to rappel off the dry boulder while in his kayak! He started lowering himself slowly; however, once over the edge, he lost control and fell, landing on Richard's head. Fortunately, no damage was done and they both completed the tense ferry.

A short distance downstream of Atom Bomb Falls, we encountered a second attraction. Curtain Falls is a 30-foot river-wide vertical waterfall formed in bedrock. Below this waterfall, the river runs over a runnable 150-foot, 20-degree, giant sliding falls into a massive standing hole. We quickly portaged this and the next 10 rapids. A mile below Curtain Falls, we started running some rapids again. We made good time to the lake, arriving half an hour before dark. Where the river met the lake, there was a half-mile-long logjam, the longest any of us had ever seen. We reached the end of the logjam at dark; before us lay 13 miles of paddling (across the lake), and the shuttle.

Nineteen portages and 15 hours after leaving the put-in, we reached the Bidwell Bar Bridge. It was midnight. Running the shuttle was out of the question. Lars and Richard spent a cold night tending a fire made from road signs. I was even a bit chilled in my down sleeping bag. The day dawned none too soon for the cold pair. Lars flagged down a ride and got the shuttle done. We called it a victory as we drove towards home.

—CS

BALD ROCK CANYON UPDATE

Things have changed in Bald Rock Canyon since 1980. In '84 and '85 I ran Bald Rock as high as 2,800 cfs with various groups. At these flows the "regular" rappel-portage was impossible, so we found a new route. Straight across the river from the rappel-portage area is a 10-foot-high vertical drop. We ran this into a boiling pool and "beached" our boats in a narrow channel between the left wall and a boulder. From here begins the portage, easy compared with what's just been accomplished. This route was on its way to becoming standard, as was running Bald Rock at higher flows. The flood of '86 put a stop to that.

Lamentably, the flood of February '86 left the Atom Bomb Falls area more difficult and dangerous than before. At flows between 1,400 cfs and 1,800 cfs the rappel-portage is now nothing short of death-defying. It looks like the strongest paddler would have a 50% chance of making the ferry. Failure would probably be death.

The aforementioned 10-foot-high vertical drop is the only choice, but this too has changed for the worse. The landing from this 10-foot ski-jump is severe. The pool surges unpredictably, due to a greater volume of water coming up from underneath the boulder. The narrow channel, where you must beach your boat, now carries a steady flow of water. Three feet beyond the crack, where you must now wedge the nose of your boat, the water pours into a swirling cauldron. It looks like a huge bathtub drain in action. Big enough for a human to disappear into, but wide enough somewhere for only short sticks to pass completely through. We tested it. Good balance is needed to safely stand up and exit one's boat. To lose balance and pitch into the water could spell curtains. More than ever, I urge anyone interested in this run to attempt it only in the company of someone who knows it well.

On a less foreboding note, Bald Rock Canyon was run twice at low flows in late spring of '86. At these levels (500 cfs–700 cfs) the run is much easier, though rockier. The original rappel-portage at Atom Bomb Falls is easy. No rope work is necessary and the ferry is safe and sane.

—LH

Lars Holbek in Bald Rock Canyon, 1984. ***John Armstrong***

NORTH FORK YUBA RIVER
(Sierra City to Downieville)

DIFFICULTY	FLOW	OPTIMUM	MILES	PORTAGES
IV (one V)	500-1200	1200	13	0
IV+	1200-2500			
V	>2500			

PUT IN:	Bridge near Wild Plum Campground (4,240 ft.)
TAKE OUT:	Downieville (2,820 ft.)
SHUTTLE:	13 miles
RAFTS:	YES (difficult)
AVERAGE GRADIENT:	109 fpm
GAUGE:	The *Inflow to Bullards Bar* is measured at a point about 20 miles below the take-out. You'll have about half this number at the put-in (flow phone).
BOATING SEASON:	Spring
WATER SOURCE:	Natural
USFS and *TOPO MAPS*:	Plumas NF; *Downieville* (7.5 series)

The North Fork of the Yuba River is a classic. The combination of unimpeded flow, excellent rapids, beautiful scenery, plentiful camping, and the quaint little town of Downieville all add up to a super river. Sierra City to Downieville is the best whitewater this river has to offer.

The first 5 miles of this run are nonstop action. The only break between the class IV+ rapids is either fast class II or a very short pool. Three miles down the run, you'll encounter a 7-foot dam named Gillespie. At appropriate levels (500-1,000 cfs) it can be ski-jumped on the extreme left—be sure to get up a good head of steam. Please avoid getting trashed by the keeper in the middle of the drop; cut into the eddy.

On your first trip down, expect to scout around 6 to 9 times, depending on your personal fright factor. At high levels, above 2,500 cfs, the river really stomps. I once survived a run at 5,000 cfs, but we had several portages and scouted about 15 times. I don't recommend it.

At mile 5, the road reappears and the character of the rapids change. At mile 7 awaits Ladies Canyon, the most fearsome drop on the run. It can be portaged with considerable effort on the left, or a partial portage around the murderous hole is possible on the right. Personally, I run it down the gut. A class IV run-out adds to the excitement. Take a look at this section before you put in. Find Ladies Canyon Creek and look downstream from the road—you can't miss it. Below the class IV, the river mellows out for awhile. Enjoy it while you can, as you'll soon encounter an intense little canyon with some tough class IV+. Below this canyon, it's a piece of cake to Downieville.

To get to the take-out, drive from Nevada City on Hwy. 49 toward Downieville. When you get to Downieville, pull into the parking lot on the right; the river is a short walk from here. The Shangri-La bridge, 4 miles upstream, is an alternative take-out.

To get to the put-in, continue on Hwy. 49, 12 miles to the tiny town of Sierra City. After driving through town, keep your eyes peeled for the road to Wild Plum Campground, a right turn. Motor about a mile to the bridge across the river. Park and put in on river left.

—*CS*

NORTH FORK YUBA RIVER (Rosassco Canyon)

DIFFICULTY	FLOW	OPTIMUM	MILES	PORTAGES
IV+	700-1500	1200	4	0
V	>1500			

PUT IN: Downieville (2,880 ft.)
TAKE OUT: Goodyears Bar (2,640 ft.)
SHUTTLE: 4 miles
RAFTS: NO
AVERAGE GRADIENT: 60 fpm
GAUGE: The *Inflow to Bullards Bar* is measured at a point about 16 miles below the take-out. You'll have a bit more than about half of this (flow phone).
BOATING SEASON: Spring
WATER SOURCE: Natural
USFS and *TOPO MAPS*: Plumas NF; *Goodyears Bar, Downieville* (7.5 series)

Rosassco Canyon isn't a particularly great run, but it's worth doing if you're already in the area. It's included here for the sake of completeness. You can make up your own mind, as the best rapid and the potential portage are easily visible from the road.

The river runs mellow class II-III for the 1.5 miles down to the potential portage at the beginning of Rosassco Canyon. After making your personal decision, either portage on the left or run the narrow slot on the left. Below here is a series of class IV-V rapids (depending on the water level) known as Cathy's Carry, followed by Giant Slalom. The portage isn't too tough. My vague recollection is that the river is class II-III from here down to Goodyears Bar. Take out on river right below the bridge.

To get to the put-in, drive out of Nevada City on Hwy. 49 toward the petite town of Downieville. Once you hit town, look to your right for the parking lot—this is it. The river is a short distance to the right. To get to the take-out, turn around and drive 4 miles on Hwy. 49 to the Goodyears Bar bridge. It's on your left.

—*CS*

NORTH FORK YUBA RIVER (Goodyears Bar)

DIFFICULTY	FLOW	OPTIMUM	MILES	PORTAGES
IV (one V−)	700-2500	1500	8.5	0
IV+	>2500			

PUT IN:	Goodyears Bar (2,640 ft.)
TAKE OUT:	Hwy. 49 Bridge (2,220 ft.)
SHUTTLE:	9 miles
RAFTS:	YES (commercial run)
AVERAGE GRADIENT:	49 fpm
GAUGE:	The *Inflow to Bullards Bar* is measured at a point about 6 miles below the take-out. You'll have most of this (flow phone).
BOATING SEASON:	Spring
WATER SOURCE:	Natural
USFS and *TOPO MAPS*:	Plumas NF; *Goodyears Bar* (7.5 series)

This is an excellent intermediate run. If you can handle Chili Bar, you're ready for this one. The lack of crowds, good rapids, clean water, and nice scenery combine to create a lovely trip. The only rapid out of character is Mixmaster, a fun class V− drop, found towards the bottom of the run. The rapid just below Mixmaster, a sneakable big hole, can get a bit sticky at higher levels. The faint-hearted may opt to portage this one also, something easily done on both rapids. All of this action can be viewed from the road which follows the entire length of the run.

To find the take-out, drive from Nevada City toward Downieville on Hwy. 49 until the bridge. It's also possible to end your journey at either Fiddle Creek Campground (0.5 mile upstream) or Indian Valley Campground (2 miles upstream). To find the put-in, continue 9 miles beyond the bridge on Hwy. 49 to Goodyears Bar. Here you'll find a road to the right and a bridge across the river. Put in below the bridge.

—*CS*

NORTH FORK YUBA RIVER
(Bullards Bar Dam to Middle Fork of the Yuba)

DIFFICULTY	FLOW	OPTIMUM	MILES	PORTAGES
V	500-1500	1000	2.3	0

PUT IN: Bullards Bar Dam (1,335 ft.)
TAKE OUT: Englebright Lake—confluence with Middle Fork of the Yuba (1,150 ft.)
SHUTTLE: 20 miles (1-mile hike)
RAFTS: NO
AVERAGE GRADIENT: 80 fpm
GAUGE: Call Flood Operations (Appendix III) and ask for the release from Bullards Bar Dam, which is the put-in.
BOATING SEASON: Spring
WATER SOURCE: Spill
AAA and *TOPO MAPS*: Feather and Yuba River Region; *Challenge, French Corral* (7.5 series)

This short section offers an alternative approach to running the Middle Fork of the Yuba River. Rather than putting in at Hwy. 49, one can paddle from the New Bullards Bar Dam. There isn't any access at the confluence, so one must continue down the Middle Fork to Englebright Reservoir. This approach has its good and bad points. On the plus side, there are no portages (the Middle Fork has 2 upstream of the confluence), it's shorter, and at times it has water when the Middle Fork is dry. On the minus side is the mile-long hike to the water. Having done the trip both ways, I'd say the whitewater on the North Fork is a little better than that on the Middle Fork above the confluence. Try it both ways and decide for yourself.

The river flows through a beautiful forested canyon. Viewing the river from the road at the top of the canyon is prevented by the steep canyon walls. Between those walls, you'll find some good class IV rapids with an occasional easy class V. The whitewater really picks up below the confluence (see Middle Yuba, Route 49 to Englebright).

To get to the put-in, drive north on Hwy. 49 from Nevada City to the Middle Fork of the Yuba. Just past the bridge over the Middle Fork, turn left on Moonshine Road. Follow this road to the E-20 Road and turn left. It's a few miles farther to New Bullards Bar Dam. Drive across the dam, take the first left, and drive or walk (the road was blocked by a landslide in '83) about a mile to the gate across the gravel road. Walk down this gravel road, which is on the river right, to the base of the dam. To get to the take-out, refer to the Middle Fork of the Yuba description. There is also a potential take-out at the Colgate Powerhouse, which is 1.5 miles upstream of Englebright Reservoir.

—*CS*

MIDDLE FORK YUBA RIVER (Plumbago to Route 49)

DIFFICULTY	FLOW	OPTIMUM	MILES	PORTAGES
III-IV+	600-1200	1000	21.7	5
IV-V	1200-2000			

PUT IN:	**Plumbago Crossing (2,970 ft.)**
TAKE OUT:	**Route 49 Bridge (1,430 ft.)**
SHUTTLE:	**30 miles**
RAFTS:	**NO**
AVERAGE GRADIENT:	**71 fpm; 81 fpm to Foote Crossing; 62 fpm to Route 49**
GAUGE:	**No gauge, but runnable during peak run-off in a big water year.**
BOATING SEASON:	**Spring**
WATER SOURCE:	**Spill**
USFS and *TOPO MAPS*:	**Tahoe NF; *Alleghany, Pike, Camptonville* (7.5 series)**

After running the Middle Yuba River below Route 49, I wanted to explore more of this great river, and decided to run the stretch below Plumbago. I put in from the north via Alleghany. Due to impassable roads, I had to walk the last five miles to the put-in. Since then, I've talked with boaters who said they'd four-wheeled to Plumbago Crossing from the south.

After a few hours of walking, I arrived to a surging 700 (?) cfs; the river looked pushy. I made 4 portages in the stretch to Foote Crossing, one of them in 2 parts around a class VI gorge that contains an interesting passage under a huge boulder. There were a few portages around ugly ledge holes, and lots of stomping class IV. The river seemed on the verge of gorging up all the time.

Below Foote Crossing is great, but there are not as many class IV rapids. The 40-foot "Our House" dam, 4 miles below Foote Crossing, is the only portage on the lower half and has a dizzying view from the top.

The south side put-in is reached by driving north on Route 49, 11 miles from Nevada City, to the road that leads to North Columbia and Moores Flat. Refer to your maps.

The take-out is the Route 49 bridge.

—LH

MIDDLE FORK YUBA RIVER (Route 49 to Englebright)

DIFFICULTY	FLOW	OPTIMUM	MILES	PORTAGES
IV-V	600-1000	800 (put-in)	12	6

PUT IN: Route 49 (1,430 ft.)
TAKE OUT: Englebright Lake (550 ft. at Colgate Powerhouse)
SHUTTLE: 14 miles
RAFTS: NO
AVERAGE GRADIENT: 73 fpm; mi/mi: 30, 85, 35, 90, 105, 135, 100, 125, 70, 85 . . .
GAUGE: No gauge, but runnable during peak runoff in a big water year.
BOATING SEASON: Spring
WATER SOURCE: Spill
AAA and *TOPO MAPS*: Lake Tahoe Region; ***Camptonville, Challenge, French Corral*** (7.5 series)

Expecting a good run, hopefully with some challenging rapids, Chuck, Richard, Mike Fentress, and I put in on this run in April 1982. Eight hours later, as we carried our boats up to the car, we shook our heads in amazement. We hardly believed that here, hidden in the foothills, was one of the most fantastic class V runs any of us had ever done.

Finding the correct flow is a problem. Only in big run-off years will one see more than a few hundred cfs in the Middle Fork. At our put-in, we had about 700 cfs. In the first 4.5 miles to the junction with the North Yuba, there are many good rapids and 2 portages. Here the North Yuba, under the influence of Bullards Bar Reservoir, brought in another 700 cfs; the flow was then about 1,400 cfs.

Just below this confluence is a huge rapid that we carried. The next 5 miles is a fantastic stretch of whitewater. All of us flipped at least once, and Chuck took his first swim in many years, fortunately one of little consequence.

At 10.5 miles the action subsided, and water surging out of Colgate Powerhouse on the right doubled the flow. Below here, a mile of big but easy water flows into the reservoir. Paddle about a half mile of flat water to the take-out.

The put-in is at the Route 49 bridge, 17 miles north of Nevada City.

To find the take-out at the drowned Rice Crossing, drive about 1 mile north from the Bridgeport bridge (see South Yuba, Route 49 to Bridgeport) to a dirt road that leads off left. This turnoff is about halfway to French Corral. The dirt road contours around the hill and drops down to Englebright. The last 0.5 mile is too rutted to drive, so boats must be carried up to the car.

—LH

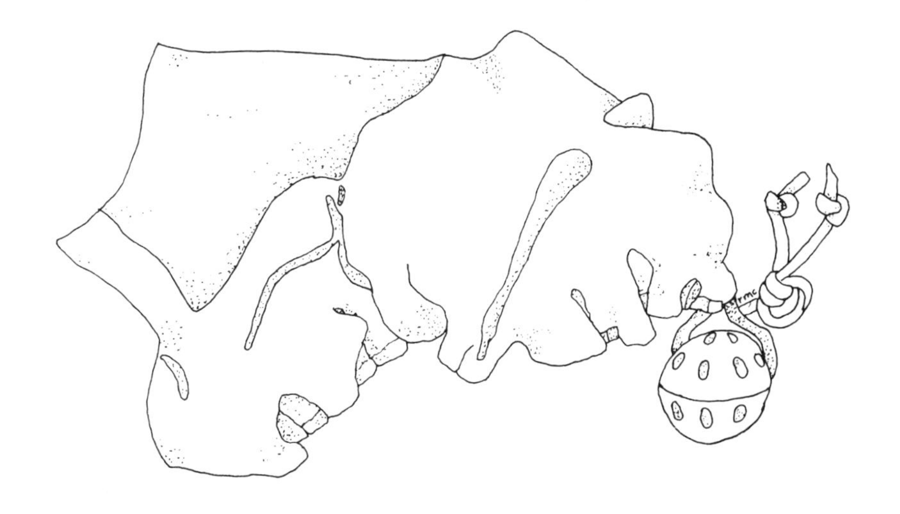

SOUTH FORK YUBA RIVER
(Kingvale to Indian Springs Campground)

DIFFICULTY	FLOW	OPTIMUM	MILES	PORTAGES
IV+	400-1000	800	8.7	6

PUT IN: Kingvale (6,040 ft.)
TAKE OUT: Indian Springs Campground (5,440 ft.)
SHUTTLE: 9 miles
RAFTS: NO
AVERAGE GRADIENT: 69 fpm
GAUGE: Call Flood Operations (Appendix III) and ask for inflow to Spaulding Reservoir, 5.5 miles below the take-out.
BOATING SEASON: Spring
WATER SOURCE: Natural
USFS and *TOPO MAPS*: Tahoe NF; *Soda Springs, Cisco Grove* (7.5 series)

Although I've never heard of anyone else having run this stretch of the South Yuba River, every kayaker driving along I-80 near Donner Pass must have looked with curiosity at it. Over the years, surely someone must have run it before Richard and I got to it in 1983.

The river is flat below the put-in, and there is no action until it comes close to the freeway. Here it goes under an access road bridge; the first rapid follows immediately. Shortly afterwards, the freeway crosses the river and a section of rapids with narrow drops follows. Below here is a campground on the right; we saw many people fishing on the weekend. Just below is a cataract. Get out early enough on the right to avoid entering the narrow granite passageway that leads to the initial cascade. At the bottom of this portage, near a house built within range of spray from the falls, get back in and paddle to the next portage.

Below this second portage the river eases for a bit, then goes under the frontage road. This is followed by a steep rapid which should be scouted. Just before going under a high bridge (the eastbound freeway), there is another portage. Between the 2 directions of I-80, a few exciting sliding falls come up; the second is the largest. Soon the river goes under westbound I-80 and flows on the north side of the freeway. The maze continues! Westbound I-80 crosses the river again. In the shadow of the freeway is the start of a horrible waterfall that must be portaged. The river is again between the two directions of freeway. Within view is a large drop that is portaged on the right. Below here a rocky, sharp drop lies just above the Eagle Lakes Road

Chuck Stanley below portage #24 on the North Stanislaus above Boards Crossing, 1982. ***Lars Holbek***

bridge. The river goes down a class III± section, is crossed by westbound I-80, and drops over a hideous waterfall just above the take-out. To avoid the last 3 portages, one can carry up to a turnout on eastbound I-80 at the horrible waterfall.

The put-in is just off the frontage road at the Kingvale exit, 6 miles west of Donner Pass.

To reach the take-out at Indian Springs Campground, take the Eagle Lakes Road exit on I-80. Follow this to the north side, above and out of the river's view, to the campground 0.5 mile downstream.

—LH

SOUTH FORK YUBA RIVER (Indian Springs to Lake Spaulding)

DIFFICULTY	FLOW	OPTIMUM	MILES	PORTAGES
IV-V–	400-1000	800	5.5 (2 on lake)	4

PUT IN:	Indian Springs Campground (5,440 ft.)
TAKE OUT:	Lake Spaulding (5,010 ft.)
SHUTTLE:	6 miles
RAFTS:	NO
AVERAGE GRADIENT:	123 fpm; mi/mi: 140,110,75
GAUGE:	Call Flood Operations (Appendix III) and ask for inflow to Spaulding Reservoir, the take-out.
BOATING SEASON:	Spring
WATER SOURCE:	Natural
USFS and *TOPO MAPS*:	Tahoe NF; *Cisco Grove, Blue Canyon* (7.5 series)

I first heard of this run when Reg Lake, John Googins and Vic Tishous did the first descent in 1980, but it wasn't until 1983 that I finally got down it.

Billy Clyde and I encountered several good rapids and a few rigorous portages. If one doesn't mind a little struggling through the brush, a jaunt down this canyon is worthwhile. The run consists of 3.5 miles on the river, followed by a 2-mile paddle across Lake Spaulding.

Within a mile of the put-in is a 20- to 25-foot waterfall that we portaged on the left. Below here, rapids lead to a jumbled cataract. Since our excursion was during high water, and eddying out above this mess looked doubtful, we continued the portage.

Many rapids required scouting, and we portaged a few steep slides. The last few rapids stand out as some of the best. The very last drop was a 10-foot turning affair that practically landed in the slack water of Lake Spaulding.

The put-in is the campground described as the take-out for the previous run, Kingvale to Indian Springs Campground.

To reach the take-out, take the Route 20 exit from I-80 and go 2.3 miles to a right turn for Camp Spaulding. One mile down this road is a parking area at the lake.

— *LH*

SOUTH FORK YUBA RIVER
(Washington to Edwards)

DIFFICULTY	FLOW	OPTIMUM	MILES	PORTAGES
III-IV	700-2000	1500	14	1

PUT IN:	**Washington (2,590 ft.)**
TAKE OUT:	**Edwards Crossing (1,940 ft.)**
SHUTTLE:	**25 miles**
RAFTS:	**NO (portage, brush)**
AVERAGE GRADIENT:	**46 fpm**
GAUGE:	**Call Flood Operations (Appendix III) and ask for release from Spaulding Reservoir, 11 miles above the put-in.**
BOATING SEASON:	**Spring**
WATER SOURCE:	**Spill**
USFS and *TOPO MAPS*:	**Tahoe NF; *Washington, North Bloomfield* (7.5 series)**

This pleasant intermediate run is the easiest on the South Yuba. Aside from the 12-foot waterfall, the run sports many class II-III rapids, and some class IV's. Some of the rapids are fairly brushy because of the lack of natural flow. This run has excellent scenery, but there are few obvious landmarks by which to gauge one's progress.

The waterfall is at mile 10.5, well after the river has changed from the initial gravel bed appearance and has dropped into a small gorge. It comes in a fairly easy section, and is not hard to spot, but pay close attention until you reach it. On river right, one can portage a few hundred feet along the gorge rim to a safe launching pad some 15 feet above the river. One can also portage on the left and put in at river level.

To reach the put-in, take the Route 20 exit from I-80 and drive west 15 miles to the Washington turnoff. Alternatively, approach from Nevada City, driving east on Route 20 to the Washington turnoff. It is 6 miles down to this old mining town.

To reach the take-out, go north on Route 49 from Route 20 on the eastern edge of Nevada City. Take Blue Tent Road to the right in a few hundred yards. There is a fire station here. A "T" intersection is reached in 0.6 mile. Turn right here and go 6 miles to Edwards Crossing.

— *LH*

SOUTH FORK YUBA RIVER
(Edwards to Purdons Crossing)

DIFFICULTY	FLOW	OPTIMUM	MILES	PORTAGES
III-IV	800-2000	1500	4	0
IV+	2000-3000			

PUT IN: Edwards Crossing (1,940 ft.)
TAKE OUT: Purdons Crossing (1,680 ft.)
SHUTTLE: 12 miles
RAFTS: YES
AVERAGE GRADIENT: 65 fpm
GAUGE: Call Flood Operations (Appendix III) and ask for release from Spaulding Reservoir, 25 miles above the put-in.
BOATING SEASON: Spring
WATER SOURCE: Spill
USFS and *TOPO MAPS*: Tahoe NF; *North Bloomfield, Nevada City* (7.5 series)

This beautiful run, with its many playspots, is pleasant by itself or can be combined with the Purdons Crossing to Route 49 run to provide a much more serious undertaking. Release from Lake Spaulding in late spring is usually quite short in a normal year. Generally, at the height of the run-off, one can arrive here to find this inviting, clear river with ample water.

A great surfing wave, one of many to come, lies just below the bridge. Rapids are frequent throughout the run, mostly class III with an occasional IV. About halfway down, an old broken dam creates a big drop. Scout from either bank.

The put-in for this run is the take-out for the run just upstream (see the Washington to Edwards description).

At the "T" intersection mentioned in the Washington to Edwards run description, turn left to reach the take-out. Go 0.5 mile to the next intersection and turn right. This road leads down to Purdons Crossing.

—LH

SOUTH FORK YUBA RIVER
(Purdons Crossing to Route 49)

DIFFICULTY	FLOW	OPTIMUM	MILES	PORTAGES
V	800-1500	1500	4	4
V+	1500-3000			

PUT IN: Purdons Crossing (1,680 ft.)
TAKE OUT: Route 49 (1,180 ft.)
SHUTTLE: 15 miles
RAFTS: NO
AVERAGE GRADIENT: 125 fpm; mi/mi: 90, 125, 125, 155
GAUGE: Call Flood Operations (Appendix III) and ask for release from Spaulding Reservoir, 29 miles above the put-in.
BOATING SEASON: Spring
WATER SOURCE: Spill
USFS and *TOPO MAPS*: Tahoe NF; *Nevada City* (7.5 series)

On our first venture down this run, Richard Montgomery and I came to curse the damkeeper(s) who chose that day to open the flood gates, doubling the flow while we slept.

We'd put in at Washington and made good time to Purdons. Below here the rapids pick up and are steep to an old, 12-foot-high dam. After portaging this, we had lunch and the obligatory snooze. I awoke to Richard's yelps and realized the water had risen sharply—our boats and gear were beginning to float away. In a panic we gathered our gear, and after scrutinizing the now raging torrent, tentatively deemed it safe for continued travel. Only moments later I questioned our decision, as I bounced around in a big hole I had mistakenly bombed into.

We finally eddied out together and saw the growing terror in each other, but decided to continue with caution. It took us four hours to run this 4-mile maelstrom through the Devil's Slide area and frankly, we were a bit out of control. The 0.5 mile above Route 49 drops 100 feet! With a more reasonable flow, this is a much better run.

The put-in for this run is the take-out for the Edwards to Purdons run. To reach the take-out, from the put-in, drive back to Route 49 and turn right (north). It is 8 miles to the bridge over the South Yuba.

—LH

SOUTH FORK YUBA RIVER
(Route 49 to Bridgeport)

DIFFICULTY	FLOW	OPTIMUM	MILES	PORTAGES
IV-V	1000-2000	1500	7.2	2

PUT IN: Route 49 (1,180 ft.)
TAKE OUT: Bridgeport (530 ft.)
SHUTTLE: 13 miles
RAFTS: NO
AVERAGE GRADIENT: 90 fpm; mi/mi: 110, 70, 75, 75, 100, 120, 90
GAUGE: Call Flood Operations (Appendix III) and ask for release from Spaulding Reservoir, 29 miles above the put-in.
BOATING SEASON: Spring
WATER SOURCE: Spill
AAA and *TOPO MAPS*: Lake Tahoe Region; *North Bloomfield, French Corral* (7.5 series)

This run is basically a continuation of the Purdons to Route 49 stretch, though the gradient tapers off a half mile below the Route 49 bridge.

One mile below the bridge is a flow gauge on river left. This can be checked before embarking, though eyeballing the flow at the put-in should be sufficient. To reach the gauge, drive from the bridge about 0.5 mile towards Nevada City to a steep dirt road that leads down to the right. Walk down here. This road comes out at the river just upstream of the gauge. We've made this run at 8 and 8.5.

Don't be dismayed by the horrendous view from the bridge. This section to the gauge is where the first portages are encountered. The rapids on this run are big and steep. Some miles downstream is a river-wide 8-foot ledge with a dangerous hole. At 1,500 cfs (8 on the gauge), this ledge can be cleanly ski-jumped beyond the grips of the hole. A section of sliding falls with radical standing waves lies below the ledge. The sliding falls is followed by a river-wide roller and severe turbulence; just below this is a big drop that causes a dangerous-looking recycling hole. This is commonly portaged on the right. The last big rapid, Tigertail, is about a mile above the take-out. A few rapids are hard to scout due to vertical walls, and portaging would be difficult. The action on this superb run abates only shortly before the take-out bridge comes into view.

The put-in is the same as the take-out for the previous run. To reach the take-out, go north on Route 49 from the put-in 4 miles to Birchville Road. Turn left here and follow to Pleasant Valley Road. Turn left again and follow to the river.

— *LH*

YUBA RIVER
(Englebright Dam to Hwy. 20 Bridge)

DIFFICULTY	FLOW	OPTIMUM	MILES	PORTAGES
III (one IV)	1500-3500	2000	6	0

PUT IN: Englebright Dam (260 ft.)
TAKE OUT: Parks Bar, Hwy. 20 Bridge (200 ft.)
SHUTTLE: 8 miles
RAFTS: YES (note put-in carry)
AVERAGE GRADIENT: 10 fpm
GAUGE: *Release from Englebright Reservoir*, the put-in, is what you'll be on (flow phone).
BOATING SEASON: Summer Fall
WATER SOURCE: Power Power
AAA and *TOPO MAPS*: Lake Tahoe Region; *Smartville* (7.5 series); *Wheatland* (15 series)

If you are currently enjoying the whitewater action that accompanies a big water year in the Sierras, read no further. However, if you're suffering through one of California's periodic low-water years, you're in luck. This run may not have a lot of whitewater, but it does have a reliable power release. During the late summer and early fall, this section sees a fair number of boaters.

Getting to the river is the major chore. The first time I shot the run, we walked down a quarter-mile-long staircase to the powerhouse. I don't recommend this route. A better plan is to put in on the reservoir next to the dam and paddle to the river right shore. From there, it's a half-mile walk, or drag for those so inclined, on a road. Once on the water, you can look forward to the Narrows, which consists of a couple of easy III's with some OK playing. Be sure to milk these rapids for all they're worth. After the preliminary rapids, 1.5 miles below the put-in, is the big one: Ground Chuck, named when Chuck Koteen had his face slightly remodeled in the rocky wave at the bottom of the drop. Despite the ominous name, this is a fun rapid with a fast bouncy chute leading to a big wave. There is a rock just under the surface on the right side of the big wave, so watch out. Below Ground Chuck is 6 miles of very dull class I "whitewater."

To get to the put-in, drive down Mooney Flat Road, off Hwy. 20, to Englebright Reservoir. There should be signs. Drive to the public access near the dam. From there, paddle and carry to the base of the dam. The take-out is where Hwy. 20 crosses the river. A short distance downstream of the bridge, on the river right, is Parks Bar, a public access point and a convenient take-out.

—*CS*

NORTH FORK AMERICAN RIVER (Generation Gap)

DIFFICULTY	FLOW	OPTIMUM	MILES	PORTAGES
III-IV+	600-1200	1500	12.3	0
IV-V	1200-2000			(recommend 1)

PUT IN: Tadpole Creek (2,820 ft.)
TAKE OUT: Colfax-Foresthill Road (900 ft.—Chamberlain Falls take-out)
SHUTTLE: 30 miles (3-mile hike with 2,400-ft. drop)
RAFTS: NO
AVERAGE GRADIENT: To Euchre Bar, 75 fpm; mi/mi: 80, 80, 60, 60, 90, 75, 90, 55, 120, 70, 145, 55
GAUGE: *Inflow to Lake Clementine* is 40 miles below the put-in. You'll get something like half of this number at the put-in (flow phone).
BOATING SEASON: Spring
WATER SOURCE: Natural
USFS and *TOPO MAPS*: Tahoe NF; *Duncan Peak, Westville, Dutch Flat* (7.5 series)

The put-in for this excellent run is an arduous 3-mile downhill hike. The run is usually done in conjunction with the 2 runs downstream, Giant Gap and Chamberlain Falls. This combination eases the shuttle logistics and provides a 30-mile run. One has to go at least to the end of Giant Gap to take out on a road. Running the entire North Fork provides an excellent 2-day run with a short shuttle.

Most of the run consists of exciting rapids, and the entire stretch maintains a fairly even gradient. Somewhere past the midpoint, the river starts to gorge up, and a difficult section called the "Dream Gap" follows. The top rapid is runnable. The second drop has been run cleanly on the right, as well as carried (grunt!) high on the left. About one-half mile above Euchre Bar is a steep, right-turning rapid that we dubbed "F-14," when a pair of USAF jets roared by while we were scouting. This terrifying experience caused the four of us on the first descent to drop to our knees and clutch our helmets for safety. We decided the rapid was wimpy compared to the airborne menace, and ran it without incident.

To reach the put-in, take the main paved road running NE out of Foresthill along the Foresthill Divide, and go 20 miles to Secret House Campground.

John Armstrong

Continue another 2 miles to the head of Secret Canyon. Where Secret Canyon's drainage crosses the road, turn left onto a rocky road. A quarter mile up this road is the start of the Beacroft Trail, which leads to the put-in. In the summer of 1982, logging crews were widening and leveling the road in this area, and supposedly it's to be paved.

At the bottom of the trail there is an old cabin. At this point, the river is just leaving a gravel bar bed and dumping into a narrow gorge over a nasty 10-foot falls. By putting in on a sloping ledge, and sliding into the river just below the falls, a portage around the whole gorge can be avoided.

Take out at the end of either the Giant Gap or Chamberlain Falls run, described in the following pages.

—LH

NORTH FORK AMERICAN RIVER (Giant Gap)

DIFFICULTY	FLOW	OPTIMUM	MILES	PORTAGES
III-IV+	600-1200	1000	14.5	0
IV-V	1200-3000			

PUT IN:	**Euchre Bar (1,900 ft.)**
TAKE OUT:	**Colfax-Iowa Hill Rd. (1,110 ft.)**
SHUTTLE:	**19 miles (2 mile hike to put-in)**
RAFTS:	**YES (difficult)**
AVERAGE GRADIENT:	**54 fpm: 60, 35, 40, 120, 85, 100, 75, 45, 40 . . .**
GAUGE:	***Inflow to Lake Clementine* is 28 miles below the put-in; you'll get most of this at the put in (flow phone).**
BOATING SEASON:	**Winter Spring**
WATER SOURCE:	**Natural Natural**
AAA and *TOPO MAPS*:	**Lake Tahoe Region; *Dutch Flat, Forest Hill, Colfax* (7.5 series)**

This now classic run was the scene of intensive exploration in the early seventies. At that time, it was on the edge of what was considered navigable, even with extensive portaging. In 1975, Chuck Stanley and Richard Montgomery made the run without portages at 800 cfs. Since then, it has been run in excess of 3,000 cfs, and today paddle rafts reportedly bomb down with abandon.

The 3-mile Giant Gap is a fantastic journey in a deep, vertical-walled gorge with class IV-V rapids. Below the Gap, hard rapids continue for some time. Eventually the difficulties ease, and this lower section contains some great playing holes.

To reach the put-in, take the Alta exit on I-80, 25 miles east of Auburn, and follow signs towards Casa Loma. In one mile, turn right at a sign for Casa Loma/Euchre Bar Trail. One-half mile from here cross the railroad tracks, and 1.3 miles farther, cross the tracks again at a sign for Euchre Bar. In 0.6 mile, the dirt road forks. Follow the left branch a few hundred yards to the trailhead.

Take the Colfax-Grass Valley exit on I-80 to reach the take-out. Go to Canyon Way on the south side of the freeway and drive west a few hundred yards to a left turn at Colfax-Iowa Hill Road. Follow this to the river for either the Giant Gap take-out or the Chamberlain Falls put-in.

—*LH*

GIANT GAP By Richard Montgomery

Through a series of beer-assisted readings of Charlie Martin's *Sierra Whitewater* stretching from 1974 to 1977, Chuck and I were inspired to run everything that the earlier author had said couldn't be. Giant Gap was to be the first big test of our dream.

In our first attempt, early in the spring of '75, despite our years of training, we were stopped cold. By the rapids? No, we couldn't find the put-in. This disappointed us, and the wasted gas practically impoverished us, but impelled by our neurotic desire for glory, and aided by our discovery of topographic maps, we returned a month later to the head of the visibly marked Euchre Bar trail which had eluded us earlier.

That early pioneer (John Ramirez), described in Martin's account, left Oakland at 2 a.m. on a Saturday morning and finally put in at 1 p.m. that afternoon, with two hours of sleep and nothing to eat since breakfast. Inspired by his example, Chuck and I got to the head of Euchre Bar trail at 3 p.m. the afternoon of the day before we were to make the run. We carried one boat down the steep mile-and-a-half trail to the river that afternoon and got to bed that night at 8 p.m., long past Chuck's bedtime.

We carried the other boat down the next morning, getting in the water at 8 a.m., with about 800 cfs and nothing to eat since oatmeal at 6:30. While putting on our sprayskirts in the cool morning, amid the singing canyon wrens, we could not help but think of the flock of experts stopped and demoralized by the Giant Gap, which lay downstream. As we paddled through the Shangri-La of Green Valley, we had to get out of our boats several times to relieve ourselves in anticipation.

As the walls of the Gap began to enclose us, we got more nervous. We eddy-hopped down the first few class IV's, looking for the big ones around the corner. As we ran more and more rapids without scouting, we became increasingly nervous and puzzled.

Finally, we came to our first scout, a nasty ledge across the whole river, except for a small tongue against the right wall. This is the infamous "Ledge" about halfway into the Gap and the most feared rapid there nowadays. The loss of several paddles and a few unintentional overnight stays are attributable to this drop. To scout it, we had to wade across a shallow pool at the brink, and then crawl along the right wall. The tongue proved runnable and we went on, wondering when things would get really serious.

I began to think they wouldn't. Chuck insisted they had to. On we went, eddy-hopping down the easy V's and IV's after the Ledge. The Gap started opening up and we started hooting and hollering.

We got to the take-out at 1:30 that afternoon. It was my turn to hitchhike the shuttle. I brought along our spare canoe paddle so people would know what we'd just done, but it wasn't much fun hanging on to it when I got picked up by a dirt-biker going into the Euchre Bar trail. At the Safeway that afternoon, we treated ourselves to heroic portions of ice cream and beer!

A NIGHT AT THE GIANT GAP HYATT

Room 109.

As you pass out of the steepest part of this run, below Giant Gap at about mile 9, look to your left. You will see many rocks. Look for a particularly hard one, with many jagged points. It will be sloped, and, if it is raining, it will be wet. Michael Snead, Rimbeaux and myself unexpectedly booked a night here on our first trip down Giant Gap in 1981. Thanks to a fashionably late start, we arrived quite a bit past sundown. By the time we checked in we'd already run the last couple of rapids in the pitch dark. Unrecommended. As are the accommodations. Single-sized, quartzite mattress, no phone, and *very* drafty. (But is there a shower? You bet.)

By midnight, after our shower had started, the three of us lay huddled together on this rock for warmth, our collective macho quotient hovering near zero. It was one of those . . . long ones.

Next morning, still shivering, we paddled out the remaining two miles. Once on top, to our utter lack of surprise, we discovered it had snowed on our car.

We didn't realize it at the time, but it turned out we had spent an hilarious night down there! It was our paddling buddies that told us. When we related to them what had happened, they immediately started to chuckle, and then when we got to the part about the snow, they just about fell in the aisles!

"Har, har," they said, "har, har."

— *John Cassidy*

NORTH FORK AMERICAN RIVER (Chamberlain Falls)

DIFFICULTY	FLOW	OPTIMUM	MILES	PORTAGES
III-IV	800-1500	1500	4.8	0
IV-V	1500-4000			

PUT IN:	Colfax-Iowa Hill Rd. (1,110 ft.)
TAKE OUT:	Colfax-Foresthill Rd. (900 ft.)
SHUTTLE:	12 miles
RAFTS:	YES (commercial run)
AVERAGE GRADIENT:	44 fpm
GAUGE:	The *Inflow to Lake Clementine*, 14 miles below the put-in, is about what you'll get (flow phone).
BOATING SEASON:	Winter Spring
WATER SOURCE:	Natural Natural
AAA and *TOPO MAPS*:	Lake Tahoe Region; *Colfax* (7.5 series)

This run has been a favorite among California kayakers for many years, and is now quite popular among rafters. It is relatively short, with good steep drops in a granitic riverbed. It makes a great continuation if one is coming out of Giant Gap or Generation Gap.

The rapids "Chamberlain Falls" and "Staircase" have a history of grabbing people when they're least expecting it. In Nosestand Rapid, one can achieve just about any configuration of vertical postures.

This run, although easier and of a lesser gradient than the two upper runs, displays a higher concentration of sieve/strainer hazards. There are a few stories of swimmers who have been temporarily caught underwater between boulders; one should be aware of this potential.

The put-in for this run is the take-out for Giant Gap, explained in the previous description.

To reach the take-out from Sacramento, take the Weimar Cross Road exit on I-80. Go east 2 miles on Canyon Way to a road sign that reads, "Foresthill 13." Follow this road 4 miles down to the river.

From Truckee, take the Placer Hills–Canyon Way Exit. Go west 1 mile on Canyon Way to Yankee Jim's Road. Follow this down to the river.

—LH

Breeching. *C. Stanley*

NORTH FORK AMERICAN RIVER (Ponderosa Way Run)

DIFFICULTY	FLOW	OPTIMUM	MILES	PORTAGES
II+	500-1500	1200	5	0
III	>1500			

PUT IN:	**Colfax-Foresthill Bridge (900 ft.)**
TAKE OUT:	**Ponderosa Way Bridge (795 ft.)**
SHUTTLE:	**10 miles (3 miles OK dirt road)**
RAFTS:	**YES (commercial run)**
AVERAGE GRADIENT:	**21 fpm**
GAUGE:	**The *Inflow to Lake Clementine*, a few miles below the take-out, is about what you'll get (flow phone).**
BOATING SEASON:	**Spring**
WATER SOURCE:	**Natural**
AAA and *TOPO MAPS*:	**Lake Tahoe Region; *Colfax* (7.5 series)**

This section of the North Fork is a good beginner run that is enjoying increased popularity with both kayakers and rafters. The scenery is a pleasant wooded canyon. The rapids are mostly big gravel bar affairs—shoot them right down the "V."

To get to the put-in, refer to the Chamberlain Falls take-out description.

To get to the take-out, drive east from Auburn on I-80 to the Weimar exit. From Weimar, drive east on Canyon Way a mile to Ponderosa Way. Turn right and drive 5 miles to the river.

—CS

MIDDLE FORK AMERICAN RIVER (Tunnel Run)

DIFFICULTY	FLOW	OPTIMUM	MILES	PORTAGES
IV	800-1500	1200	17	1

PUT IN: Ralston Afterbay (1,080 ft.)
TAKE OUT: Spring Garden Road (700 ft.)
SHUTTLE: 25 miles (5 miles of fair dirt road)
RAFTS: YES (commercial run)
AVERAGE GRADIENT: 23 fpm
GAUGE: The *Release from Oxbow Powerhouse*, at the put-in, is what you'll be on (flow phone).
BOATING SEASON: Spring Summer
WATER SOURCE: Spill/Power Power
AAA and *TOPO MAPS*: Lake Tahoe Region; *Michigan Bluff, Foresthill, Georgetown, Greenwood* (7.5 series)

This is a marginal run that has one major redeeming feature: water in the dry summer months. When all else fails, the Tunnel Run often will have a boatable flow due to the power release below Ralston Dam. The two major drawbacks to the run are the long sections of flat water and the long shuttle. When you're desperate, these burdens are worth bearing. I didn't list a difficulty above 1,500 cfs for a reason. If the Middle Fork is up above the maximum release level, a ton of other better rivers will also be running. Why waste your time here?

The action on this river occurs in fits and starts. There are several sections of good whitewater, between which lay giant sections of flat water. There is a potential portage around Tunnel Chute and one certain portage around Ruck-A-Chucky rapids. After you embark in the powerhouse pool below Ralston Dam, there is consistent class III and IV action for two miles. About two miles below the powerhouse awaits Tunnel Chute. Here the river makes a large oxbow around a huge rock outcropping. Goldminers decided to blast a tunnel through the rock, thus short circuiting the oxbow. They also blasted a narrow slot through solid granite in order to coerce the river to flow into the tunnel. The tunnel is big and flat; the slot is narrow and ultra-wicked. Gunter Hemmersbach, in a glass boat, broke a couple of feet off the end of his kayak when he was spun sideways by the extreme turbulence. At the bottom of the slot is a 6-foot drop into a monster hole. This rapid is not for the faint-hearted. There is an easy portage on the left. Below Tunnel Chute, the river is class III (with one class IV) or flat until Ruck-A-Chucky rapids. Ruck-A-Chucky is

John Armstrong running a drop on the Tuolumne River below Tuolumne Meadows. ***Lars Holbek***

an irrigated pile of giant boulders: it's not a pleasant sight. The best portage is on the river left. The route is a bit precarious but nothing horrible. I'd rate it a "moderate" portage. I've heard a rumor that the commercial rafters (there are a few trips run each year) have rigged up some sort of portage cable around this section. Below Ruck-A-Chucky there are several good class IV drops with some fun 4-foot vertical drops. Below these, it's flat down to the take-out on McKeon Road.

To get to the put-in, drive from Auburn on the Auburn-Foresthill Road toward Foresthill. Just as you're entering "downtown" Foresthill, turn right on Mosquito Ridge Road. Follow this to French Meadow Road, where you turn right and drive down to your first right and follow it to the river.

To get to the take-out, retrace your tire tracks down toward Auburn. About six miles past Foresthill, turn left on McKeon Road (marked Spring Garden Road on the AAA map) and drive 5 miles of dirt road to the river.

—*CS*

RUBICON RIVER (Lower Run)

DIFFICULTY	FLOW	OPTIMUM	MILES	PORTAGES
V−	500-1000	1200	20.3	2
V	1000-2000			(recommend 5)

PUT IN:	Ellicott Bridge (3,350 ft.)
TAKE OUT:	Ralston Afterbay (1,150 ft.)
SHUTTLE:	32 miles (slow paved road)
RAFTS:	NO
AVERAGE GRADIENT:	108 fpm; mi/mi: 60, 120, 130, 120, 120, 120, 140, 80, 110, 85, 160, 100, 95, 145, 80, 150, 65, 70 . . .
GAUGE:	Runnable during the peak run-off of a big water year when Hell Hole Dam is spilling (PG&E knows when this is happening, if you can get them to tell you).
BOATING SEASON:	Spring
WATER SOURCE:	Spill (rare)
USFS,AAA, and *TOPO MAPS*:	Eldorado NF; Lake Tahoe Region; *Robb's Peak, Devil Peak, Tunnel Hill, Michigan Bluff* (7.5 series)

I'd heard of the Rubicon for years before Lars, Richard, and I made the first descent in the spring of '82. Many a group of brave paddlers considered the challenge, some even attempted the run, but all failed. It wasn't a lack of courage, skill, guts, determination, fortitude, valor, intrepidness, resoluteness, audacity, prowess, or moral righteousness that kept them from success. No, it wasn't that; it was a lack of water.

As we all know, rivers are made of water and rocks; this river always has rocks, and it seldom has water. The problem is Lower Hell Hole Dam which diverts much of the flow. The river only flows when the dam is spilling, which only occurs in the spring during big water years.

Was the Rubicon worth the wait? I'd say yes. It is an excellent self-supporting 2-day wilderness trip. We saw no one the entire length of the run. The heavily wooded canyon provides excellent scenery. We had no trouble finding adequate camping. Along the entire length of the run, one can't help but notice the abrupt change in vegetation 50 feet above the canyon floor. This phenomenon was caused by the failure of the original Hell Hole Dam in 1964. All of the big trees were washed away in the flood.

The difficulty of the whitewater was mixed; I recall many sections of class III and IV rapids with an occasional class V tossed in. On the first and only descent, Richard and I cowered at the sight of 5 rapids, which we promptly portaged; Lars stood tall and ran all but 2 drops. In general, the hard rapids were easily scouted and could be portaged without undue effort. However, I recall one major drop that we ran that would be difficult, but possible, to schlep around.

One rapid worthy of note is One-in-a-Million, a series of stairsteps that ends in an awesome drop. Another super rapid is a 15-foot vertical falls which Lars and I ran without mishap. Poor Richard didn't fare as well. What befell wasn't tragic, but rather comical. The falls on the right had a small bench 3 feet above the pool that turned the water 90 degrees, sending it shooting straight downstream. Lars and I ran the falls over the bench; we hit the pool in a shallow dive. Richard elected to explore a more glorious route—he went right down the middle. He hit the pool in a vertical nose dive to China. He completely disappeared only to surface sideways in the falls,

Chuck Stanley running a 15-foot waterfall on the lower Rubicon River, 1982. ***Lars Holbek***

Richard Montgomery and Chuck Stanley in "One in a Million" on the first descent of the lower Rubicon River, 1982. ***Lars Holbek***

his head being pummelled by the jet of water shooting off the bench. After several panic-stricken seconds, Richard was pushed into the pool below. We were too busy laughing to tell him what had happened.

While on the subject of the Rubicon, I should mention our run from Hell Hole Dam to Ellicott Bridge. We had a flow of around 200 cfs at the put-in and 400 cfs by the bridge. At this flow, the run is a pain in the arse. We had many (let's guess 10) portages, although none were long or difficult. The scenery is fine. At the time, we declared the run to be totally lacking in redeeming qualities, hence we swore a solemn vow never to return. However, now that time has fogged my memory, I'd bet the run might be worth a second try with a decent flow. Another consideration is the mile-long walk down the face of the dam to the river. If you want to run this section, you'll have to figure out the shuttle yourself.

To get to the take-out for the lower run, drive out of Foresthill on Mosquito Ridge Road to French Meadow Road (this is the road to Ralston Afterbay). Turn right on French Meadow and drive down the canyon and across the Middle Fork of the American. Continue onward to the powerhouse on the Rubicon—judge the water flow here. To get to the put-in, continue up French Meadows Road and follow your map to the bridge that crosses the river 20 miles upstream. The roads in this area are very confusing—both AAA and USFS maps are recommended. We spent a fair amount of time peering at maps and scratching our heads while making our way to the put-in.

—*CS*

SOUTH FORK AMERICAN RIVER (Lovers Leap Run)

DIFFICULTY	FLOW	OPTIMUM	MILES	PORTAGES
V	500-1200	1000 (take-out)	9.6	3

PUT IN: Strawberry (5,720 ft.)
TAKE OUT: Kyburz (4,060 ft.)
SHUTTLE: 10 miles
RAFTS: NO
AVERAGE GRADIENT: 171 fpm; mi/mi: 160, 120, 110, 150, 190, 210, 210, 250, 180, 80
GAUGE: No gauge, but runnable before and after the spring peak of a normal year.
BOATING SEASON: Spring
WATER SOURCE: Natural
USFS and *TOPO MAPS*: Eldorado NF; *Pyramid Peak, Kyburz* (7.5 series)

This run has the distinction of being perhaps the steepest in the state with very few portages. In June 1979, Richard Montgomery, Mike Schlax, and I, in a 2-day effort, ran the stretch from Strawberry to the 30-foot falls 0.5 mile above Eagle Rock Picnic Area. From the falls, we basically portaged to Eagle Rock. This, the steepest section, has never been run. In June 1982, Richard and I ran from Eagle Rock to Kyburz. On subsequent trips we simply took out at the 30-foot falls. By doing this, one can make a 7-mile run with a minimum of one portage. Everyone should choose carefully which rapids to run or scout. Commonly, 2 days are taken for this run; the amount of scouting and deliberation consumes much time and energy. The numerous roads

Rodeo contestant, Trinity River Rodeo. ***Pinky Collamer***

leading down to summer cabin tracts provide access for previewing sections of the river.

Just below a bridge, about a mile below the put-in, is a 10-foot drop called "Derb's Decision." Some distance below here is a recognizable rapid called "Hole in a Box"; this drop sports a powerful reversal with exits blocked by boulders. "Auto End-on" consistently requires a direct nose hit to get through. "Next Year" is one rapid that has always been portaged. "Supra-orbital," perhaps the biggest runnable rapid, was named for the gash I sustained on my brow while going over a drop upside down.

The hamlet of Strawberry, gateway to the popular Lovers Leap climbing area, is 80 miles east of Sacramento on Route 50. Just past Strawberry Lodge, the secondary road crosses the South American. This bridge provides a legal put-in.

—*LH*

SOUTH FORK AMERICAN RIVER (Kyburz to Riverton)

DIFFICULTY	FLOW	OPTIMUM	MILES	PORTAGES
III-IV+	700-1200	1200	9.6	2
IV-V	1200-3000			

PUT IN: Kyburz (4,060 ft.)

TAKE OUT: Route 50 Bridge (3,200 ft.)

SHUTTLE: 10 miles

RAFTS: YES (below class VI rapid)

AVERAGE GRADIENT: 90 fpm; mi/mi: 100, 110, 110, 150, 80, 80, 85, 55, 60, 30

GAUGE: *Flow at Kyburz*, the put-in, is what you'll have (flow phone).

BOATING SEASON: Spring

WATER SOURCE: Natural

USFS and *TOPO MAPS*: Eldorado NF; *Kyburz, Riverton* (7.5 series)

This run has been a favorite of California boaters since Walt Harvest and Noel Debord made the first run in 1965. The accessibility and good whitewater make it a natural target for river-runners. Occasionally, adventurous fools in K-Mart rubber duckies are lured onto this run because of its proximity to Route 50.

The first 4 miles are significantly steeper than the rest of the run and there are a few hazards in this stretch. They consist of logjams, which shift from year to year, and a class VI rapid. Shortly below the confluence with the Silver Fork is a 4-foot diversion dam. This is runnable but should be examined. The class VI rapid comes shortly below Sand Flat Campground. Portage on the right.

The lower half of the run has many excellent play areas. Just above one of the access bridges are several fantastic, side-surfing holes that are quite safe below 1,200 cfs. Unfortunately, the incessant Route 50 traffic detracts somewhat from this run.

In the winter of 82/83, a huge slide dammed the river 5 miles below Kyburz, creating a reservoir for several days. The mud dam later collapsed, destroying the roadbed and littering the river downstream with logs. In June '83, we saw the disaster site from the newly constructed road, though we did not make the run. The new rapid is ugly and strewn with huge logs; it looks to be at least class V. Use extreme care on the river below here, as other new hazards undoubtedly exist.

The put-in is at the bridge just past the grocery store and post office in Kyburz, located some 70 miles east of Sacramento.

The take-out is the Route 50 Bridge 10 miles downriver.

—LH

SOUTH FORK AMERICAN RIVER
(Riverton to Peavine)

DIFFICULTY	FLOW	OPTIMUM	MILES	PORTAGES
III-IV	700-4000	1500	3.5	0

PUT IN: Route 50 Bridge (3,200 ft.)
TAKE OUT: Peavine Ridge Road (2,960 ft.)
SHUTTLE: 4 miles
RAFTS: YES
AVERAGE GRADIENT: 69 fpm; mi/mi: 40, 80, 80, 40
GAUGE: *Flow at Kyburz*, 10 miles above the put-in, is what you'll have (flow phone).
BOATING SEASON: Spring
WATER SOURCE: Natural
USFS and *TOPO MAPS*: Eldorado NF; *Riverton* (7.5 series)

This run is essentially a continuation of the lower part of the Kyburz run, though the river begins to drop into the deep canyon that exists for the next 10 miles. Many good rapids of moderate difficulty are found on this run.

Put in at the take-out for the Kyburz to Riverton run, the Route 50 Bridge.

To reach the take-out, take the eastern of the two Route 50 exits for Pacific House. Just east of the market and gas station, a dirt road leads down to a closed bridge that spans the South Fork.

—LH

SOUTH FORK AMERICAN RIVER (Golden Gate)

DIFFICULTY	FLOW	OPTIMUM	MILES	PORTAGES
V+	700-1500	1000	9.4	5

Very dangerous above 2000

PUT IN: **Peavine Ridge Road (2,960 ft.)**
TAKE OUT: **Forebay Road (1,860 ft.)**
SHUTTLE: **12 miles**
RAFTS: **NO**
AVERAGE GRADIENT: **117 fpm; mi/mi: 60, 70, 170, 190, 170, 200, 90, 80, 50, 20**
GAUGE: ***Stream inflow to Slab Creek Reservoir*, the take-out, is what you'll have (flow phone).**
BOATING SEASON: **Spring**
WATER SOURCE: **Natural**
USFS and *TOPO MAPS*: **Eldorado NF; *Riverton, Pollock Pines, Slate Mtn.* (7.5 series)**

In Charlie Martin's book, *Sierra Whitewater*, this run is described as "a novel substitute for jumping off the Golden Gate Bridge" and "accessible only by helicopter."

Chuck, Richard and I had never seen anything that approached the definition of class "VII." We had to find out if it existed. We wondered if there wasn't a gem flowing down there, the undiscovered "classic."

We ran the Golden Gate at the start of a week of river exploration, after which we descended Bald Rock Canyon and the Bear River below Route 49. (The latter turned out to be a portage-fest, recommended for those who thrive on lower extremity exertion.)

On our first run, almost to our disappointment, we found the canyon to be negotiable. Any rapid can be portaged with only average difficulty, and there are no vertical-walled canyons. Nonetheless, this run is on the far end of the kayaking spectrum and should not be approached with a cavalier attitude. At high water, the river is very pushy; I'd venture to call it unrunnable above 2,000 cfs.

Late March 1980 found us at the Peavine Bridge, with the river low and just starting its spring flush. The first 2 miles are a good warm-up for the intensity that lies ahead. The next 4.5 miles contain many difficult, dangerous rapids. Five or six of the major rapids are probably portaged more than they are run. "Straight Shot," "Drainpipe," "Taco Bell" (the last place you'd ever want to be), and "Brain Fade" have all been run with varying degrees of success. A steep rapid ends at the confluence of Silver Creek at mile 6.5. Below here the gradient eases, though there are still big rapids. A 15-foot waterfall, "F-111," is usually portaged.

The put-in is the take-out for the Riverton to Peavine run. To reach the take-out, turn off at the eastern exit for Pollock Pines from Route 50. Go north, past the Safeway, and turn left on the main street. In a few blocks, turn right on Forebay Road and drive 8 miles down to the bridge.

—LH

STRAIGHT SHOT

To name a rapid is an awesome responsibility. All those that follow in your footsteps will be forced to utter those hallowed words you've chosen to denote the collection of rocks, waves, holes, and fear that constitute a class V rapid. I can think of few rapids more aptly named than "Straight Shot," a class V rapid on the Golden Gate run of the South Fork of the American River.

It was on the first descent of "The Gate" that Richard Montgomery, in one of his heroic moods, elected to run a 6-foot vertical drop without thoroughly scouting. He landed in 2 feet of water. The boat stopped with a loud jarring smack on the rocks.

All was not well with Richard; he had a pained expression on his face, due to a distorted ankle. As a result, Richard was no longer able to portage unassisted. He was reduced to hobbling, while Lars or I carried his boat. The pain made him reluctant to even scout if it involved much walking. He relied on our verbal reports of what lay below.

This system worked well enough for a while. To scout Straight Shot, we had to walk on a smooth sloping granite slab 40 feet to get a view of the rapids. Richard elected to stay with his boat. I took one look and wimped out. Massive boulders force the river width down to 10 feet. Between these jutting shores the water fights; twisting boils carom off the walls with awesome force. A sideways kayak would be instantly folded like a Tijuana Taco.

Richard Montgomery prepares one taco to go at Straight Shot.
Lars Holbek

I got into position to take movies as Lars backpaddled at the lip of the rapid. Richard, while in his boat, peered downstream at the drop that was just out of his sight. While in the pool, Lars assured Richard that the rapid was an easy "Straight Shot" down the middle. I filmed as Lars fought his way through the boiling maelstrom. He managed to thread the needle. To save time, I unfortunately elected not to record Richard's descent. I quickly packed up the camera and began my portage.

As I was putting on my spray skirt, my view of the rapid was blocked, but I could clearly see Lars in position to photograph from a midstream boulder. As he raised his camera, I knew Richard must have begun his run. All appeared well until Lars lowered his camera and his eyes bugged out in disbelief. Seconds later, Richard and his "tacoed" boat swam into my sight. He had bridged sideways momentarily before the kayak bent in half and ejected him.

Several frantic seconds later, we had Richard safely to shore just above the following class V rapid. A swift kick to midsection of the Hollowform and a short rest for the wounded warrior and we continued the battle.

— CS

SOUTH FORK AMERICAN RIVER (Slab Creek)

DIFFICULTY	FLOW	OPTIMUM	MILES	PORTAGES
IV+	500-1500	1500	7	1
V	1500-2500			

PUT IN: Slab Creek Dam (1,600 ft.)
TAKE OUT: White Rock Powerhouse (1,000 ft.)
SHUTTLE: 10 miles
RAFTS: Possible
AVERAGE GRADIENT: 89 fpm; mi/mi: 110, 100, 100, 150, 60, 50, 60
GAUGE: The *Release from Chili Bar*, less 3,500 cfs diversion. EXAMPLE: When Chili Bar release is 5,000 cfs, Slab Creek will be running 1,500 cfs. Runnable during the peak of a normal year (flow phone).
BOATING SEASON: Spring
WATER SOURCE: Spill
AAA and *TOPO MAPS*: Lake Tahoe Region; *Slate Mtn., Garden Valley* (7.5 series)

Slab Creek lay waiting to be paddled for many years. Macho river explorers desperately searched up and down the state for elusive first descents while Slab Creek rested a few miles upstream of Chili Bar. I always wondered about the possibility of a run between the Golden Gate and Chili Bar, but I never got around to getting out the topo maps. Two separate groups finally planned the run in the spring of '82. Louis Debret and Tom Anderson made the first run April 20, one week before a group from the Loma Prieta Paddlers traversed the section. The word has spread quickly and now many paddlers have made the trip.

The whitewater on this section of the South Fork is excellent, as there are many class III and IV rapids. Depending on the flow, expect to stretch your legs while scouting a few rapids. Below the Mosquito Ridge Road bridge awaits Mother Lode Falls, a tough class V that is normally portaged with moderate effort. I know of one heroic run by Vince Hayes—all others have sniveled down the left bank defeated. When drifting the flat water, feel free to gaze upon the lovely granite canyon. The rapids are formed by the same material; large smooth granite boulders provide the whitewater action.

The water for this run spills from Slab Creek Dam. PG & E is able to divert 3,500 cfs out of the river bed; the remainder of the river's flow spills the dam. The water level can be easily determined from the flow at Chili Bar.

Simply subtract 3,500 cfs from the Chili Bar flow and you have it.

Finding the put-in and take-out for this run is a bit tricky. When I ran the river with Lars and Vince Hayes, we missed the turn to the put-in. A friendly local led us to the unmarked road that leads to the put-in, Slab Creek Dam. The take-out is a bit easier to find, but the road isn't marked on the AAA map. Both roads are found on the Eldorado National Forest map. One can also access the river at the Mosquito Ridge Road bridge, 3.3 miles down the run.

To get to the put-in, drive a few miles east of Placerville on Hwy. 50 and take the Schnell School Road exit. Turn left and go under the freeway up to Carson Road where you turn right. Drive 3 miles and turn left on North Canyon Road. Continue 2 miles to the Hassler Road junction. From there, it's 0.5 miles, just past a creek, to the only wide gravel road on the left. Follow this road down to a locked gate at Slab Creek Dam. It is a short walk to the river.

To get to the take-out, drive north on Mosquito Road out of Placerville 2 miles and turn left on Meadow Lane (this sign is small, so keep an eye out). A few miles down this road is a locked gate barring access to White Rock Powerhouse. It's a 10-minute walk to the river.

—CS

SOUTH FORK AMERICAN RIVER (Chili Bar)

DIFFICULTY	FLOW	OPTIMUM	MILES	PORTAGES
III+	700-1500	2000	5.8	0
III-IV	1500-10000			

PUT IN:	**Route 193 (930 ft.)**
TAKE OUT:	**Coloma (750 ft.)**
SHUTTLE:	**9 miles**
RAFTS:	**YES (commercial run)**
AVERAGE GRADIENT:	**31 fpm**
GAUGE:	**The *Release from Chili Bar* is just above the put-in. This is the flow you'll be on (flow phone).**

BOATING SEASON:	**Winter**	**Spring**	**Summer**	**Fall**
WATER SOURCE:	**Spill/Pwr.**	**Spill/Pwr.**	**Power**	**Power**

AAA and *TOPO MAPS*: **Lake Tahoe Region; *Garden Valley, Coloma* (7.5 series)**

The Chili Bar run is probably the most popular whitewater run in the western United States. Due to its centralized location, reliable dam release, and good rapids, hundreds of boaters congregate here on summer weekends. Seen from the air on Memorial Day Weekend, the run might look like an unbroken chain of rafts being expelled from cars at the put-in, and sucked back in at the take-out. On weekends such as these, the scavenging kayaker is likely to find a fantastic array of beers, sodas, and suntan lotions in the eddies.

This run has long been a learning and practice area for rafters and kayakers, and the hole at the put-in is a favorite play spot.

The put-in is reached by driving north on Route 49 from Placerville. On the edge of town, turn onto Route 193 and go 3 miles downhill to the river. A fee is charged to put in.

The take-out can be reached by a variety of ways, but the easiest is to go north on Route 49 until the town of Coloma. The park just downstream from the main part of town is a good take-out, but be prepared to pay another fee.

—LH

Paul Stone, First Threat, Chili Bar. ***Chuck Stanley***

SOUTH FORK AMERICAN RIVER (Coloma to Lotus)

DIFFICULTY	FLOW	OPTIMUM	MILES	PORTAGES
II	500-1500	1500	3	0
II+	1500-3000			
III	>3000			

PUT IN: Coloma Park (750 ft.)
TAKE OUT: Lotus Campground (680 ft.)
SHUTTLE: 3 miles
RAFTS: YES (commercial run)
AVERAGE GRADIENT: 24 fpm
GAUGE: The *Release from Chili Bar* is 6 miles above the put-in. This is the flow you'll be on (flow phone).

BOATING SEASON:	Spring	Summer
WATER SOURCE:	Spill/Release	Release

AAA and *TOPO MAPS*: Lake Tahoe Region; *Coloma* (7.5 series)

This is an excellent first whitewater kayaking trip. The rapids are quite straightforward yet will pose a variety of challenges for the beginning paddler. Lotus Ledge hole, which is about a mile downstream of the Hwy. 49 bridge, has put many upstarts back in their places. There are many access points along the stretch in case some neophyte gets cold feet.

The best put-in is at Coloma State Park, which is on Hwy. 49 in Coloma. Here you'll find ample parking and flush toilets. Be prepared to pay a fee to put in or take out. To get to the take-out, drive north on Hwy. 49 a mile or so, and turn left on Lotus Road. Drive 1.5 miles to Bassi Road and turn right. It's a mile to Camp Lotus, which has camping, flush toilets, and a small store. Again, be prepared to pay a fee to put in or take out.

—*CS*

SOUTH FORK AMERICAN RIVER (The Gorge)

DIFFICULTY	FLOW	OPTIMUM	MILES	PORTAGES
III+	800-2000	2000	11.2	0
III-IV	2000-10000			

PUT IN:	**Lotus Campground (680 ft.)**
TAKE OUT:	**Folsom Lake (440 ft.)**
SHUTTLE:	**15 miles**
RAFTS:	**YES (commercial run)**
AVERAGE GRADIENT:	**21 fpm**
GAUGE:	**The *Release from Chili Bar* is 9 miles above the put-in. This is the flow you'll be on (flow phone).**

BOATING SEASON:	**Winter**	**Spring**	**Summer**	**Fall**
WATER SOURCE:	**Spill/Pwr.**	**Spill/Pwr.**	**Power**	**Power**

AAA and *TOPO MAPS*: **Lake Tahoe Region; *Coloma, Pilot Hill* (7.5 series)**

On this run, the river flows through the rolling foothills for about 7 miles before entering the last gorge on the South American River. The ride through the gorge is relatively easy but fun. At high water, the gorge can be very exciting.

The put-in is at Camp Lotus, or at the Route 49 bridge a few miles upstream. Camp Lotus is reached by turning onto Lotus Road from Route 49 in Coloma, and driving one mile to Bassi Road. A mile down Bassi Road is the campground entrance. A fee is charged to put in or take out here.

The take-out is on Folsom Lake, and is reached by driving north on Route 49 about 7 miles, then turning left on Salmon Falls Road near Pilot Hill. Follow Salmon Falls Road to the lake. A large take-out area has been constructed here, complete with bathrooms and a parking lot that doesn't drain rain water. When the reservoir is full, there is over a mile of flat water to the take-out.

—LH

COSUMNES RIVER (Upper Run)

DIFFICULTY	FLOW	OPTIMUM	MILES	PORTAGES
IV	500-1500	1200	10.5	1
IV+	1500-2500			
V	>2500			

PUT IN: Hwy. 49 (770 ft.)
TAKE OUT: Latrobe Road (340 ft.)
SHUTTLE: 15 miles
RAFTS: NO
AVERAGE GRADIENT: 41 fpm; 100 fpm first two miles, the rest is 25 fpm
GAUGE: The *Flow at Michigan Bar*, a bridge about 6 miles below the take-out, is about what you'll get (flow phone).
BOATING SEASON: Winter
WATER SOURCE: Natural
AAA and *TOPO MAPS*: Lake Tahoe; *Fiddletown, Latrobe* (7.5 series)

The Cosumnes is a good Sierra winter run, if such a thing can be said. The low-elevation Sierras, in general, can be boated in the winter; the water is still just as wet, but the weather is cold. Every time I paddle Chili Bar on a 55-degree rainy day, I can't help but remember how much better it is in the summer.

So what's different about the Cosumnes? Well, it doesn't run in the summer and has a very short spring season due to its low elevation drainage. Since the Cosumnes doesn't flow during the summer, you won't be distracted by any fond memories of warm whitewater frolicking.

The crux of the run is a hassle-free put-in and take-out. The access to the river at Latrobe Road is hindered by overzealous enforcement of contrived parking and trespass laws by the local sheriff. A commando take-out or put-in on the river left is your best bet if you must use the Latrobe Road access. All the trouble is due to the popularity of the area with bikers and other fun types whom the locals desire to send elsewhere. I recommend running both the upper and lower runs in a single shot; it's long, but just think of the exercise benefits.

The whitewater on this section is short but sweet. As the gradient warns, the first two miles are fairly continuous class IV; the section terminates with Old and Grey, a runnable class VI. The name of the falls comes from John "Tiger" Holland's announcement that he'll be "old and grey" when some brave soul attempts to run the awesome 30-foot double falls. There is an easy portage on the right. Afterwards, the river falls a bit flat; check out the OK scenery while you paddle off that winter fat.

To get to the take-out, drive east from Sacramento on Hwy. 16. About 11 miles past the Hwy. 16 bridge over the Cosumnes, you'll get to Latrobe Road; turn left here and drive to the bridge. If you leave a car here, you'll get a ticket. The put-in is the Hwy. 49 bridge over the river.

—CS

COSUMNES RIVER (Lower Run)

DIFFICULTY	FLOW	OPTIMUM	MILES	PORTAGES
III+ (one IV)	800-1500	1500	10	1
IV	>1500			

PUT IN: Latrobe Road (340 ft.)
TAKE OUT: Hwy. 16 (100 ft.)
SHUTTLE: 12 miles
RAFTS: NO
AVERAGE GRADIENT: 24 fpm
GAUGE: The *Flow at Michigan Bar*, a bridge about 6 miles below the put-in, is what you'll get (flow phone).
BOATING SEASON: Winter
WATER SOURCE: Natural
AAA and *TOPO MAPS*: Lake Tahoe Region; *Latrobe, Folsom SE* (7.5 series)

As mentioned in the Upper Cosumnes description, there is a considerable chance of confrontation with either the law or a landowner at the put-in (Latrobe Road). I recommend either running both the upper and lower sections together, thus avoiding Latrobe Road, or executing a commando put-in (CoPI). To successfully execute a CoPI, the sportsmen arrive at the put-in fully dressed and prepared to paddle. Once the car halts, they grab the boats and beat a hasty path to the water while the shuttle bunny (a person dressed in a rabbit suit) speeds off in the get-away car, drawing away any interference. Whatever you do, good luck.

Once in the water, one can look forward to a wicked waterfall (exit stage right 0.5 miles below the put-in!), after that a nice class IV, and about 6 decent class III rapids; the rest is flat. Enjoy the scenery.

For you daredevils out there, I'll mention that the falls were run at 7,000 cfs, with excellent style, by Super Kid Vince Hayes. Watch out for the hole at the bottom. There is a diversion dam towards the end which is easily portaged on the right.

To get to the take-out, drive east out of Sacramento on Hwy. 16 until you reach the bridge over the Cosumnes. There is a good parking area and take-out on river left. To get to the put-in, drive east from the take-out on Hwy. 16 until you see Latrobe Road; turn left here. Drive until you cross the river. If you leave a car here, it will get a ticket!

—CS

NORTH FORK MOKELUMNE RIVER (Fantasy Falls Run)

DIFFICULTY	FLOW	OPTIMUM	MILES	PORTAGES
IV-V	500-1200 (inflow)	800	24.9 (4.9 across reservoir)	35

PUT IN: Route 4 Bridge (7,060 ft.)
TAKE OUT: Salt Springs Reservoir (3,950 ft.)
SHUTTLE: 45 miles (dirt and pavement)
RAFTS: NO
AVERAGE GRADIENT: 156 fpm; mi/mi: 285, 195, 70, 140, 240, 290, 150, 100, 160, 40, 100, 200, 120, 200, 100, 80, 190, 170, 170, 100
GAUGE: Call Flood Operations (Appendix III) and ask for inflow on Salt Springs Reservoir, the take-out.
BOATING SEASON: Spring
WATER SOURCE: Natural
USFS and *TOPO MAPS*: Stanislaus NF; ***Markleeville, Silverlake, Big Meadow*** (15 series)

Several winters ago, as I skied down Deer Valley into the Mokelumne Canyon, the idea of paddling these upper reaches struck me. After looking at topos, and realizing how hideously steep this section is, my obsession waned. By June 1981, however, the gradient didn't seem so ridiculous;

Chuck Stanley in a narrow gorge, first day of Fantasy Falls run, 1981.
Rick Fernald

Chuck, Richard, Don Banducci, Rick Fernald and I put in on a measly 300 cfs.

Going fairly quickly, and putting in long days, the run took us 4 days. Five of the portages are a quarter mile or longer, though none are technical. Keep the boat light, as it will often be on your shoulder.

Around mile 16, which was the end of our third day, are a pair of spectacular falls. The 2 miles above the falls are probably the most uninterrupted section of rapids on the river; "Fantasy Falls" provides a spectacular finale. We ran only the lower of the 2 waterfalls, a drop of 22 feet.

The last 4 miles to the lake contain some good rapids and portages around awesome drops. A series of class IV rapids drops right into the lake.

A strong tailwind created waves on the water, and we surfed the 5 miles across the reservoir to the dam.

Put in at the bridge across the Mokelumne River, 13 miles east of Bear Valley on Route 4.

A USFS map is essential for finding the take-out, and even with a map we had trouble. Seven miles west of Bear Valley on Route 4, turn north at Cabbage Patch Maintenance Station and find your way through the maze of dirt roads that lead to the Mokelumne below Salt Springs Reservoir. There are signs along the way to ease the confusion. It is possible to shuttle on the other side of the canyon, via Routes 88 and 89, but this greatly lengthens the shuttle.

—LH

Dieter King running F-111 Falls on the Golden Gate Run, South Fork American River.
Chuck Stanley

NORTH FORK MOKELUMNE RIVER
(Bear River to Tiger Creek)

DIFFICULTY	FLOW	OPTIMUM	MILES	PORTAGES
III-IV	700-1500	2000	14.8	1
IV-V	1500-4000			

PUT IN:	**Near Bear River (3,140 ft.)**
TAKE OUT:	**Tiger Creek Afterbay (2,340 ft.)**
SHUTTLE:	**20 miles (dirt)**
RAFTS:	**YES**
AVERAGE GRADIENT:	**54 fpm: 100 fpm in last 2 miles**
GAUGE:	**Runnable during peak run-off in a normal year.**
BOATING SEASON:	**Spring**
WATER SOURCE:	**Spill**
USFS and *TOPO MAPS*:	**Stanislaus NF; *Blue Mtn.* (15 series)**

In the first 10 miles, the rapids are moderate, the scenery pleasant. The rapids get longer and more difficult as the run progresses, and shortly before entering the "gorge" there are a few long class IV rapids.

The last 2 miles of this gorge is a granite canyon containing several big rapids. The last one is often portaged. Shortly below this is a 15-foot dam that requires a carry. The river slows down quickly and is soon impounded by the small Tiger Creek Afterbay.

To reach the take-out, go east on Route 88 from Jackson. Two miles past the town of Pioneer, take the turn-off for the Tiger Creek and Mokelumne River areas. This turn is to the right, next to Buckhorn Lodge. It is 2 to 3 miles to Tiger Creek.

To reach the put-in from here, drive up the dirt road that parallels the canyon on the north side. There are signs along the way, and turns are marked. Put in at the first campground after crossing the Bear River.

—LH

NORTH FORK MOKELUMNE RIVER
(Tiger Creek Dam Run)

DIFFICULTY	FLOW	OPTIMUM	MILES	PORTAGES
IV	600-2500	1500	3	0
IV+	>2500			

PUT IN: Below Tiger Creek Dam (2,220 ft.)
TAKE OUT: Red Corral Road (2,020 ft.)
SHUTTLE: 3 miles (good gravel road)
RAFTS: YES
AVERAGE GRADIENT: 67 fpm
GAUGE: Runnable during peak run-off of a normal year, when Tiger Creek dam spills (PG&E knows when this happens, if you can get them to tell you).
BOATING SEASON: Spring
WATER SOURCE: Spill
AAA and *TOPO MAPS*: Lake Tahoe Region; *West Point* (7.5 series)

This is a nice little run if you happen to be in the area and are short on time. The whitewater is fun class III with a few class IV rapids. The forested granite canyon provides very pleasant scenery, and the short, easy shuttle is hard to beat.

In general, the rapids on this section are class III with 3 easy class IV's. The major exception is the last rapid before Red Corral Bridge, a solid class IV drop, and a sensible place to scout at low flows.

To get to the take-out, drive east from Jackson on Hwy. 88 until you reach Red Corral Road. If you get to Pioneer, you've gone too far. Turn right on Red Corral Road and drive until you reach the take-out bridge. To get to the put-in, drive upstream on the river right on a gravel road until you reach Tiger Creek Dam. There is a side road that leads down to the river 100 yards below the dam. Put in here.

—*CS*

MOKELUMNE RIVER (Electra Run)

DIFFICULTY	FLOW	OPTIMUM	MILES	PORTAGES
II	500-1000	1200	3	0
II+	1000-1500			
III	1500-3000			
IV	>3000			

PUT IN: Electra Picnic Area (675 ft.)
TAKE OUT: Hwy. 49 Bridge (600 ft.)
SHUTTLE: 3 miles
RAFTS: YES
AVERAGE GRADIENT: 25 fpm
GAUGE: *Inflow to Pardee Reservoir*, 2 miles below the take-out, is pretty much what you'll have (flow phone).
BOATING SEASON: Spring Summer
WATER SOURCE: Spill/Power Power
AAA and *TOPO MAPS*: Lake Tahoe Region; *Mokelumne Hill* (7.5 series)

If you happen to be a novice paddler, searching for good runs in this book, I'm sure you've concluded that this book was a ripoff. I admit our book doesn't include a plethora of beginner runs, but this section of the "Moke" is a good one. It's an excellent run for the slightly experienced sportsperson.

Due to the semi-reliable summer water releases, good scenery, clean water, excellent road access, and straightforward class II rapids, the river enjoys a wide popularity with budding paddlers and tubers. An added attraction is the annual slalom and wildwater races held each spring. The only drawback of the area is the lack of camping. Camping at one of the inviting beaches along the river will result in being rousted by the sheriff at midnight. The narrow paved road follows the entire length of the run, providing several access points.

The whitewater is excellent for paddlers with some experience (i.e., some sort of pool roll and can paddle straight). Most of the rapids are simple down the middle riffles, which require little maneuvering of the boat. Two rapids of note are The Chute, a fast narrow chute with some crisp waves; and S-turn, a fast rapid that ends in a boiling pool. Both rapids have slow pools above them, which facilitates getting out to scout or portage, for those so inclined. The Chute is about halfway down the run. S-turn is about a quarter mile above the Hwy. 49 bridge. For those into cheap thrills, there is the Afterbay Dam, located just upstream of the Electra Picnic Area. I've run it over the top at 4,000 cfs and through the slots (when all of the boards are removed) at lower flows. I don't recommend either stunt to the inexperienced. Just below the dam is a fun play spot named Maytag Hole. It's an easy paddle up from the Electra put-in to the hole.

To get to the take-out, drive south on Hwy. 49 from Jackson about 4 miles to the river crossing. Electra Road is the turn-off on the left just before the bridge. Just after crossing the bridge across the river, turn left into a dirt parking area. This is the traditional take-out. In recent years, there have been problems with the landowner. An alternative, and recommended, take-out is just below S-turn rapid. To get there, drive up Electra Road, on the river right, about a quarter mile. Look for a small trail to the river; there is very marginal parking on the side of the road here. To get to the put-in, continue on Electra Road until you reach the picnic area. Here you'll find a parking area and a short walk to the water. The put-in has an excellent beach and swimming area (the water is cold). There is an outhouse at the picnic area.

—CS

NORTH FORK STANISLAUS RIVER (Boards Crossing Run)

DIFFICULTY	FLOW	OPTIMUM	MILES	PORTAGES
IV–V	500–1500	1200	7.5	0

PUT IN: **Sourgrass Bridge (3,960 ft.)**
TAKE OUT: **Utica Ditch Diversion Dam (3,380 ft.)**
SHUTTLE: **18.5 miles (steep dirt road to take-out)**
RAFTS: **YES**
AVERAGE GRADIENT: **77 fpm; mi/mi: 100 fpm in last 2.5 miles**
GAUGE: **Runnable during normal runoff**
BOATING SEASON: **Spring**
WATER SOURCE: **Natural**
USFS and *TOPO MAPS*: **Stanislaus NF; *Board's Crossing, Dorrington, Stanislaus* (7.5 series)**

The rapid at the put-in is exemplary of the many good rapids downstream. The Board's Crossing Bridge lies 1.5 miles below Sourgrass. Between here and Calaveras Big Trees, 3.3 miles farther, the rapids are mostly class III–IV. There is a good drop directly under the Big Trees Bridge. This is a common take-out. The remaining 2 miles to the Utica Dam contains several classic class IV–V rapids.

To reach the take-out from Angels Camp, drive approximately 18 miles to Avery. Turn right on Moran Rd. and go 1 mile to Love Creek Rd. Turn right here and go 4 miles to a "Y". Take the right fork and climb .5 mile to a 4-way intersection atop a ridge. Go straight here, on road 5N63, and drop steeply .5 mile to the river. Two-wheel drive vehicles may have trouble getting out if the road is muddy.

To find the put-in, backtrack to Moran Rd. Turn right and go 4 miles to Hwy. 4. Turn right here and go 4.4 miles to Board's Crossing Rd. Turn right again and go 5 miles to the Sourgrass Bridge.

—LH

DUCKIES TO HELL

This was 1974, more than ten years ago, and that might be part of the explanation. Back then, I thought the Stanislaus, American, and Tuolumne Rivers had all the whitewater in the state, and, what's worse, I thought duckies were for sissies.

It was a single trip, on the Chamberlain Falls section of the North Fork of the American River, that cured me of both illusions.

It must have been in early June. A trip was forming on the spur of the moment and Ed Maloney and I grabbed the only craft we could find, a $39 K-Mart inflatable. While everyone else was out scouting Chamberlain, Staircase and all the rest, Ed and I were submarining that little boat through the teeth of every hole we could find. After two years of wrestling with commercial ton loads and 11-foot oars, it was a revelation; I was a changed man.

I was also primed for more. I figured if the North Fork of the American had been good, probably the North Fork of the Stanislaus would be even better. (This would not be the last time that my powers of brilliant deduction would lead me into trouble.)

So thinking, I pulled together a group of friends who apparently found my logic persuasive (that's the kind of crowd I hung around with back then) and we set out for Candy Rock, a favorite hang-out for nudists on the North Fork of the Stanislaus about 6 miles up from its confluence with the main stem.

We got there on a brilliant June morning to find the river running springtime high. All we could see were rocks, blue sky and fast-moving water. We'd brought along two duckies for this first descent, but we'd neglected to bring any pumps. No problem, though; we just blew them up ourselves. It took a little while, but by taking turns, we got them both up to somewhere between dead flat and "squooshy."

Still reeling from the effort, we all jumped on board and tore off downstream.

It was instant chaos. Our paddles turned out to be totally useless. We went careening from boulder to boulder, over falls, down chutes, squeezing between half-width slots. We'd wash out, wash in, jump highside, spin off a rock and take off again. At one point, I tried to stop us by hanging onto a rock. The boat took off and left me half-beached. I washed away and ended up augured in at the bottom of a little falls, where I stayed put for quite a little while. Finally, I crawled up on a rock, stranded out in the middle of all this craziness. After some time of looking hopelessly at the nearest shore rock—a good 12 feet of jet-stream away—Rimbeaux showed up on it. He was able to shakily plant a foot down low on the side of the rock for a handhold and I made one of those "Ooooh sh____!" kinds of jumps. It worked, though. Couldn't believe it.

A hundred yards downstream, we found our little group and the two duckies. People were looking a little stunned. Mine, apparently, had not been the only story.

At this distance in time, I can't remember how the thinking must have gone, but we all must have figured the worst was over, because back we went, little toy paddles in hand, earnestly looking downstream as we screeched out of that eddy.

I don't know how long it took, but, after awhile, the river started breaking up into discernible rapids, one of which I remember we called "The Forces of Kaos." It had a four-cushion, three-bank, in-the-corner-pocket kind of route that we both uncontrollably followed to the letter. Another one I called Last Tango Falls, and Rimbeaux and I didn't run it. But Sparky and Jimbo sure did. You bet.

Rimbeaux and I had scouted this particular stretch, and we came upon a narrow, vertically walled cattle chute, which the river tore through, terminating in a 12 footer with an indeterminate bottom.

Nasty, nasty!

Jimbo and Sparky were still upstream and we thought, getting out to scout as we had. But just as we were turning away, we looked up, and what should we see. Here they came, rub-a-dub-dub.

We started hollering and waving like mad, but there was little they could do. Sparky tried. He leaned out and dug his fingernails into the granite, but it was hopeless. Rimbeaux is a bit squeamish; he averted his eyes, but I watched them shoot over the lip, and when they hit the bottom, they both just tore right through the floor of that boat. By the time Rimbeaux peeked again, they were both spinning around in the pool, Jimbo looking a bit dazed and wearing his little duckie like an inner tube.

And so we had to sorrowfully abandon one of our little K-Mart fleet. Sparky and Jimbo started hoofing it, and Rimbeaux and I put back in.

At this point, things start to jumble all together. I remember one place where we ended up stuck in a hole for what must have been five minutes, with me hanging onto the bowline in the downstream current, acting like an (ineffective) sea-anchor. I think Sparky finally got us out with a tree limb.

It was quite a while later, long after we started wondering when we'd ever get out of there, when we saw a trail sign on the right bank, pointing straight up. We pow-wowed for a bit and decided we'd try the walk out. It was nearly dark and shore hiking over some very rough terrain didn't look too feasible.

So began the second part of our little epic. Pitch black, radical hillside, no flashlight, no food, no gear of any kind, and not much idea of where we were. But when the rest of us started fading, Jimbo strode to the fore.

The trail was a joke, consisting entirely of tree blazes spaced out at hundred-foot-or-so intervals. Jimbo would locate each of them by "feel" alone. When he'd find one, he'd call us all over, we'd slump down at the bottom of the tree, and, all by himself, he'd fan out doing his Braille search for the next one. It was yeoman work. But we finally got to the point where we couldn't go on. The blazes petered out, and we were dead. We laid down in a huddle and waited for the dawn.

When it finally came, we groggily got back to our feet and hit the trail again. It didn't take too long to find the North Fork flume and, once there, the highway. By 7:30, we were back at our house at Vallecito, where we devoured a cake that had been baked for Rimbeaux's birthday, which we'd celebrated the night before on the hillside. By 8:30, Jimbo, Sparky and I were back in the truck for a commercial river trip put-in (that's how we made our living back then), and by 11:30 we had our group of Los Angelenos all loaded up and headed for Widow-maker.

It wasn't until noon that it finally all caught up with us. I fell asleep at my rowing seat while lunch was being fixed, and I didn't wake up until someone was shaking me, and asking where I thought Sparky and Jimbo were. Nobody had seen them since we pulled in.

I finally found them, sound asleep and slumped over some rocks up on Knight's Creek like a couple of old sea lions.

— *John Cassidy*

MIDDLE FORK STANISLAUS RIVER (Dardanelles Run)

DIFFICULTY	FLOW	OPTIMUM	MILES	PORTAGES
IV-V	300-600 (put-in)	500	9	4

PUT IN: Baker Campground (6,220 ft.)
TAKE OUT: Clark Fork bridge (5,360 ft.)
SHUTTLE: 10 miles
RAFTS: NO
AVERAGE GRADIENT: 95 fpm; mi/mi: 60, 105, 50, 110, 100, 120, 80, 90, 150
GAUGE: PG&E monitors the inflow to Donnell's Lake, which is what you'll have. Runnable during the peak of a normal year.
BOATING SEASON: Spring
WATER SOURCE: Natural

USFS and *TOPO MAPS*: **Stanislaus NF; *The Dardanelles* (7.5 series)**

Although I've never made this run, I feel quite familiar with the area. I used to camp out with my dad and brother in the 60's at the first gorge mentioned in this description. We would spend a week or so fishing and clambering about in the surreal gorges. We rarely caught fish, but, when bored, we would tie a stick to our line and let it dangle in one of the crashing waterfalls. The severe pull from the water's force supplied all the excitement we needed, and made up for the lack of fighting rainbows.

The following description was written by John Magneson.

> **On August 28, 1982, Steve Arrowsmith, Eric Magneson and I put in at upper Baker Campground on a barely floatable volume of water. The 5-mile stretch from Baker Campground to the Route 108 bridge was for the most part class III, except for 2 unrunnable gorges in the last 2 miles. The first one appears abruptly below Eureka Valley Campground. We carried this on the river right to a point halfway around the gorge, where we could launch into a deep pool just above a class V rapid that we named "Zig-zag." The last boat into the water got a push-off from a friendly fisherman.**
>
> **Directly below Zig-zag, we portaged a narrow, rocky drop on river right. The distance to the next gorge, about a mile, has a few class III rapids.**
>
> **We hadn't scouted the second gorge from the road beforehand, and we made the mistake of pulling out on the left about 100 yards earlier than necessary. As we portaged, we saw a good eddy on river left just above the gorge that will save us some walking next time.**
>
> **The stretch from the Route 108 bridge to the Clark Fork confluence started with a short carry around the first 2 drops. The next 2 miles were fairly easy class III and IV, except for a pine tree across the river. Around Dardanelle, we came upon 2 children sitting quietly on a rock island holding onto a small yellow ducky at the top of a class III rapid. We ferried them to shore and wondered what we would find further on. We didn't find any more kids, but did find that the river progressively increased to class V. These last 2 miles were filled with challenging, continuous rapids that reminded us of Cherry Creek's "Miracle Mile Rapid," except on the Middle Fork the river bed and boulders are on a smaller scale. The last rapid above the Clark Fork bridge, "Tightrope," combines some of the best qualities we found on this run, including a presumably ever-present driftwood log that almost blocks the route.**
>
> **We were so jazzed by this run that instead of taking out at**

the bridge, we decided to continue to the Clark Fork confluence. We took out just above the confluence on the river right and hiked up to the main road via an old dirt road.

To reach this run, drive 50 miles east on Route 108 from Sonora to the Clark Fork turn-off. One-half mile down this road is the bridge across the Middle Stanislaus just above "Tightrope." The put-in is 9 miles farther up Route 108, at the turn-off for Kennedy Meadows.

—LH

MIDDLE FORK STANISLAUS RIVER (Donnells Run)

DIFFICULTY	FLOW	OPTIMUM	MILES	PORTAGES
IV-V	400-800	700	6	3

PUT IN: Clark Fork Road (5,360 ft.)
TAKE OUT: Donnells Lake (4,900 ft.)
SHUTTLE: 10 miles
RAFTS: NO
AVERAGE GRADIENT: 115 fpm; mi/mi: 120, 80, 140, 120
GAUGE: PG&E monitors the inflow to Donnells Lake, the take-out. Runnable during the peak of a normal year.
BOATING SEASON: Spring
WATER SOURCE: Natural
USFS and *TOPO MAPS*: Stanislaus NF; *Dardanelles Cone* (15 series)

From the Donnell Vista on Route 108, one can see Donnells Lake and part of the gorge that empties into it. I have never kayaked this stretch, but, as a youngster, I hiked some miles down this river with my father. I remember the glow of mystery that struck me years later when I thought of this canyon.

The following description was written by Mike Schlax.

This is an excellent run—quite technical, hard, and continuous, but not terrifying. We made 2 or 3 portages. I highly recommend it for scenery and good whitewater. This run is 4 miles on the river, 2 across the lake.

The put-in is the Clark Fork bridge, 3 miles east on Route 108 from Donnell Vista on Clark Fork Road.

Three miles west from Donnell Vista is the road that leads to the dam. If this is closed, it's possible to drive up to Donnell from Beardsley Reservoir. Mike reports that the road was blocked when he made the run, and that the alternate route was a long way to go for such a short run.

—LH

MIDDLE FORK STANISLAUS RIVER (Sand Bar Flat Run)

DIFFICULTY	FLOW	OPTIMUM	MILES	PORTAGES
IV-V	800-1500	1200	6	4

PUT IN: Sand Bar Flat Dam (2,720 ft.)
TAKE OUT: Mount Knight (1,800 ft.)
SHUTTLE: 30 miles
RAFTS: NO
AVERAGE GRADIENT: 153 fpm; mi/mi: 250, 200, 120, 110, 130, 110
GAUGE: Runnable when Sand Bar Flat dam spills an adequate amount (PG&E knows when this happens, if you can get them to tell you). Basically runnable during the peak of a normal year.
BOATING SEASON: Spring
WATER SOURCE: Spill
USFS and *TOPO MAPS*: Stanislaus NF; *Crandall Peak, Stanislaus* (7.5 series)

This run must be done with the 8-mile stretch below it, if one is to avoid a 2-mile hike out at the Mount Knight trail. Because this run appears to be in a realm of its own, it is described separately, instead of as a possible extension of the Mt. Knight to Camp 9 run.

The only people I know of who have run this stretch are Rick Fernald and Mike Schlax. I have stayed away from this run because of class V poison oak. The following description was written by Mike.

> **Every aspect of this run is arduous. The put-in at Sand Bar Flat Reservoir was very hard to find at night, and we found the USFS maps to be of minimal assistance.**
>
> **Don't be dismayed by the put-in rapid. Just paddle across**

the reservoir and carry along the right bank through several hundred yards of poison oak and boulders. The next few miles consist of continuous class IV-VI water, requiring much scouting. The luxuriant, abundant poison oak and large boulders make for very strenuous going on land. The river eases for a while before the "Lunch Counter," a beautiful class V-VI rapid that we portaged.

Easier but still difficult rapids follow, complicated by many dangerous brush and tree hazards. A large, river-wide falls marks the end of the upper section, and the start of the Mt. Knight run.

Some of our portages are certainly runnable. The steep and remote nature of this run, and the few portages, make it an exciting experts' challenge.

Go up Highway 108 to a turnoff for Fraser Flat Campground. Follow this road to a four-way intersection with 4N01, and take the northeast branch of this group. Follow along until a road leads off to the left. Take this to the river.

Instructions to the take-out at Camp 9 and Mt. Knight are in the following Mt. Knight run description. One may wish to hike out at Mt. Knight to camp, continuing on the lower stretch the next day.

—LH

MIDDLE FORK STANISLAUS RIVER (Mt. Knight Run)

DIFFICULTY	FLOW	OPTIMUM	MILES	PORTAGES
V−	1200-2000	2000	8	3
V	2000-3000			

PUT IN:	Mt. Knight Trail (1,800 ft.)
TAKE OUT:	Camp 9 Powerhouse (1,080 ft.)
SHUTTLE:	14 miles dirt (2 miles trail)
RAFTS:	NO
AVERAGE GRADIENT:	90 fpm; mi/mi: 170, 80, 70, 55, 60, 95, 110, 80
GAUGE:	Runnable when Sand Bar Flat dam spills an adequate amount (PG&E knows when this happens, if you can get them to tell you). Basically runnable during or near the peak of a normal year.
BOATING SEASON:	Spring
WATER SOURCE:	Spill

The Stanislaus River, about 4 miles upstream of Parrott's Ferry. Neither gone nor forgotten. *Ty Childress*

USFS and *TOPO MAPS*: **Stanislaus NF; *Crandall Peak, Strawberry, Liberty Hill* (7.5 series)**

New Melones Dam didn't get it all. The Middle Fork of the Stanislaus is still a good run above Camp 9. The scenery is nice wooded canyon and the whitewater borders on excellent. A major drawback is the 2-mile hike down to the river.

The run starts out with a bang; within the first mile, there are 2 easy portages around runnable class V+ drops. The following 4 miles are nice class III and IV. A mile before the confluence with the North Fork, the rapids pick up again; there is one short portage just above the confluence. The North Fork normally has the same flow as the Middle Fork. Below the confluence, the granite boulders give way to bedrock; some super rapids result.

The story of the first descent of the Middle Fork is an excellent example of how not to run a trip. The first problem was timing. By coincidence, there were two groups attempting the run on the same day. The first group included myself, Bob Porter, Dave Blau, and Walt Garms; the second group included Richard Montgomery and Lars. These groups were separate but not equal.

The first major disaster occurred at the trailhead; Walt left his helmet at the take-out. He jumped into Bob's car, which Bob claims has never been the same since, and drove fast to get his helmet. The rest of us set out for the river. About two-thirds of the way down, Walt caught up to us. Meanwhile, Lars and Richard had arrived at the trailhead and were shocked to see that other paddlers had the same first descent in mind. They rummaged through Walt's car to find out who these run robbers were. They didn't know Walt but were somewhat placated by eating all the doughnuts we left in the car. Once fed, the pair set out in hot pursuit.

About one-third of the way down, there is a small flat area where the trail becomes ambiguous; here the pair made a big boo-boo. With Richard boldly leading the way (having been down the trail some years before), they walked straight across the flat—rather than bearing to the left as one should—and into the bush. The farther they went, the steeper the hill got.

As they neared the river, they were reduced to clinging to the brush for life and limb. On the steepest section of the hill, Richard slipped and was sent hurtling downhill. Only a desperate grab at the nearest poison oak bush saved him from injury, but his boat continued. It sustained a 4-inch slice on the bottom. They had no duct tape to cover the leak, but feared not—they had matches for a fire in case of a bivouac. Richard checked to make sure the matches were OK. Alas, he'd put them in with his peanut butter sandwich. The pair reached the river a mess, and spent a demoralized hour picking stickers out of their socks before venturing onto the water. They reached the take-out at dusk.

To get to the take-out, drive down the Camp Nine road from Vallecito. When you get to the river, cross the bridge and drive upstream to the powerhouse on the river left. Be sure to judge the river flow above the powerhouse; remember that 2 miles upstream the North Fork doubles the flow. The shuttle entails driving on good dirt roads that are fairly well marked — if you know where you're going. A USFS map is very helpful. The put-in is found by driving up the dirt road on the river left side of the canyon. Continue until you reach the Forebay turn-off, then turn right; note the mileage at this point. Drive 7.5 miles to the unmarked trail head, which is on the left; there is a dirt road to the right that doesn't appear on the USFS map. On the USFS map, the trail begins at the base of Mt. Knight. To pinpoint it, look just to the left of the letter "M" in the words "Mt. Knight." The route to the river begins as a narrow steep road which, about a half-mile down, peters out into a trail. Follow the trail to the river. The trail section is not shown on the available topo maps or USFS maps.

— CS

SOUTH FORK STANISLAUS RIVER (Strawberry)

DIFFICULTY	FLOW	OPTIMUM	MILES	PORTAGES
V–	400-700	700	11.7	1
V	700-1200			

PUT IN: Hwy. 108 bridge (5,300 ft.)
TAKE OUT: Lyons Reservoir (4,214 ft.)
SHUTTLE: 17 miles (3.7 miles OK dirt road)
RAFTS: NO (too small and brushy)
AVERAGE GRADIENT: 93 fpm; mi/mi: 80, 95, 160, 120, 130, 180, 90, 40, 45, 45, 40
GAUGE: Runnable when Pine Crest Lake spills an adequate amount (PG&E knows when this happens, if you can get them to tell you). Runnable during or near the peak of a normal year.
BOATING SEASON: Spring
WATER SOURCE: Spill (rare)
USFS and *TOPO MAPS*: Stanislaus NF; *Strawberry, Crandall Peak, Twain Harte* (7.5 series)

This is a nice little run if you're in the area and enjoy running big creeks. As with all creeks, judge the water level at the take-out. The most memorable feature of this run is the brush. On my one and only trip, we were led by Mike

Stemler; he had the river wired. Above each blind rapid, he would give us an involved description of where to go. Invariably, the story would end with "at the bottom go left of the log all the way across the river." We were forced to follow due to the severe brush growth on the banks which prevented scouting. Most of the eddies were also filled with brush. This condition persists for about a third of the run. The rest is open and pleasant.

The river has a small boulder bed with semi-continuous rapids. In general, I'd call it tight IV with a couple of class V's thrown in. At mile 3 is a 20-foot dam which has been run by Mike, but I recommend a carry on the left. At mile 6 there is a small gorge that causes a long class V rapid. This can be portaged on the right or run. Below here, the river is mostly class III. Take care to avoid barbed-wire fences; there is a bad one just above Lyons Reservoir.

To get to the put-in, drive east on Hwy. 108 from Sonora to the little resort of Strawberry. Cross the river (it looks like a big creek) and park on the right. To get to the take-out, drive down the hill on Hwy. 108. When you're 1.5 miles past Miwok Village, look for signs to Lyons Reservoir on the right. Follow the dirt road to the reservoir; once there, continue upstream on the reservoir left until the road ends. The distance from Hwy. 108 to the end of the road is 3.7 miles. Once again, watch out for the barbed-wire fences. Please be especially careful of the one just above the reservoir.

—*CS*

STANISLAUS RIVER (Goodwin Dam)

DIFFICULTY	FLOW	OPTIMUM	MILES	PORTAGES
III–IV++	500-1000	2000	4	0–3
III–V–	>1000			

PUT IN: Goodwin Dam (280 ft.)
TAKE OUT: Knights Ferry (160 ft.)
SHUTTLE: 6 miles
RAFTS: YES (note potential portage)
AVERAGE GRADIENT: 30 fpm
GAUGE: The *Flow at Orange Blossom*, 5 miles below the take-out, is what you'll have (flow phone).
BOATING SEASON: Summer
WATER SOURCE: Irrigation release
AAA and *TOPO MAPS*: Yosemite National Park; *Knights Ferry* (7.5 series); *Copperopolis* (15 series)

All whitewater enthusiasts in California are well aware of the long battle to save the popular Camp 9 section of the Stanislaus. The bitter battle was fought through elections, the courts and eventually civil disobedience. Today, the canyon lies in a watery grave. An interesting footnote to the battle was an Army Corps of Engineers' offer to mitigate the loss of the Camp 9 section by developing the stretch of river from Goodwin Dam to Knights Ferry into a viable whitewater run. A group of kayakers (Charles Martin included) was escorted down the river by the Corps to determine the feasibility of the run.

The section was pronounced trash for 2 reasons: first was the presence of 2 (then) unrunnable rapids, second was reluctance to give up the Camp 9 run by accepting this run as mitigation. As time wore on, the Corps won and they didn't bother to develop the lower run, either. It was with this knowledge that I set out in the summer of '83 to paddle the Goodwin Dam run—I was not optimistic.

Paddlers who suffer difficulty recounting the day's paddling activities after a couple of beers will have no such problem here. One has to remember only 3 hard class IV and a few class III rapids on the entire run. The fact that each rapid has its own personality simplifies matters even further. The first rapid of note has been dubbed Surf City by yours truly. I've seen some awesome surfing on this 3-foot wave. After a short pool is Mr. Toad's Wild Ride. When I first saw this drop I was scared, a solid class V for sure. The problem is an undercut wall at the bottom of the rapid. After watching 5 out of 7 boats effortlessly float the entire rapid upside down with no damage, I changed my tune; let's call it an easy V. Since then I've heard a couple of nasty stories about people smacking into the undercut wall—please be careful. About a mile later is Off Ramp (called Matterhorn by the locals), an 8-foot waterfall. This is easily run right down the middle if the water is just the right level (around 2,000 cfs). If the water is too low, you'll have run the gnarly chute on the left (watch out for the Matterhorn rock) or join me portaging on the right (it's easy)! If the water is too high, the falls form a killer, river-wide hole! Be sure not to bumble down this one. Last but not least is Haunted House. Here the river plunges into a killer hole, followed by a nasty little head wall. We're talkin' wild action! I portaged this the first 2 times I ran the river, but after watching enough successful runs I went for it and discovered it's a piece of cake, if you miss the hole. If you don't miss the hole, you're in for the ride of your life! After this there's a fun ender hole, followed by a bunch of flat water and class I.

The shuttle on this run is refreshingly easy, and a welcome relief if you've run the Tuolumne shuttle the day before. To get to the put-in, drive east on Hwy. 120 out of Oakdale to Tulloch Road, turn left (the only way to go), and drive until you reach the second cattle guard. Here you'll find marginal parking and a gate. The Army Corps is planning to improve the parking situation at the put-in; we'll see what happens. You've gone too far if you can see Goodwin Dam from the road. Grab your boat and gear and crawl through the gate. Cross the canal on the small bridge and walk upstream along the canal until you reach the Golden-Gate-style suspension bridge. The easiest put-in entails partially crossing the bridge to the support tower on the far side of the river. Once there, lower the boats and climb down the tower (10 feet) to the ground. It's easy.

Getting to the take-out is a bit tricky, but not too tough. The road is off a loop of old Hwy. 120 that has been short-circuited by the new highway; thus, the shuttle road can be accessed from either end. When traveling from the west (i.e., the Bay Area) on Hwy. 120, turn left (north) on Knights Ferry road, drive a few hundred yards to a dirt road, and turn left. Continue about a mile to a small river access park on the left—this is the take-out. If you're approaching from the east (i.e., the Tuolumne River), turn right on Knights Ferry Road (the eastern access). Drive past a bar and continue about a mile to the dirt road, turn right, and go a mile to the Army Corps River Access parking lot.

—*CS*

TUOLUMNE RIVER (Grand Canyon Run)

DIFFICULTY	FLOW	OPTIMUM	MILES	PORTAGES
IV-V	500-1200	1200 (inflow)	32 (8 on reservoir)	6 miles

PUT IN: Tioga Road Bridge in Tuolumne Meadows (8,590 ft.)
TAKE OUT: Hetch Hetchy Reservoir (3,795 ft.)
SHUTTLE: 65 miles
RAFTS: NO
AVERAGE GRADIENT: 200 fpm: many sections >400 fpm
GAUGE: Call Flood Operations (Appendix III) and ask for inflow to Hetch Hetchy, the take-out.
BOATING SEASON: Summer
WATER SOURCE: Natural
AAA and *TOPO MAPS*: Yosemite; ***Tuolumne Meadows, Hetch Hetchy Reservoir, Lake Eleanor*** (15 series)

This stretch of the Tuolumne was perhaps the last "obvious" High Sierra run to be done, and predictably had the most portaging. On our August 1983 descent from Tuolumne to Hetchy, we portaged at least 25 percent of the 24 miles on the convenient trail that parallels much of the river.

Lars Holbek on the Grand Canyon of the Tuolumne. ***Chuck Stanley***

HYDRA

Lars Holbek running Chuck Steak Falls, Clavey River. ***Chuck Stanley***

Chuck Stanley running a sliding falls on the Tuolumne River below Tuolumne Meadows. ***Lars Holbek***

Richard Montgomery on Cherry Creek. *Chuck Stanley*

Exiting the Grand Canyon of the Tuolumne. *Chuck Stanley*

Those who want to see this canyon will find it much easier without a boat on the shoulder. Those who want to push the art of running 300-foot, 25-degree granite "schlidin'" falls will find themselves in paradise.

Our group of Chuck, Richard, John Armstrong, Reg Lake, Royal Robbins, and I wanted only to descend as much of the river as possible in kayaks. We made the journey in 2 long days; the 8-mile reservoir crossing at the end of the run was aboard one of the boats that operates under the City of San Francisco.

The most appealing section is from Tuolumne Meadows to Glen Aulin, at 6.5 miles, where there are many runnable slides and falls, and the rugged surroundings are spectacular.

Portages are long above the Muir Gorge; below, shorter and easier. The Muir Gorge portage is 2 miles long and requires nearly 1,000 feet of elevation gain.

In addition to the arduous nature of this run are the dim legalities. Only two weeks before we made our run, the Park Superintendent closed the Tuolumne within Yosemite to all boating, allegedly for environmental and safety reasons. To avoid conflict, we put in earlier than one might normally like.

Hetch Hetchy is also closed to boating, save for the City of San Francisco which runs a limited number of fishing charters during the summer. We were picked up by one of these boats shortly after beginning the traverse of the drowned Hetchy Valley. The captain offered us and our boats free passage to O'Shaughnessey Dam. He explained to us that non-acceptance would result in a $50 fine from the ranger, whom he would gleefully call if we insisted on paddling the distance.

If you're crazy enough to do this run, you won't need to have shuttle details explained.

—LH

TUOLUMNE RIVER (Cherry Creek)

DIFFICULTY	FLOW	OPTIMUM	MILES	PORTAGES
V	600-1500	1200	6	0
V+	>1500			

PUT IN: Cherry Creek (2,160 ft.). A permit is required; see appendices for information.

TAKE OUT: Lumsden Falls (1,500 ft.)

SHUTTLE: 12.5 (8 miles OK dirt road)

RAFTS: YES (Extremely difficult!)

AVERAGE GRADIENT: 110 fpm

GAUGE:	The *Release from Holm Powerhouse* is the flow at the put-in. Less than a mile downstream, the Main Tuolumne kicks in an additional 200 cfs UNLESS Hetch Hetchy is spilling, at which time you'll get all the spill. This generally only happens during the peak. Basically runnable at its optimal before or after the peak when Holm's release averages around 1,000 cfs and the Main is just putting in its 200 cfs fish release (flow phone).
BOATING SEASON:	Spring Summer
WATER SOURCE:	Spill/Power Power
USFS and *TOPO MAPS*:	Stanislaus NF; *Jawbone Ridge*, *Duckwall Mountain* (7.5 series); *Lake Eleanor* (15 series)

Are you a macho man (or woman)? Cherry Creek is a hurdle all prospective macho class V river runners must overcome. This is where they come to strut their stuff or to get stuffed while strutting.

Lars Holbek on the Cherry Creek run of Tuolumne River. *John Armstrong*

John Armstrong in the Mushroom Rock rapid on Cherry Creek ***Lars Holbek***

This is the most popular class V run in the state; on any given summer weekend, you'll probably find one or two groups of paddlers fighting their way down, not to mention the commercial raft trips. The reason for the popularity is three-fold: first is the semi-reliable summer water release; second is the great whitewater; third is its proximity to the famous Lumsden-to-Wards Ferry run. This popularity has provided ample raw material for blood-and-guts river stories. To my knowledge, no one has been seriously damaged, other than a shoulder dislocation, but many paddlers have been banged and bruised. Others have been forced to hike out after they've wiped out on the water. This river is class V, and class V rivers are dangerous!

Do not judge the river difficulty at the put-in. The first couple of rapids on Cherry Creek are trivial. The major rapids are spread evenly along the entire length of the trip, with some of the toughest being in the last mile. There are two big class V drops, Mushroom Rock and Lewis' Leap, which are portaged by a fair number of paddlers. There are nine more rapids that are easy class V. In the last mile, you'll find 3 class V rapids—Son of Chamberlain, Lewis' Leap, and Flat Rock Falls—I hope you aren't tired.

The shuttle on this run is not fun. The best plan is to shanghai a driver. Failing that, the easiest way to get to Lumsden Falls, the take-out, is to drive down Lumsden Road. To get to Lumsden Road, drive east from Groveland on Hwy. 120, 7.5 miles to Ferretti Road. Turn left and drive about a mile to the cattle guard, cross it and turn right onto Lumsden Road. Drive 7 long, dusty, rocky, winding, and crummy miles to the bridge that crosses the main Tuolumne (not the South Fork).

Once at Lumsden, the best way to get to the put-in is to continue upstream on Lumsden Road, 12.5 miles to the Cherry Creek put-in. I'm going to attempt a description, but I highly recommend getting the USFS map. To get to the put-in, cross the river at Lumsden Bridge and head upstream. In 4 to 5 miles, at a "T" intersection, turn right. There is a USFS guard station on the right. Continue 0.5 mile and drive through Jawbone Creek (it's usually hub-cab deep). At the next major intersection, you'll hit a paved road (marked 3N1DS); turn right again. Follow this to a crossroads, and turn right. Follow this paved road to the bridge across Cherry Creek. Once across the creek, drive about 1.5 miles to a small, unmarked, paved road on the right that leads to Holm Powerhouse. It's a very hard right turn. Good luck.

If you are successful at shanghaiing a driver, drive directly to the put-in; take Hwy. 120 east out of Groveland to Cherry Oil Road (just past the South Tuolumne), turn left, and follow signs to Early Intake. Drive across the Tuolumne (you can put in here if you want) and drive about a mile to an unmarked left turn. Follow the paved road a short distance to Cherry Creek. If you cross Cherry Creek, you've gone too far. There is marginal camping at the put in.

—CS

LUMSDEN FALLS

Lumsden Falls is the awesome class VI rapid that marks the end of the Cherry Creek run. Easily viewed from the bridge or road, Lumsden has held an awful attraction for boaters for years, largely because it's right there on the edge. Anyone who's had a clean, controlled run down Cherry Creek has looked very closely at this drop, but only one boater (that I'm aware of) has truly run it under control.

Gordon Patchin is a Right Stuff boater. He may not be the absolute greatest, but he's pretty darn good—and he hates to portage. Really hates it. Which is an important prerequisite to paddling over something like Lumsden Falls.

For years, while driving down Lumsden Road to the Cherry Creek run, I'd mentally run the falls, stroke by stroke. But each time, I'd take another look, shake my head, and shoulder my boat.

When Gordon ran it, I was on the bridge, taking pictures and enjoying a post-Cherry Creek beer. He ran it just the way I'd always done it in my head. Watching him, I felt for a moment like I was in there with him.

Gordon made it look easy, almost irritatingly so. I wanted a little bit of excitement, if only to justify all those years of good sense of mine. But no, he had to shoot the thing with no sweat. Show-off.

For those of you who know the rapid, he ran the leftmost of the two "tongues" on the river right. After getting launched off a rock at a very fortuitous angle, he hit the hole near the middle of the rapid nearly sideways. He was then shot out of there, clean as a whistle, down the main ramp, into the big hole at the bottom well to the left of the undercut wall. As he entered it, he deliberately flipped to avoid a potential collision with the overhang. He flew through the hole like it wasn't even there and rolled up with a joyous hoot!

As Chuck Yeager might have put it, "It can be done . . . but I'm not sure I'd recommend it."

—CS

RICHARD'S HOLE

Richard Montgomery is an excellent paddler with a bad reputation as a Hollowform abuser. While on a pilgrimage to Colorado in '74, Richard destroyed his "guaranteed indestructible" Hollowform. When he attempted to exercise his guarantee, Tom Johnson, the boat's designer, declared Richard a "registered boat abuser" and refused him a replacement. Hearing this, Richard had perverse visions of action with his favorite boat and some Vaseline. However, the true source of the problem lay in his delight in bombing down vertical class V drops without bothering to scout. He felt it was much better style to stay in his boat and peer over the brink.

Having paddled often with Richard, I've witnessed several spectacular wipeouts that his boat scouting has generated. The best of these might have happened in a place we ended up calling Richard's Hole.

Richard's Hole, on the Cherry Creek run, is an ultra-wicked river-wide reversal backed up by a large boulder. The water hits the rock and recycles 20 feet. The entrance to the rapid is a 7-foot slide with a narrow runnable tongue on the extreme right, against a wall. Richard ran the rapid blind, right down the middle.

From above, I saw him hit the hole. His wildly sculling paddle told me he was in trouble. After a brief struggle, the hole won. Luckily, Richard quickly washed free and got to shore. By now, I was out of my boat and watching his boat being pummelled. The boat would do some wild acrobatics and then be sucked under, only to surface by the rock and be cycled back in for more action. This process was repeated over and over. The first item out of the boat was the lunch. Then came the rear floatbags and the spare paddle. This was followed by the front floatbags. Next was the front and rear mini-cell walls. Then the boat folded in half, which freed the plastic seat. Finally, after ten minutes, the shell washed free.

As I got back into my boat to retrieve Richard's equipment, he sat on the shore dejected. Amazingly, I was able to find all the parts of the boat in the large pool around the corner and got the boat itself in the nick of time at the lip of Lewis' Leap (the biggest class V rapid on the river). Several swift kicks had that boat straightened out and we were back on our way down the river.

—CS

TUOLUMNE RIVER (Lower)

DIFFICULTY	FLOW	OPTIMUM	MILES	PORTAGES
IV−	600-1500	2500	18	0
IV	1500-4000			
IV+	4000-8000			
V	>8000			

PUT IN: Lumsden Campground (1,440 ft.)

TAKE OUT: Wards Ferry Bridge (850 ft.)

SHUTTLE: 30 miles (4.5 miles slow dirt road)

RAFTS: YES (commercial run)

AVERAGE GRADIENT: 35 fpm

GAUGE: The *Flow at Meral's Pool* is your most accurate gauge, but occasionally this gets left off the recording. The *Inflow to Don Pedro* is always there, but this is a figure somewhat inflated (by 10-25%?) by its inclusion of some significant tributaries as well as the outflow from Moccasin Powerhouse.

BOATING SEASON: Spring — Summer

WATER SOURCE: Spill/Power — Power

USFS and *TOPO MAPS*: Stanislaus NF; *Jawbone Ridge, Groveland, Standard, Moccasin* (7.5 series)

I'm tired of writing this book and wish I was shooting Sunderland's Chute at 15,000 cfs! That would be a thrill. But instead I'm sitting in front of this dumb word processor, typing my life away for your benefit. I know you don't care, so it's on with the show.

The "T" is another classic: great rapids, great scenery, and great camping. The river flows the entire spring and summer due to water releases, but watch out for Black Sundays late in the season when they can pull the plug and reduce the flow to a trickle. The Tuolumne has been spared the fate of the South Fork of the American River (i.e., a zillion rafters) by the implementation of a permit system. As of this writing ('83-'84), boaters are required to call ahead to the Groveland Ranger Station [(209) 962-7825] and book a permit. You can pick it up the day of the trip in Groveland, have it mailed, or make special arrangements to have it left out on the ranger station porch if you're arriving after hours. You can also show up at the ranger station and try to get a permit the day of your trip. This only works when the river is either very high—>5,000 cfs—or very low—800 cfs. When the river flows in the 1,200-4,000 cfs range, it's hard to get in on the weekends. Vince Hayes, Gordon Patchin, and I had no problem getting a permit when we ran the "T" at the record level of 13,500 cfs on July 4, 1983. Our record was short-lived, as Bob Porter and John Paris ran the river on July 5, 1983, at 14,000 cfs. At these levels, the section is class V!

The river can be one day, or two if you want to camp; the commercial rafters stretch it out to three days (they drift a lot). A two-day Tuolumne trip is really nice.

The first 5 miles down to Clavey Falls is continuous class III and IV action separated by medium-length pools. Most of the rapids are easily boat scouted. It is wise to scout Clavey Falls on the right. You'll know you're there when the Clavey River enters on the right and the river disappears downstream.

There are many ways to run the "big drop"; be sure to note the big hole at the bottom. Many a boater has seen the error of his ways and wished to repent, while in that hole. Below Clavey Falls, the river mellows out, and there are long sections of class I and II between the few good rapids left. The thrillseekers will enjoy riding Steamboat Hole. The river hits the reservoir with a thud!

There is normally a one-mile flat-water paddle which is garnished with the infamous logjam. During "normal" water years, the logjam is easily traversed by kayaks, and determined rafters can make it in half an hour. After a big flood year, the logjam is unbelievable. In 1982, it was so bad that a group of commercial rafters abandoned their rafts in the middle of it! Determined kayakers paddle through in 45 minutes to 1.5 hours under these conditions. Rafts must be towed by the log barge (inquire at the USFS when you get your permit).

To get to the take-out, drive up Hwy. 120 towards Groveland. Before the main part of town, turn left on Wards Ferry road; follow the signs to Sonora until you reach the bridge across the reservoir. To get to the put-in, drive through Groveland and continue east on Hwy. 120 for about 7.5 more miles. Turn left on Ferretti Road, drive about a mile, then turn right onto Lumsden Road just past the cattle guard. Follow the dirt road 4.5 dusty miles to the River. There is an obvious parking area and put-in trail. Some kayakers prefer to drive a little further to the campground to put in. A further option is to continue upstream to Lumsden Falls Bridge. This adds about 2 miles and the class IV thrill of Horseshoe Falls.

—CS

Richard Montgomery, in search of a river. Near Glen Aulin. ***Chuck Stanley***

SOUTH FORK TUOLUMNE RIVER

DIFFICULTY	FLOW	OPTIMUM	MILES	PORTAGES
IV–V	400–800	600	6	12

PUT IN:	**Hwy. 120 Bridge (3,520 ft.)**
TAKE OUT:	**Rainbow Pool Picnic Area (2,700 ft.)**
SHUTTLE:	**7 miles**
RAFTS:	**NO**
AVERAGE GRADIENT:	**137 fpm; mi/mi: 40, 80, 120, 270, 160, 150**
GAUGE:	**Runnable during normal runoff**
BOATING SEASON:	**Winter/Spring**
WATER SOURCE:	**Natural**
USFS and *TOPO MAPS*:	**Stanislaus NF; *Lake Eleanor* (15 series)**

Though the Tuolumne River has been declared wild and scenic, Turlock Irrigation District (TID) and Modesto Irrigation (MID) still have plans for the south and middle forks of the Tuolumne and the Clavey rivers. They seek to build small, but devastating hydro projects on these streams, and as yet, it is all still under study.

While this stretch of river is not exactly a classic kayak and raft run, it is a priceless example of relatively untrampled nature that we should not allow destroyed by insatiable water interests.

The river is too small for rafts, though Tahiti/Cherokee inflatables could probably make the run under expert guidance. Competent kayakers can navigate the canyon if they're willing to portage.

At the Hwy. 120 bridge the river looks inviting. Large oaks and pines form a canopy over the river. Shortly below the put-in, the river enters a small granite gorge, somewhat reminiscent of the Lovers Leap run on the South Fork American.

Following an easy portage or two, the river opens up at Harden Flat and the river is slowed by a small reservoir. Less than a half mile farther one will arrive at a 25-foot-high dam, the cause of the reservoir.

Below this mandatory portage, the river runs through a steep, rugged canyon for the remaining 4 miles to Rainbow Pool. I made at least 10 portages in here on a solo run. Utilizing the safety net that companions can provide, many of these rapids are probably runnable. There is a portage around two spectacular waterfalls, 20 feet and 35 feet respectively.

Shortly before the take-out the gradient tapers off. Rainbow Pool Waterfall, an "easy" and apparently safe 20-foot-high drop, is the last on the run.

Below Rainbow Pool the South Fork of the Tuolumne drops over 1,200 feet in the 3 miles to its union with the Main Tuolumne .5 miles above Lumsden Campground. The second mile of the three drops 600 feet over many large waterfalls. Hiking this gorge as far as one dares at low summer flows is well worth the effort.

To reach the take-out from Groveland, drive approximately 13 miles east on Hwy. 120 toward Yosemite. On the west side of the Hwy. 120 Bridge is the road that leads down to Rainbow Pool.

To find the put-in, continue 7 miles on Hwy. 120 to the next bridge across the South Fork Tuolumne.

—LH

Lars Holbek running Rainbow Pool Waterfall, South Fork Tuolumne.
Suren Holbek

NORTH FORK TUOLUMNE

DIFFICULTY	FLOW	OPTIMUM	MILES	PORTAGES
IV–V	400–1000	700	12 (3 miles on Tuolumne River)	4

PUT IN: Riverside Campground (2,150 ft.)
TAKE OUT: Wards Ferry, North Fork of the Tuolumne at Confluence (830 ft.)
SHUTTLE: 12 miles
RAFTS: NO
AVERAGE GRADIENT: 182 fpm down to Tuolumne confluence; mi/mi: 175, 180, 170, 150, 215, 110, 175, 195 . . .
GAUGE: No gauge, runnable after storm or very early part of spring runoff (low elevation drainage).
BOATING SEASON: Winter Spring
WATER SOURCE: Natural Natural
USFS and *TOPO MAPS*: Stanislaus NF; *Tuolumne, Standard* (7.5 series)

One of the major chores of MACHO class V first-descent types is finding a decent river to run first. By the spring of '85, Lars and I had run out of classic first-descents. We were reduced to scouring our "to do" lists for first-descent action. As anyone who has floated by the North Fork while running the main "T" can attest, this creek doesn't look promising at the confluence. The sight of bushes in the middle of the "river" always cools my jets. The view from the put-in is worse—a narrow little creek with over-hanging trees. To compound matters, the creek is a bit steep: 171 fpm down to the confluence. Running this type of water is simply a matter of paddling through the bushes and portaging a million rapids through the poison oak. We're old enough to know better!

Thus, it was with a sense of foolishness that Lars, Richard Montgomery, Dieter King, Walt Garms and I set out on the glorious first descent. At the lovely put-in campground, we braced ourselves for the day's events with a shot of Wild Turkey and a quick beer. We felt the need to add the thrill of impaired skills and judgement to this exercise of brush-creek kayaking.

My expectation of bumping my head on overhanging trees was fully realized in the first mile of the run. At one point, Dieter was stuck upside down between a stick (not big enough to call a log) and a rock. Typical brush creek whitewater action.

Perhaps due to the effects of the Wild Turkey, I can't recall how far downriver the first major shoals were. But believe me, they were there! Rather than typical junk creek rapids, the North Fork turned out to have many big classic class V drops. A quick look at my NF "T" slide show reveals at least 10 major shoals with beautiful, big, clean drops. However, there are several long "classic junk creek rapids." These class V boulder gardens demand 8 to 10 distinct moves to get to the final drop where it is imperative to be in exactly the right spot. I recall one such rapid where the route included jumping a small log just before going through an archway formed by two big boulders which was followed by a zigzag route down a series of boulder cascades—tricky stuff. The major rapids are dispersed throughout the run, separated by pleasant sections of continuous, rocky class II–III rapids. As usual, there were several portages tossed in. Lars did the run with 4 portages, while the rest of us walked from 5 to 9 rapids.

The first three portages are short-to-medium and at river level; nothing too traumatic. The last portage is about 2 to 3 miles upstream of the confluence. It's a semi-major project. Here Lars decided to portage on the right; he reported easy going. Unfortunately, the rest of us chose the left. It took us half an hour climbing over and around giant poison oak-infested boulders—not recommended. Using Lars' route on the right, it should take around 10 to 15 minutes. About a mile upstream of the confluence is a 12-foot waterfall which Lars ran (and hit head on!). Dieter and I wallowed through the p.o. once again, while Richard and Walt did an elegant seal launch on the right. Adventure doesn't come cheap.

Once you hit the confluence with the main Tuolumne, you can look forward to about 3 miles of class II paddling down to Wards Ferry.

Despite the one funky portage, I declare the North Fork of the Tuolumne well worth paddling and plan to return. If you plan to run the NF, please note that there is no road access between the put-in and take-out. Get an early start or be prepared to go camping!

To get to the take-out, drive up Hwy. 120 toward Groveland. Before the main part of town, turn left on Wards Ferry Road and follow the signs to Sonora until you reach the bridge across the reservoir (Wards Ferry). To reach the put-in from the take-out, continue driving toward Sonora on Wards Ferry Road. After a few miles, turn right on Yosemite Road and go 2.5 miles to a "T" intersection. Turn right here and go 3 miles to the town of Tuolumne. Just past the park, in the center of town, turn right, go 2 blocks and turn left. Drive a few blocks and veer right. In less than a mile, the road forks. The left branch leads to Twain Harte and Route 108, the right to Cherry Lake and the North Fork of the Tuolumne River. Take the right branch, drive about 2.3 miles to the river, where you turn right onto the bridge, and cross the river. Continue a few hundred yards to Riverside Campground.

—*CS*

CLAVEY RIVER (Upper Run)

DIFFICULTY	FLOW	OPTIMUM	MILES	PORTAGES
V+	500–1000	800	8.5	6

PUT IN:	Upper Bridge (3,425 ft.)
TAKE OUT:	Lower Bridge (2,375 ft.)
SHUTTLE:	18 miles
RAFTS:	YES (see text)
AVERAGE GRADIENT:	123 fpm; mi/mi: 215, 120, 130, 80, 70, 110, 140, 150, 30
GAUGE:	Runnable during normal runoff
BOATING SEASON:	Winter/Spring
WATER SOURCE:	Natural
USFS and *TOPO MAPS*:	Stanislaus NF; *Duckwall Mtn.* (7.5 series)

The upper Clavey River is a difficult and beautiful run in a wild setting. It is a high-quality test piece for advanced and expert boaters. Since 1984, this run has often been done as a warm-up for the lower Clavey. Because they are relatively far off the beaten track, it's tempting to do both while in the area. Also, the upper Clavey is somewhat easier than the very demanding lower run, so it can serve as a gauge of one's ability to survive the lower Clavey.

In spring 1986, Beth Rypins, Julie Munger and other members of ALL WET! (Women's Exploratory Team) rafted the upper Clavey in a 12-foot Sotar. They reported a splendid adventure, but many portages and much scouting. It appears that raft companies may soon begin commercial exploratories on this run, a welcome presence in the face of looming dam threats.

Previous to the flood of '86, the upper Clavey was often done with only two short portages. On descents of the run in spring '86, I added at least 5 to that, most of them in the first mile. Despite new portages, this run is still high on my list of classics.

I advise putting in early, being prepared, and enjoying the run. The following is an account of my first trip down the upper Clavey in 1984:

Richard Montgomery and I made the run with 2 portages—the first just below the put-in and the other a quarter mile above the take-out. With 5 or 6 additional portages, the class V "teeth" could be pulled from the run, making it possible for the confident class IV boater.

Chuck Stanley "kayaking" down the Grand Canyon of the Tuolumne, 1983. ***Lars Holbek***

Richard and I got into an extreme boat-scouting mood on this run, as we often do when the river allows it. After a time we were boating on pure intuition, barely needing to give the rapids more than a glance as we entered them.

When we boated closely there was a certain pressure on the lead boat. If the lead boat paused too long, the other would pass, assuming the favored position. Richard is a master at boat scouting; I have seen few people who approach his keen level. When in the lead, I felt the pressure to maintain the fluidity of the descent, yet go fast enough to avoid being passed. We fell into a dance-like trance.

Richard was ahead and caught an eddy above another of the myriad class IV rapids. After casually casting his head around, barely allowing time for his eyes to focus on anything, he pushed backwards out of the eddy with a strong reverse sweep. As he swept over the initial 3-foot drop he had a peaceful, almost drowsy look on his face. I revelled in our joint mastery and movement.

The tail of his boat hit a submerged rock and his descent stopped abruptly! The change in expression that shook his face defies description. A combination of surprise, fear, annoyance, and frustration tortured his facial muscles. His paddling strokes were nothing short of maniacal, desperate, and spastic. He was scrappling for control! Over he went, in shallow water. He rolled instantly, his face now puckered and twitching in an effort to rid his eyes and nose of water. In the pool below, I pulled up alongside him. Barely containing my mirth, I assured myself that he was unharmed. He looked at me and said, "Well, I guess we're getting a bit too mellow."

Directions to the take-out for this run (1N01 bridge) are described as the put-in for the lower Clavey run.

To reach the put-in from the take-out, drive up the road on the east side of the canyon (river left). In 7 miles, a partially paved road joins from the right. Continue a few miles farther to a major paved road (3N01) and turn left. In 5 miles you'll come to the main road between Tuolumne City and Cherry Lake. Turn left here and go 3 miles to the bridge over the Clavey River. The best put-in is on river left, downstream side of the bridge.

If you wish to drive directly from Tuolumne City to the upper put-in (i.e. you have a shuttle driver), follow directions to the North Fork Tuolumne put-in. Instead of crossing the North Tuolumne, stay on the main paved road (1N04) that follows that river. Follow this 15–20 miles to the upper Clavey put-in.

—LH

CLAVEY RIVER (Lower Run)

DIFFICULTY	FLOW	OPTIMUM	MILES	PORTAGES
V+	600–1200	800	20.8 (12 miles on Tuolumne)	

PUT IN:	**Lower Bridge (2,375 ft.)**
TAKE OUT:	**Wards Ferry (1,170 ft. at Tuolumne confluence)**
SHUTTLE:	**27 miles**
RAFTS:	**NO**
AVERAGE GRADIENT:	**137 fpm; mi/mi: 135, 120, 130, 150, 130, 120, 170, 160, 95**
GAUGE:	**Runnable during normal runoff**
BOATING SEASON:	**Winter/Spring**
WATER SOURCE:	**Natural**
USFS and *TOPO MAPS*:	**Stanislaus NF; *Duckwall Mtn., Jawbone Ridge* (7.5 series)**

The 17 miles of the Clavey River above its confluence with the Tuolumne River at Clavey Falls is a stretch that no high gradient/low volume whitewater enthusiast should miss.

Before 1984 the Clavey was shrouded in mystery. In 1980 Dennis Johnson, that tight-lipped pioneer of many "secret" runs, ran the two sections of the Clavey with Rob Kirby. From the few distorted rumors that circulated after their descent, I deduced that they had done the upper run and then the lower. Allegedly, they took two days on the 8.8 mile lower run, portaged over 20 times, and subsisted on only a few peanut butter sandwiches. Evidently, they considered the 8.4 mile upper run the more worthwhile of the two.

Stories like this had the effect of scaring off even the most dedicated billygoats. I was rather thankful that someone had gone in there before me and shook hands with all the inpenetrable poison oak that I assumed grew there. For years I would warn any parties considering the Clavey, "Look, Dennis and Rob are good paddlers. They ran upper Mill Creek with no portages (a respectable accomplishment), yet experienced dozens of portages on the Clavey."

The scare stories worked for a time, but then even I began to doubt them. As my list of "runs to do" in the state dwindled to less than one column, and my lust for new experiences raged, I finally gave in. "What the heck, I thought. I haven't had a crippling case of poison oak in years (maybe I'm immune by now?) and those old portaging dents in my shoulders are nearly healed."

I easily convinced Chuck Stanley to go, and in the splendid company of John (Bubba) Armstrong, Gordon (Vegemite) Patchin, and Walt Garms, we set off on the lower run on April 15, 1984 at 6:45 a.m. The flow at the bridge seemed 600–800 cfs and we judged it "medium" after negotiating the first few rapids.

Only a few minutes below the put-in, a 6-foot-high drop in a narrow gorge forced us to scout. We all portaged, though on a later trip I successfully ran it. Below here, the river runs through "just another of the 100+ class IV rapids." This one is dangerous; jagged remains of a steel bridge lurk just above the water, almost in the main channel. Next the river bends to the left and charges down a narrow canyon—most of these rapids can be scouted from the boat. Beyond here the river melds into a blur. Only the most prominent rapids defy storage in that limitless gray matter file labeled "class IV pool/drop."

Below the narrow canyon are several long, complex, and steep boulder fields. After perhaps a quarter mile of steep eddy-hopping requiring very precise boat placement, a rapid ends in a steep drop. I was first, and bore all my senses in on the last eddy on the left, above an obviously serious drop. I barely made it. Below I saw a sliding drop, questionable in the center but easily runnable on the extreme left into a green eddy. I bopped over the drop, eddied out in a little cove, and got my camera out. Chuck followed without incident.

I looked up to see Bubba careening down the middle of the rapid backwards, with little hope of catching the critical last eddy that he was quickly approaching. He broached against a boulder that forms part of the last drop and his entire boat slowly slid under water. As I looked on in amusement (it happened too fast to get excited) his boat folded behind the seat and began to slide off the boulder. He poured over the middle of the nasty drop upside down, underwater, and in a bent boat. As usual his halo stayed on and he rolled up unscathed.

I dropped back into the little cove to put my camera away. Just as I finished I heard Chuck screaming for help. I looked up and saw Gordon, the nose of his boat pinned in the center of the drop I had thought questionable. I grabbed my throw rope and sprinted to the rescue. Halfway there I realized that Chuck was just standing there, snapping photos of Gordon. Judging the situation "stable" I got my camera again, and only after several shots of Gordon in animated poses did we get about the business of rescue.

Gordon handed us his paddle and we handed him the end of a throw-rope. He bent forward, allowing the river to completely submerge him, and passed the rope under the bow of his boat. Straining against the power of the river, he sat up and gave us the end. We gave his paddle back and then tugged until the boat came loose. We dropped one end of the line and it slid harmlessly over his bow as he drifted into the eddy. I dubbed the rapid "Double Doom."

Gordon Patchin pinned on the Clavey River.

Chuck Stanley

Hunter Bend, easily spotted on maps as the point where the river leaves its southerly course for a final turn to the west, is a rough halfway landmark on the lower Clavey run. Three or four major class V rapids lead to Hunter Bend. Two in particular twist around bends in the river in which the bottom can't be seen from the top.

Below Hunter Bend the river eases a bit—the pools are longer and the rapids generally boat-scoutable. It doesn't last long. After scouting or portaging a few more big rapids, we came to a rapid created by a massive slide on the right. We ran this one, portaging the 20-foot cataract at the bottom.

About a mile and a half above the confluence with the Tuolumne river are two steep drops in narrow "gorgettes." On our run we took the chicken chute on the upper of the two, though this was essentially an "in-boat portage." We successfully ran the 10-foot drop in the next rapid.

The flat stretches were longer and we saw occasional glimpses of the Tuolumne Canyon. A faint trail was visible a few hundred feet up on the river right. Following a few bouldery drops, the Clavey made a final left turn and ran 300 yards straight home to the Tuolumne. A 10-foot waterfall into a 10-foot-wide channel marked the last portage—or the last chance for a big adrenaline surge.

The take-out at Wards Ferry is described on page 164.

To reach the put-in from Wards Ferry, drive north towards Sonora. After a few miles turn right on Yosemite Road and go 2.5 miles to a "T" intersection. Turn right here and go 3 miles to the town of Tuolumne. Just past the park in the center of town, turn right, go 2 blocks and turn left. Drive a few blocks and veer right. In less than a mile the road forks. The left branch leads to Twain Harte and Route 108, the right to Cherry Lake and the Clavey River. Take this right branch and follow it to the North Fork Tuolumne River. Cross the bridge and follow the well-marked dirt road (1N01) about 15 miles to the lower bridge across the Clavey: take-out for the upper run/put-in for the lower run. From Wards Ferry to this bridge the total distance is 27 miles, and driving time about 75 minutes.

The flood of Feb. '86 changed at least 20 rapids on the lower Clavey. The author portaged 4 he'd never portaged before. Several others were more difficult than before. Extra caution is urged on this run.

—LH

CLAVEY RIVER DAM PROPOSAL

In August 1986, a reconnaissance report was completed for Tuolumne County and Turlock Irrigation District (TID) concerning their proposed damming of the Clavey River at mile 18 (less than 2 miles above the upper put-in).

They seek to build a 400-foot roller-compacted dam, creating a 90,000-acre foot reservoir. The water will travel through a 12-mile, 11-foot-diameter tunnel to a powerhouse one-half to one mile upstream of the Tuolumne River confluence. Here the outflow from the powerhouse will be regulated by a 60-foot-high dam ensuring constant flows back into the Clavey River.

The implications of this project are devastating. River running on the Clavey would be severely reduced, unless scheduled releases are planned into the project. Spilling would occur in wet years, but we all know how hit or miss that can be. The fishery would be severely depleted in not only the Clavey, but on Reed and Hull Creeks, where diversions are planned. Outflow to the Tuolumne would be cold, adversely affecting the swimming holes on the Clavey where so many commercial passengers frolick. The powerhouse is planned to be underground, but the 60-foot dam will be an eyesore visible from within the Tuolumne's wild and scenic corridor.

Project director John Mills is open to any and all comments and ideas from users and lovers of the Clavey River. I urge everyone to express their concerns to him ASAP. Contact FOR in Sacramento for updates on the project's status. John Mills, 2 S. Green St., Sonora, CA 95370, (209) 533-5700.

—*LH*

MERCED RIVER (Merced Gorge)

DIFFICULTY	FLOW	OPTIMUM	MILES	PORTAGES
V+	800–1600	1000	4.8	7

PUT IN: Routes 120–140 Junction (3,800 ft.)
TAKE OUT: Arch Rock Entrance Station (2,800 ft.)
SHUTTLE: 4.8 miles
RAFTS: NO
AVERAGE GRADIENT: 208 fpm; mi/mi: 300, 80, 220, 240, 160
GAUGE: You'll have 70%–90% of ***Inflow to McClure*** depending on tributary inflows

BOATING SEASON:	**Winter/Spring**
WATER SOURCE:	**Natural**
USFS and *TOPO MAPS*:	**Stanislaus NF; *Yosemite* (15 series)**

Without doubt this is one of the most radical stretches of "runnable" whitewater in California. One of the most spectacular sights I've ever seen is 10,000 cfs charging down this canyon in peak spring runoff. I've looked inquisitively at this stretch since 1974, while on climbing trips to Yosemite. As my ability to read rivers grew in the late 70's I began to realize that someday I'd have to run this gorge. All through this period I ran the class III–IV Merced from El Capitan Bridge to the 120–140 Junction, but never dared continue. In '82 I hiked the less-visible lower stretch from Arch Rock to El Portal, some 2.5 miles, and decided it marginally feasible with 15 portages.

Finally, in June '84, having pioneered the Golden Gate without portages the day before with Eric Magneson and Mike Schlax, we decided it was time.

Schlax and I put in during a thunderstorm with about 1,200 cfs in the river. Just below the put-in, we got out and hiked several hundred yards, getting back into the river below a 30-foot waterfall. Below here, all went well for the remainder of the first mile—until we were accosted by a ranger. He was off-duty, but waved his radio menacingly anyway. He threatened a $50 fine if we didn't quit right there. Apparently, the Merced within YNP is closed to boating (even though Curry Co. rents duckie rafts by the hundreds to tourists for floating through the valley).

I met with the chief ranger that autumn and pled my case. He rattled of park regulation numbers, complained that Yosemite was zoo enough already, and suggested I kayak elsewhere. I told him that I'd already been everywhere "elsewhere" and that this was the last gem. He stonewalled me.

We essentially gave up our quest, though thoughts of doing a midwinter descent in camouflaged gear were discussed. It wasn't until May '86 that the spark was renewed by Tom Meager, a fellow kayaker within the NPS. He had spoken with the chief ranger and found that it really wasn't against the law to kayak the Merced. Somehow he broke through the stone wall and got us "permission" to do it.

In early July of '86 Chuck Stanley, Eric Magneson, Dieter King and I embarked, with a park service "escort" of Tom Meager and Lloyd Price filming from shore. On this run we had 1,600 cfs, a bit much, and arrived exhausted at Arch Rock 6 hours later. We declared the run an "expert's classic". I thought it comparable to the Golden Gate, with road access and more portages.

Two weeks later Eric and I ran it at 800 cfs. We found this flow a tad low, but still good. I recommend this run *only* to experts who want the extreme.

To reach the put-in drive to the junction of Routes 120 and 140 in Yosemite National Park. Put-in below the 20-foot diversion dam. The take-out is 5 miles downhill on Route 140.

—LH

MERCED RIVER (El Portal to Briceburg)

DIFFICULTY	FLOW	OPTIMUM	MILES	PORTAGES
III-IV	1000-2000	1500	16	0
III-V−	2000-4000			
IV-V	>4000			

PUT IN:	**El Portal (1,900 ft.)**
TAKE OUT:	**Briceburg (1,120 ft.)**
SHUTTLE:	**16 miles**
RAFTS:	**YES (commercial run below Indian Flat Campground)**
AVERAGE GRADIENT:	**50 fpm; mi/mi: 110, 100, 95, 40, 70, 55, 40, 55, 35, 45, 25, 20, 30, 30, 20, 20**
GAUGE:	**The *Inflow to McClure* is 14 miles below the take-out (flow phone).**
BOATING SEASON:	**Spring**
WATER SOURCE:	**Natural**
USFS and *TOPO MAPS*:	**Stanislaus NF; *El Portal, Kinsley, Feliciana Mtn.* (7.5 series)**

This section has something for paddlers of all skill levels: daredevils can put in at El Portal and pull foolish showboating stunts in full view of the crowds flocking to Yosemite; more level-headed and responsible individuals will put in at the bridge a mile below the Chevron Station and run the solid class IV section; the mild-mannered can put in at Indian Flat Campground and run the class III (one fun IV, at Ned's Gulch) down to Briceburg. The higher the water, the more "F" action available: that is, more fright, fear, frolic, fun, fast, foolhardy, formidable, and far-out full-river action.

Where you belong on the river can be easily discerned: simply look out your car window as you drive along. Most of the river is visible from the road. Be forewarned: a few of the big rapids on the upper 3 miles are obscured by trees. The Merced is an excellent high-water (i.e., 10,000 cfs) run. Remember that full rivers always look much easier from the car than from the boat. I once ran from the Chevron station at 15,000 cfs with my buddy "Big Water" Bob Porter. From the shore, it appeared to be no big deal, but, once on the water, we were shocked by the power and blinding speed of the river. Despite having thoroughly scouted the section, I was amazed. I barely had time to figure my position in the rapid, and had no time to look ahead to see where I was going. The only safe procedure was to pick large objects, such as trees on the shore, to key off.

At lower flows, the river from El Portal to the bridge is technical class IV+. There are many steep drops with only short pools between them. Below the bridge, the river is class IV down to Indian Flat Campground. There are pools separating the somewhat long sections of whitewater. Below here, the river is fun class III with many good play spots.

To get to the take-out, drive towards Yosemite on Hwy. 140. Take out where the road first meets the river. There is a small bridge here. Rafters will prefer to cross the bridge to the river right. Drive downstream on the dirt road until you see a likely take-out. The commercial companies take out here. To get to the various put-ins, continue driving towards Yosemite on Hwy. 140. It's 16 miles to El Portal.

—CS

MERCED RIVER (Briceburg to Bagby)

DIFFICULTY	FLOW	OPTIMUM	MILES	PORTAGES
II-IV	800-2000	1500	13.4	1
III-V	>2000			

PUT IN: **Briceburg (1,130 ft.)**
TAKE OUT: **Route 49 at Lake McClure (850 ft.)**
SHUTTLE: **30 miles**
RAFTS: **YES (commercially run)**
AVERAGE GRADIENT: **21 fpm**
GAUGE: **The *Inflow to McClure* is the take-out (flow phone).**
BOATING SEASON: **Spring Summer**
WATER SOURCE: **Natural Natural**
AAA and *TOPO MAPS*: **Yosemite; *Feliciana Mtn., Bear Valley, Hornitos* (7.5 series)**

This is the last stretch of whitewater on the Merced before it is impounded by Lake McClure and has been a popular kayak run for years. Since the murder of the Stanislaus Canyon, it has seen increased use by commercial rafters.

The first 3 to 4 miles are mostly swift and easy, with an occasional good class III rapid. The river eases for a bit but then picks up; rapids lead to an old, broken weir. Shortly below here, the river narrows and careens through the longest rapid on the run, "Quarter Mile." It can be scouted or portaged on the convenient old Yosemite Railroad bed that lies on the right. A short distance below this class IV rapid is North Fork Falls. This is actually a waterfall of 12 to 15 feet on the right and a very steep rapid on the left. Portage ramps exist on the right, above and below the waterfall, to ease the rafters' laborious predicament.

The North Fork of the Merced comes in on the right just below the waterfall. There are beautiful, warm swimming holes a few hundred yards upstream. Below the North Fork, the river is quite easy to the reservoir. When the lake is full, there are 3 miles of flatwater to Bagby, the boat launch at Route 49. Often a sizeable logjam exists on the upper end of the reservoir, though this is usually navigable without undue agony.

Put in at the Briceburg bridge, where Route 140 leaves the river and climbs over the divide to Mariposa.

To reach the take-out, drive to Mariposa, some 15 miles south of the put-in on Route 140. Go north on Route 49 at the edge of town, and drive 15 miles to Bagby.

—LH

NORTH FORK FALLS

by Barry Wasserman

It was probably 1976, one of the drought years in California, and my friend Jimbo and I were utilizing our modest kayaking skills to run the Merced. The water was low—500 cfs—and it was our first trip down this river.

"No problem," we were told. "It's easy at low water, though you do want to keep an eye out for North Fork Falls. You have to carry around that, for sure. It's unrunnable."

So, no sweat, an easy run with a mandatory portage. There's no pressure if you're told a rapid is unrunnable. What puts your adrenal glands on alert is a comment such as, "Well, it's pretty long and nasty. You better take a good look at it." But that wasn't our problem here. We just had to make sure to take out above this unrunnable falls and walk around it.

And off we went, floating the first few miles uneventfully, dodging rocks, and keeping an increasingly sharp eye out for the falls. Then, around a bend, maybe 30 yards ahead, we saw what we'd been looking for. An abrupt drop like North Fork Falls notifies you of its presence by the way it hides itself beyond the river's horizon. Peering downstream from water level, you lose your continuous view of the current. The flowing water in front of you suddenly disappears. You know there's a blind spot where the river has dropped sharply out of sight. You can see the river again further downstream, and in this particular instance, you know for sure that hidden between the two views of the river is the unrunnable North Fork Falls.

So now, with our danger located, Jim and I relaxed and looked for a good place to eddy out and make our portage. A quick survey showed us that there were two eddies we could catch. One was about 20 yards upstream of the falls and would require a little longer portage over huge boulders. The other was conveniently but dangerously poised just to the right of a chute that hooked left and down out of sight into the falls. It took only a few seconds for both of us to see our choices and to eye each other in unspoken indecision. Lacking total confidence in my mediocre boating skills, but unwilling to veto a simple eddying-out maneuver, I met Jim's questioning eyes with a shrug as if to say, "I'm not so excited about catching an eddy two feet from death, even if it is a pretty easy move." But Jimbo, with a typical air of low-key confidence, turned downstream and drifted toward the do-or-die eddy.

With undivided attention, I watched him float to the critical spot, where the eddy was in an alcove to his right and the ominous chute to his left. Expecting, I guess, that his momentum would carry him into the eddy, Jim must have been as startled as I to see the eddy fence turn his bow and cause him to begin slowly drifting into the chute. Casual no more, Jim leaned long and hard to his right, reached for the eddy with his paddle, and tried to draw himself back to its safe confines. But it was no go. The current had him. As my own panic mounted, I watched him lean even further on his desperate draw, while his boat drifted out from under him. With fear and disbelief, I saw him fall upside-down and quietly float into the chute and out of sight.

Nothing seems more awkward and time-consuming than getting out of a kayak quickly. Once on shore, I scrambled over the boulders, keeping my eye on the river downstream of the still hidden falls, expecting to see Jim, in one form or another, floating into sight. When he failed to appear, my fright and panic increased. In the calm and silence of the canyon, I could only picture Jim dead and consumed by rock and foam. My thoughts and emotions were racing in the way that happens only when one fears that the hand of death is near.

It was probably no more than a minute since Jim's disappearance that I reached the rocks above the falls and could glimpse into the abyss. Where was he? The chute descended about 12 feet into a turbulence of whirlpools and rocks. No Jim! From this pool, most of the water moved left into another steep drop that disappeared behind a house rock. To the right, a small amount of water drifted over a rocky ledge which made a sheer drop of 15 feet into a large pool. As I scrambled downstream, now confused as well as worried by my friend's disappearance, I suddenly found him. With water pouring over his helmet as though he were part of the falls, Jim was sitting in his boat which was fixed at a perfectly vertical angle, its nose stuck solidly in the rocks at the base of the falls.

To my utter amazement, and I'm sure his, ole Jimbo was all right. He climbed out of the boat which remained implanted like a rocket ship that has crashed into Mars. After a short swim, Jim pulled himself out of the water along with a wet sponge, one float bag, and a very sheepish grin. After a lot of back slapping and head shaking, we pulled his boat out, fed it a large helping of duct tape, and floated on home.

SOUTH FORK MERCED RIVER

DIFFICULTY	FLOW	OPTIMUM	MILES	PORTAGES
III-IV	800-1500	1200	7.4	0

PUT IN:	**Snyder Gulch (1,800 ft.)**
TAKE OUT:	**Route 140 Bridge (1,380 ft.)**
SHUTTLE:	**31 miles (3-mile hike)**
RAFTS:	**NO**
AVERAGE GRADIENT:	**57 fpm**
GAUGE:	**No gauge, but generally runnable when the *Inflow to McClure* exceeds 3,000 cfs (flow phone).**
BOATING SEASON:	**Winter Spring**
WATER SOURCE:	**Natural Natural**
USFS and *TOPO MAPS*:	**Sierra NF; *Buckingham Mtn., El Portal, Kinsley* (7.5 series)**

It has been many years since I kayaked this river. Though the details are foggy, the memory of an excellent whitewater run on clean, cold Sierra water remains strong.

After minor confusion finding the trailhead, we made the 3-mile hike down to the river. I recall many good class III-IV rapids throughout the run. About halfway down, Hite Cove is on the right; a trail parallels the river from here to the take-out.

To reach the put-in, drive to Mariposa, 37 miles east of Merced on Route 140. From Mariposa, go 5 miles over Midpines Summit and turn right at Triangle Road. The Midpines Bible School is on the corner here. Drive 6.5 miles to the intersection at Darrah. Turn left here and continue 3.7 miles to a right fork onto Hite Cove Road. Follow this along Snyder Ridge about 3.5 miles to the end of the road, and the start of the trail.

This put-in description is taken from topos, rather than from notes scribbled en route. Given my recollection of difficulty in finding the put-in, I recommend carrying a USFS map and perhaps a topo.

The take-out is found by simply continuing past Triangle Road to the Merced River and along it to the South Fork.

—LH

MIDDLE FORK OF THE SAN JOAQUIN
(Devil's Postpile Run)

DIFFICULTY	FLOW	OPTIMUM	MILES	PORTAGES
V+-VI	300 (put-in)	300	32.5 (6 miles on lake)	50?

PUT IN:	**Devil's Postpile National Monument (7,600 ft.)**
TAKE OUT:	**Mammoth Pool Reservoir (3,330 ft.)**
SHUTTLE:	**210 miles**
RAFTS:	**NO**
AVERAGE GRADIENT:	**164 fpm; mi/mi: 60, 120, 220, 160, 480, 360, 310, 180, 340, 230, 170, 190, 120, 110, 80, 90, 70, 190, 180, 60, 80, 70, 130, 90, 120.**
GAUGE:	**The inflow to Mammoth Pool Reservoir, something that Consolidated Edison monitors, is what you'll have by the take-out. The flow at the put-in is much less. Generally runnable at the end of the runoff of a normal year.**
BOATING SEASON:	**Summer**
WATER SOURCE:	**Natural**
AAA and *TOPO MAPS*:	**Yosemite; *Shuteye Peak, Devils Post Pile, Kaiser Peak.* (15 series)**

This section of the San Joaquin was first run by Reg Lake, Doug Tompkins and Royal Robbins in the summer of '80. Chuck and I completed the run in three and a half long days in July '86 and came away elated and impressed. My hat is off to the first descenteers.

This is the most demanding run I've ever seen. In many places it is like Yosemite Valley, but the walls are only a river's width apart. The scenery is awesome, as are the portages. No fewer than two technical rock climbing portages are necessary. The portage through the Crucible area near Balloon Dome requires delicate friction climbing, lots of precarious rope work with people and boats, and flawless teamwork. We "blitzed" it in 5 hours.

The best boating is in the 8-mile stretch from Fish Creek to Lower Miller Crossing at Cassidy Bridge. Two of our 4-man party hiked out here due to strains and pains. By far, the most impressive stretch is the 2 miles between the bridge and Granite Creek—the Crucible of Balloon Dome Gorge. Below Granite Creek, the towering walls boggle the mind, which unfortunately is too absorbed in the endless portages to fully appreciate the beauty. This run makes Bald Rock Canyon seem like a Cub Scout campout. If you've done all the other high Sierra runs, and want more, this is for you. To quote Chuck, "You'll have to figure out the shuttle yourself. If you can't find the put-in, you'll never get down the river."

—*LH*

SOUTH FORK SAN JOAQUIN
(Paiute Creek to Florence Lake)

DIFFICULTY	FLOW	OPTIMUM	MILES	PORTAGES
−V	800–2500	2000	14	1
V	>2500		(6 miles on lake)	

PUT IN: Bridge over Paiute Creek (8,000 ft.)
TAKE OUT: River inflow to Florence Lake (7,328 ft.)
SHUTTLE: 7.5 miles (boat hiking)
RAFTS: NO
AVERAGE GRADIENT: 84 fpm; mi/mi: 150, 80, 70, 70, 30, 40, 170, 80
GAUGE: None, but Southern California Edison knows, if you can get them to tell you.
BOATING SEASON: Spring
WATER SOURCE: Natural
AAA and *TOPO MAPS*: Yosemite National Park; ***Mt. Abbot, Blackcap Mtn.*** (15 series)

During the spring of '84 Lars Holbek, John Armstrong and I discovered a known but unrun section of the South Fork of the San Joaquin. A couple of years earlier a group of paddlers, which included myself, had grand plans of running this section with the help of a helicopter as there is no road access to the put-in. An account of that failed plan is included in the description of the Mono Hot Springs-to-Mt. Tom run.

First, allow me to give you the lay of land. The put-in for the run is a bridge over Paiute Creek just upstream of the confluence with the South Fork. This section of Paiute Creek also happens to be the border of Kings Canyon National Park (boating isn't allowed within the park). The put-in is 7 miles upstream of Florence Lake (reservoir). The take-out is near the dam which is about 3 miles from where the river flows into the reservoir. Access to the put-in is provided by the John Muir Trail, which runs parallel to the river.

Thus, to get to the put-in (the bridge over Paiute Creek), one starts out at the dam and paddles the 3 miles to the river inflow. From there, continue on foot following the gently-sloped (it's up) John Muir Trail 7.5 miles to the put-in, which is at 8,000 ft. It's easy!

On our trip we arrived at the dam at around 11:00 AM, June 3, 1984. We put in on the reservoir at 11:30 sharp and arrived at the river inflow area at 12:15. At this time we hid the champagne in the ice-cold river water. From here we hit the trail.

Once on the trail, Lars and I instructed John (one of his nicknames is "Lightning") to be at the riverside by 4:00. We figured that "Lightning" would be far behind the much-swifter Stanley and Holbek and would never make it to the put-in before dark. Our instructions awakened a dynamo! From that point onward, Lars and I saw only John's backside and then finally footprints.

We reached the put-in at 4:00—totally exhausted. After a half-hour rest period, we embarked on the first descent. The river was flowing around 2,000 cfs.

Paiute Creek from the bridge down to the SF confluence is continuous class IV to V (depending on how many river-wide logs there are!). I elected to carry a few hundred yards downstream of the bridge. The first 3 miles of the South Fork are fast, continuous class II and III. The only hazards were fallen fir trees near the shore—watch out! This section ends in a small granite canyon with an inviting VERTICAL WALLED class III entrance which leads into a killer class VI boxed-in hole! We easily portaged the entire section on the river right.

Shortly below this section, the river meanders for 2 miles through Blayney Meadow. Some sections of the meadow give way to forest. Several times we were paddling through the trees looking for the route downstream. While negotiating the forested sections, we encountered many log jams, which we were able to safely jump in our boats as the water was quite slow.

The scenery is great. We saw a herd of deer grazing—a lovely sight. In the middle of the Blayney Meadows is the Muir Trail Ranch on the river right. There is a hot springs somewhere in the meadows, but we couldn't find it.

Below the meadow, the river enters a 2-mile-long granite canyon full of nonstop class IV to V− action. At 2,000 cfs there were several river-wide holes which required judicious hole-punching skills. Hit the right spot or else you'll go for a ride! I recall only one rapid which was difficult to scout due to the granite walls. Fortunately, the rapid was only class IV—no big deal. Overall, I recall tons of great rapids. Just before Florence Lake, there is a giant class V rapid which can be scouted from the footbridge which crosses the river just below the rapid. After much deliberation we all screwed up our courage and ran the drop—we're talking major thrills!

Upon entering the lake at 7:00 we paddled straight to the champagne and let the cork fly. We managed to zigzag our way to the dam for an 8:00 PM take-out.

The Florence Lake/Mono Hot Springs area is beautiful. There isn't much better scenery in California! The last 2 miles of the river before the lake is great class −V (at 2,000 cfs). I'm also sure that there is some wild white-water upstream of our Paiute Creek put-in—we were simply too exhausted to even walk upstream to take a look. An earlier start would alleviate this problem! This section of the SF is natural runoff—it runs every year. Go run it, it's great!

To get to the put-in—Florence Lake (reservoir), drive from Shaver Lake toward Mono Hot Springs. Follow this road (and the signs) to Florence Lake. There are several obvious places to park and launch your craft.

—*CS*

SOUTH FORK SAN JOAQUIN RIVER (Florence Lake to Mono Hot Springs)

DIFFICULTY	FLOW	OPTIMUM	MILES	PORTAGES
IV	500-1000	1000	7	0
V−	1000-1500			

PUT IN: Jackass Meadow Campground (7,200 ft.)
TAKE OUT: Mono Hot Springs (6,520 ft.)
SHUTTLE: 7 miles
RAFTS: NO
AVERAGE GRADIENT: 97 fpm; mi/mi: 30, 50, 150, 170, 160, 70, 30
GAUGE: You'll be running on the spill from Florence Lake, something that Consolidated Edison monitors. Generally runnable during the peak of a big water year.
BOATING SEASON: Summer
WATER SOURCE: Spill
USFS and *TOPO MAPS*: Sierra NF; ***Mt. Abbot, Kaiser Peak (15 series)***

Although I kayaked this run only a few years ago, my memory of it is vague. Perhaps this is due to the fact that I had boat-hiked the Paiute Creek-to-Lake Florence stretch the day before, and felt rather fatigued. The run is high-quality and the scenery, as described by Chuck in the other South San Joaquin runs, is exceptional.

We found the run very enjoyable and continuous. I recall no portages and only a few scouts. There are long stretches of rapids that demand good eddy-catching ability. The threat of logjams is ever-present, as trees grow down to the riverbank along much of the run. Always approach with caution, and don't run anything blind.

To get to the put-in, refer to the Florence Lake directions in the previous description. To find the take-out, backtrack several miles from Florence Lake to the turnoff for Mono Hot Springs and drive to the bridge across the river.

—LH

SOUTH FORK SAN JOAQUIN RIVER (Mono Hot Springs to Mt. Tom)

DIFFICULTY	FLOW	OPTIMUM	MILES	PORTAGES
V	500-1500	1200	11.3	0

PUT IN:	**Mono Hot Springs (6,520 ft.)**
TAKE OUT:	**Mt. Tom Heliport (5,480 ft.)**
SHUTTLE:	**20.5 miles (8 miles dirt); 4-mile hike-out**
RAFTS:	**NO**
AVERAGE GRADIENT:	**92 fpm; mi/mi: 30, 40, 40, 85, 60, 50, 60, 80, 110, 140, 200**
GAUGE:	**You'll be running, more or less, on the spill from Florence Lake, something that Consolidated Edison monitors. Generally runnable during the peak of a big water year.**
BOATING SEASON:	**Summer**
WATER SOURCE:	**Spill**
USFS and *TOPO MAPS*:	**Sierra NF; *Mono Hot Springs* (15 series)**

This is a great trip but the shuttle is a bear. As of this writing, two parties have ventured down the river. The first group successfully arranged for a helicopter pickup and had a wonderful time. The second group, which included yours truly, unsuccessfully arranged for a helicopter pickup. We had to carry our equipment-laden boats up 2,100 feet from the river, and over 4 miles, to the nearest dirt road. It took us a day to reach the road; we spent the next day getting back to our cars and running the shuttle. I don't recommend this method.

I imagine you're curious as to what lay below our take-out and impelled us to hike part of 2 days to avoid it. Looking at the mile-by-mile gradient figures ought to give you a clue. The further one goes, the "better" the whitewater becomes. Two miles below our take-out, for example, the river drops 320 fpm through a granite canyon. It's simply too much fun for me!

The river starts very slowly. The first 8 miles are scenic class III with some dull class IV. The excellent scenery makes up for the lack of rapids. At mile 9, the rapids pick up considerably. There are many excellent class IV drops and a few fun class V's. All of the rapids on the entire section were run by at least one paddler on our trip. A strong class IV paddler would have a maximum of 4 portages overall. A macho class V paddler would have a maximum of one portage.

The unique feature of the run is the high-Sierra wilderness scenery. For the first few miles below Mono Hot Springs, the river flows through a forest, occasional rock outcroppings augment the view. As the gradient steepens, the river drops into an ever-deepening granite canyon. At the heliport take-out, the canyon towers 2,000 feet above river level. The scenery is deluxe.

The hike from the heliport to the Mt. Tom road is not deluxe. Despite the fact that we actually knew our location (very unusual for paddlers looking at topo maps), we spent hours following trails that had to lead "somewhere." Unfortunately, we weren't going "somewhere;" we were going to the base of Mt. Tom.

After many group navigation pow-wows, we ended up at 6:00 p.m. in a tall forest in the rain. By group vote, we should have already reached our goal, the road at the base of Mt. Tom, about 5 times. We decided to give up for the day and camp. The ever-active Doug Tompkins decided to hike off on his own to find the road; I wished him luck as he disappeared into the wet, misty forest. My last words to him were a request for beer if he found a store.

Doug returned 20 minutes later with an old Budweiser can. It turned out we had given up a few hundred yards short of our goal. The next day, we walked and hitchhiked back to the cars at Mono Hot Springs. The trip was capped by driving up to the summit of Mt. Tom. The 360-degree view from the fire watchtower was incredible.

To get to the put-in, drive out of the Shaver Lake area to Mono Hot Springs. There is a parking lot right next to the river near the store and the restaurant. To get to the take-out, drive back the way you came to the road for Mt. Tom. Use USFS and topographic maps to figure it out yourself. It's much too detailed to describe. One tip is to take the fork to the left, the long way, when going towards Mt. Tom. The road is much better this way. The best way to run the shuttle is to charter a helicopter ride from a helicopter service in Fresno. Be sure to work out a Plan B in case the weather is bad on the pickup day.

—CS

SAN JOAQUIN RIVER (Tied for First)

DIFFICULTY	FLOW	OPTIMUM	MILES	PORTAGES
V−	600-1500	1500	7	1
V	1500			(recommend 2)

PUT IN: Mammoth Pool Dam (2,880 ft.)
TAKE OUT: Mammoth Pool Powerhouse (2,200 ft.)
SHUTTLE: 32 miles
RAFTS: NO
AVERAGE GRADIENT: 97 fpm; mi/mi: 80, 80, 100, 110, 130, 90, 70
GAUGE: You'll be running on the spill from Mammoth Pool Reservoir, something that Consolidated Edison monitors. Generally runnable during the peak of a normal year.
BOATING SEASON: Spring
WATER SOURCE: Spill
USFS and *TOPO MAPS*: Sierra NF; *Shuteye Peak*, *Shaver Lake* (15 series)

It's hard to believe that this section of the San Joaquin River wasn't run until the spring of '82. The run has excellent whitewater and very pleasant wilderness scenery. It should be on everyone's "to-do" list.

Once on the water, you can look forward to many fun class IV rapids with an occasional easy class V. In general, the rapids are of medium length (100 to 200 yds.), though there are a few long (400 yds.) tough rapids. The class V rapids can be portaged with moderate effort (river level, over boulders). There are two portages: the first is a 10-foot falls into an awful hole; carry on the right side. The second, which was run by Richard Montgomery at 2,500 cfs, is portaged on the left. The second portage is a bit exciting; at low water, wade down the extreme left chute and jump off the 10-foot falls. At higher flows (2,000 cfs), either run the left chute or jump 15 feet off a boulder into a rock-strewn pool. A rappel nut could be helpful in this situation. Don't be put off by the portages; this is an excellent run that's well worth the effort.

The first descent of this run is a story in itself. Several factions had had an eye on this run for quite a while. I got the idea in the spring of '82 and rounded up Richard Montgomery and Bob Porter. Jerry Kauffmann had the same idea and caught wind of our plans. In order to placate him, we elected to invite him on our trip. Both Jerry and I knew that Reg Lake et al. had the same run in mind. My plan was to run the river at 2,500 cfs—much too high for a first descent—knowing that the billy-goat boaters would "never" attempt such a feat. Jerry, usually less than subtle, called Reg the week before our trip and interrogated him as to what he was planning for the coming weekend. He also asked Reg to reveal his "secret contact" to get the water flow. When Reg asked what Jerry was doing, he responded with, "Buh-dee, buh-dee, uh, I'm not sure." Unknown to us, Reg marshalled his troops; Doug Tompkins, Royal Robbins, Newsome Holmes, and Reg were on the move.

As is typical on all Bob Porter kayak trips, we were eating a leisurely breakfast on Saturday morning, this time in North Fork. While I was buttering my toast, the billy-goat boys sped past the restaurant, unbeknownst to me. An hour later, we finally got Bob moving towards the river. As we drove to the put-in, I was exultant: we had a major first descent in the bag. My mood was further elevated by the excellent scenery. I was in seventh heaven, looking over the lip of the dam at the awesome spillway below.

As we neared the put-in, I saw a terrible, almost sickening sight. No, it wasn't a dead cow with maggot-covered guts spilled on the road. It was Doug's car. My premature euphoria was instantly converted to outrage. What were these guys doing on my river? We had to catch them! I tore the boats off the rack and threw my paddling stuff into my boat. My last command to the troops, as I headed off in pursuit, was to hurry. Upon reaching the river, we met their shuttle driver. He was a non-paddler, completely unaware of the race that had begun. He told us they were an hour ahead of us. Armed with this information, we set off at breakneck speed. We attacked the flatwater and ran any rapids quickly. After half an hour of paddling, I saw my prey at the end of a long pool; they were portaging a rapid. We approached the rapid and waved to our friends. They were schlepping their boats down a rock island in the river. We scouted on the left. Bob and I shot the shoals on the left, Richard ran it right, and Jerry threw his lot in with the portagers. It was a rocky class IV.

Below the rapid, we struck an uneasy truce and ran the river together. If a member of one group slowed, all members of the other group slipped ahead. The laggards would struggle to catch up. About halfway down, the first wipe-out occurred. Newsome was delayed in a ledge hole and elected to swim for his life. I saved his boat. This action worked to fuse the two groups; the truce became a peace treaty. From here on, we worked as a team. The bond was truly consummated when Doug broke out cold beer at the take-out.

To get to the take-out, drive east on Minarets Road towards Mammoth Pool Reservoir. About 12 miles from North Fork, turn right towards Chawanakee Flats; the road drops down the canyon and ends at a gate just before the river. The take-out has an outhouse, stairs to the water, and plenty of parking—it's deluxe. To get to the put-in, drive back up the canyon to Minarets Road and turn right. Follow signs to Mammoth Pool. Once you get to the reservoir, drive to the dam; just before the dam, turn right on a dirt road. The road soon becomes very narrow and nearly overgrown; just drive to the end of the line and park. Grab your boat and follow the road, which eventually becomes a trail and leads to the river in about 0.5 mile.

—CS

SAN JOAQUIN RIVER (Chawanakee Gorge)

DIFFICULTY	FLOW	OPTIMUM	MILES	PORTAGES
V	500–800	600	8.3 (2.8 miles on reservoirs)	5

PUT IN: Base of Dam 6 (2,170 ft.)
TAKE OUT: Redinger Lake (1,400 ft.)
SHUTTLE: 19.8 miles
RAFTS: probably
AVERAGE GRADIENT: 140 fpm; mi/mi: 130, 180, 160, 140, 120
GAUGE: The spill at Dam 6. Usually before and after the peak of spring runoff. SCE knows exact flows if you can contact them.
BOATING SEASON: Spring/early summer (probably 10 days each year)
WATER SOURCE: Spill
USFS and *TOPO MAPS*: Sierra NF; ***Musick Mtn., Cascadel Point*** (7.5 series)

Believe it or not, this was probably the last unkayaked classic class V run left in the Sierra. Several people were aware of its existence, but no one had yet caught it with the proper flow. Southern California Edison (SCE) has a total stranglehold on this fantastic gorge and as a result the river has water in it only during spill periods. I monitored the flow for some weeks after peak runoff before running this and found that it carried the optimum flow of 600 cfs for only 3 days. A small window indeed. There is an SCE phone number that I call for flow information, but if it were printed here they say they'd probably change the number.

SCE has a 7.5-mile-long road blasted into the side of the south cliff about 300 feet above the river. Both ends of the road are closed with locked gates, but accessing via bicycle is a cinch. From this road one can preview the run and facilitate a bicycle shuttle of sorts.

I first saw this run from my bicycle on the aforementioned road. From my vantage point I saw smooth steep granite walls with huge boulders clogging the riverbed. I saw several spots where it looked difficult to portage or scout. I envisioned a kayak run that could be descended only with the aid of rock climbing gear.

In July of '86, armed with Firé rock shoes, stoppers, friends, pitons and bolts, Eric Magneson and I returned for an attempt. We previewed the gorge, each of us on our own bike. With binoculars we scanned each major drop (that we could see). By and by we decided the gorge navigable. We reached the take-out, a sizeable powerhouse at the head of Redinger Lake. Here we stashed my bike at the top of the penstocks, and rode double back to the put-in on Eric's bike.

Already tired and somewhat sunstruck, we put in on Dam 6 Lake, the take-out for the "Tied for First" run. We paddled a mile across the lake and barged over the safety booms above the spilling 80-foot Dam 6. At the lip of the dam an airy-but-easy exit exists. We scrambled down slabs and brush to the river below.

It starts off with a bang. At 600 cfs critical control is needed to run a tight class V drop shortly below the dam. At mile 1.4 the canyon cinches down to its narrowest point. To our glee there was a route through the huge boulders. At mile 1.6 a steel stairway descends the slabs from the road to a gauge. In this area we made our first portage. Shortly below are two steep drops against the right wall. We portaged these too, as the outcome of running them looked questionable.

Continuing into the growing afternoon twilight we encountered incredibly good rapids and another portage. At mile 3.5 Stevenson Creek enters on the left and at perhaps mile 4.5 is the final portage. Below here the river begins to ease and the canyon opens up. Of all our rock gear, we had carried only slings and throw ropes. We didn't touch any of it.

We arrived at the powerhouse in gathering dusk. Eric towed my boat 1.8 miles across Redinger Lake to the Italian Bar Rd. Bridge while I climbed up the seemingly endless penstocks to my concealed bike. Seven dark and harrowing miles later I arrived at our car at the put-in and drove up, around, and down to retrieve Eric.

To reach this area find your way first to the town of North Fork, located 15 miles SE of Oakhurst or, looking on a map, 53 miles east of Merced.

From North Fork follow signs toward Mammoth Pool. In 4.4 miles turn right on Italian Bar Rd. Four miles down this road go straight at a sign that reads "Powerhouse 3." In 2.2 miles you'll arrive at the bridge where we took out. It's possible to drive on to the powerhouse, a few miles farther.

To get to the put-in drive back up to Mammoth Pool Road. Turn right and drive 9.6 miles to a right turn with a sign that indicates "Locked Gate 4 miles," and something about Dam 6. This leads to the put-in, also the take-out for "Tied for First."

Don't paddle into the shuddering, boiling turbulence at the powerhouse just upstream of the bridge! I foolishly did this at the end of a "tied for first" run and was saved only by bug-eyed, rodent-fast paddling. Without Chuck to "catch" my boat as I frantically attempted to beach my boat on the concrete shores, it may have been curtains. For a more complete understanding, go ponder the vibrating electric-like flashes that haunt the water where it exits the powerhouse.

—LH

SAN JOAQUIN RIVER (Horseshoe Bend Run)

DIFFICULTY	FLOW	OPTIMUM	MILES	PORTAGES
III (2 IV+'s)	1000-2500	1500	6	0
V−	2500-8000			
V	>8000			

PUT IN:	Redinger Dam (1,200 ft.)
TAKE OUT:	Kerckhoff Reservoir (1,000 ft.)
SHUTTLE:	7 miles
RAFTS:	YES
AVERAGE GRADIENT:	33 fpm
GAUGE:	You'll be running on the spill from Redinger Reservoir, something that Consolidated Edison monitors. Generally runnable during the peak of a normal year.
BOATING SEASON:	Spring / Summer
WATER SOURCE:	Spill/Release / Release
USFS and *TOPO MAPS*:	Sierra NF; *Shaver Lake* (7.5 series)

I haven't managed to catch this section of the San Joaquin River with an adequate flow yet. This description originates with my reliable friend Bob Porter. He's run the section at 1,000 cfs and 15,000 cfs. He reported a considerable difference in difficulty at the two levels!

I've personally only viewed the scenery in the area: it's pleasant, low-Sierra oak and digger pine country. The river flows through a small canyon lined with granite boulders, forming the rapids. At reasonable levels the river is class III, except for the 2 class IV rapids. Both of these can be portaged.

To get to the take-out, drive from Auberry to the bridge over Kerckhoff Reservoir. You can take out on the reservoir by the powerhouse. To reach the put-in, turn right after crossing the bridge and drive 5 miles to Redinger Dam. It may be possible to also take out at Powerhouse #4, 1 mile upstream of the bridge over Kerckhoff Reservoir.

—*CS*

SAN JOAQUIN RIVER (Patterson Bend)

DIFFICULTY	FLOW	OPTIMUM	MILES	PORTAGES
V	1500-5000	4000	11.5	0

PUT IN: Kerckhoff Reservoir (880 ft.)
TAKE OUT: Kerckhoff II Powerhouse (560 ft.)
SHUTTLE: 11 miles
RAFTS: NO
AVERAGE GRADIENT: 33 fpm; mi/mi: 20, 30, 20, 20, 20, 30, 70, 55, 35
GAUGE: You'll be running, more or less, on the spill from Kerckhoff Dam, something that PG&E monitors. Runnable during the peak of a big year.
BOATING SEASON: Spring Summer
WATER SOURCE: Spill Spill
USFS and *TOPO MAPS*: Sierra NF; *Northfork, Millerton Lake East* (7.5 series)

Here lies a classic example of Carl Trost's famous quote: "PG&E giveth and PG&E taketh away." Once the new Kerckhoff II Powerhouse (capacity 3,500 cfs) goes on-line, the river will only run when the storage and diversion capability of the utility company is exceeded. When only the old powerhouse (Kerckhoff I) was in use, the river often had 2,000 to 4,000 cfs between its banks during the summer months. Now that the system has been expanded, a spring or winter run would be your best bet to catch some water.

After an easy paddle across the reservoir, portage the dam on the left side. The water spilling over the dam creates a giant green falls. The next 6 miles are mostly flat or class II, with an occasional fun class III or IV rapid—there is some super playing on this stretch. At mile 7, the river turns to the left and enters a canyon; for the next 2 miles, there's one giant rapid after another. All can be run—one *must* be run.

The mandatory rapid, Binocular, is the crux of the run. At flows above 3,000 cfs, this class V rapid must be run because the portage route is under water. At flows in the 1,000 to 2,000 cfs range, a nasty drop is exposed and one must portage, with moderate effort, halfway down this rapid. This rapid can be scouted, with binoculars, from a distant vista point on the road to the take-out. At river level, the upper half of the rapid can be scouted from river left. A view of the lower half can be seen from afar, but a closer look is prevented by giant boulders. At high flows, these same boulders also block the portage route. Another rapid of note is El Limpo which upon inspection renders all but the most potent paddlers flaccid. A mile above the Kerckhoff I

Powerhouse, the river mellows out to class IV. The powerhouse adds 4,000 cfs, and a mile below is Squaw Leap Falls. Squaw Leap Falls at 10,000 cfs is one of the wildest rapids in California. It starts with a skijump off an 8-foot midstream boulder on both sides of which lie killer holes. Just after landing, one crashes a 6-foot wave and then eddies out. Fifty yards downstream lies a steep 10-foot slide into a crashing wave. If you're ready for some giant water class V action, this is the run for you!

To get to the take-out, drive east from Madera on Hwy. 145 towards Friant. From here, follow the signs to Auberry. Getting to the take-out is a bit tricky. Drive 0.5 miles past New Auberry and turn left on Smalley Road. Follow this road several miles to the Kerckhoff II Powerhouse. It's also possible to access the river at Kerckhoff I Powerhouse.

To get to the put-in, drive north out of Auberry towards North Fork. When you reach Kerckhoff Reservoir, cross the bridge and drive past the powerhouse. About 0.5 mile past the powerhouse, on the left, is a place to park and put in.

—*CS*

NORTH FORK KINGS RIVER (Balch Camp to Kings River)

DIFFICULTY	FLOW	OPTIMUM	MILES	PORTAGES
V−	400-800	700	3	0
V	>800			

PUT IN: Balch Camp (1,240 ft.)
TAKE OUT: Main Kings confluence (980 ft.)
SHUTTLE: 3 miles
RAFTS: NO
AVERAGE GRADIENT: 87 fpm; mi/mi: 100, 100, 60
GAUGE: When the *Main Kings at Rodgers Crossing* is running 2,000 to 3,000 cfs, go for it (flow phone).
BOATING SEASON: Spring
WATER SOURCE: Spill
AAA and *TOPO MAPS*: Sequoia; *Patterson Mtn.* (15 series)

To tell you the truth, this run is not worth driving to; however, if you happen to be in the area, it's well worth crashing down it in a plastic boat. Due to the dams upstream, the river typically flows in the 400- to 600-cfs range. I've made the trip about three times and have always enjoyed myself. There are lots of fun steep drops, but it's very rocky. All the major rapids can be seen from the road, which follows the river the length of the run. About halfway down is a drop into a wicked river-wide, boat-eating hole. I once fell into it sideways and ended up leaping out of my boat, while still upright in the hole, towards the outflow 10 feet downstream; I didn't make it. After several cycles around the hole, I managed to get to shore; my boat, though, didn't come out for another five minutes. We call it "Chuck's Leap."

The take-out is just upstream of the Main Kings. Drive across the Roger's Crossing Bridge and turn left. Drive a short distance to where the road turns right; there is a turnout and a dirt road going to the left, down to the North Fork. To get to the put-in, drive 3 miles upriver towards Balch Camp. Stop just before the first bridge you come to; this dried-up trickle is the North Kings. Put in here and skateboard the 50 yards to the confluence with Dinky Creek.

— *CS*

MIDDLE FORK OF THE KINGS RIVER

DIFFICULTY	FLOW	OPTIMUM	MILES	PORTAGES
V–VI	500–1500	1000	29	50?

PUT IN: Dusy Branch (8680 ft.)
TAKE OUT: Yucca Point Trail (2240 ft.)
SHUTTLE: 275 miles
RAFTS: No
AVERAGE GRADIENT: 222 fpm; mi/mi: 280, 180, 220, 340, 420, 400, 510, 360, 200, 120, 100, 250, 90, 180, 140, 290, 260, 210, 110, 190, 110, 190, 160, 260, 300, 320, 210, 230, 200.
GAUGE: The flow at *Rodgers Crossing* on the Main Kings is roughly twice what you'll see on the Middle Fork (flow phone).
BOATING SEASON: Summer
WATER SOURCE: Natural
AAA and *TOPO MAPS*: State of California; 15's: Tehipite Dome, Marion Peak, Mt. Goddard.

The put in for the classic Kings Canyon run is the take out of Middle Fork run. Everytime I've hiked down the put-in trail of the Canyon run, I've been transfixed by the inviting sight of the Middle Fork. The river emerges from the awesome canyon in a steep series of continuous rapids. What lies in the canyon upstream is unseen and unknown. A glance at a topo map confirms the worst, as the river drops 1260 feet in last 5 miles, an average of 250 fpm. A further difficulty is the 10 miles of boat dragging required to reach the put-in. Any sane river runner would quickly conclude that the Middle Kings is impossible.

The primary prerequisite for obtaining the title "macho river explorer" is a lack of sanity. The impossible is merely the undone. Many paddlers had their eye on the Middle Fork, myself included. The year before Royal Robins, Reg Lake, Doug Tompkins, and Newsome Holmes ran the section I mentioned my interest to Royal. He replied that he thought the river was much too steep—at that instant I just knew he was going to run it. When I heard the Triple Crown boys had bagged the river, a year later, in 1982, I felt as if I was robbed. But that's life in the first descent fast lane.

After hearing the river report from Reg I felt that perhaps I was lucky they beat me to the river. The awesome high country scenery is primarily viewed while schleping one's boat along the river. Class VI rapid fiends will be in heaven. Reg and the guys felt that this was the toughest river they had been down, and I don't doubt it. The walking on the upper two-thirds of the river is greatly facilitated by a trail. Getting through the final canyon isn't facilitated by a trail, but it can be done. Be prepared for extensive portaging.

If you're after paddle twirling whitewater don't look here. If your cup of tea is expedition style big mountain river taming you'll be in hog heaven!

If you think you're tough enough to tackle this section get one of your smart friends to figure out the shuttle and point you in the proper direction.

—*CS*

SOUTH FORK KINGS RIVER (Park Boundary Run)

DIFFICULTY	FLOW	OPTIMUM	MILES	PORTAGES
IV+ to VI	500–1000	1000	7.8	8
V–VI	>1000			

PUT IN: Kings Canyon National Park boundary (4,615 ft.)

TAKE OUT: Boyden Cave (3,060 ft.)

SHUTTLE: 8 miles

RAFTS: NO

AVERAGE GRADIENT: 199 fpm; mi/mi: 125, 110, 130, 200, 270, 290, 290, 140

GAUGE: The *Flow at Rogers Crossing* on the Main Kings is roughly twice what you'll see on the South Fork (flow phone).

BOATING SEASON: **Spring**
WATER SOURCE: **Natural**
AAA and *TOPO MAPS*: **Sequoia National Park; *Marion Peak Tehipite Dome* (15 series)**

In the first edition of this book, I wrote off this run with only a quick ". . . the further you go, the harder it gets, until you are reduced to walking long sections on the road." Since the first go round, I've run this section several more times and have grown to like it. The standard procedure is to boat three miles to the first real big class V+ drop (Take-out Falls) and call it a day. Sure, it's a bit short, but it beats being scared to death trying to run Horseshoe Bend! Die-hard types can continue onward and portage their way to Boyden Caves. Either way, the section offers a scenic run with an easy shuttle for those planning to run the Kings Canyon section the next day.

The run starts out with a class II–III section which leads into a tricky class IV drop, named Swirl de Whirl. From here on, there are several more good class IV rapids and one easy class V drop, a 6-foot ledge named Horseshoe Days Falls, which is described in that stupid story "One of Those Days" (see page 202). All of the major rapids can be seen from the road. The big class V+ rapid, Take-out Falls, is easily seen from the road. However, once on the water, it's easy to end up on the wrong side of the river (the left) above Take-out Falls. This leads to either an exciting ferry or an extra portage. Check out the take-out before making the run.

To get to the take-out, drive east on Hwy. 180 from Fresno towards Kings Canyon National Park. After driving through Sequoia National Park, you'll come to Boyden Caves (a tourist trap). Die-hard types can plan on taking out here. The level-headed will continue driving upstream another 4.5 miles to Take-out Falls (which is .3 miles downstream of Grizzly Creek). To get to the put-in, continue driving upstream another 3 miles to the Kings Canyon National Park boundary sign. It's a short carry through the forest to the river. It's a bust to paddle in the park.

—CS

SOUTH FORK KINGS RIVER (Horseshoe Bend)

DIFFICULTY	FLOW	OPTIMUM	MILES	PORTAGES
VI	800–1000	800	4.4	3

PUT IN: Boyden Caves (3,060 ft.)
TAKE OUT: Yucca Point Trail (2,240 ft.)
SHUTTLE: 7.5 miles (2.5 mile hike)
RAFTS: NO
AVERAGE GRADIENT: 185 fpm; mi/mi: 220, 260, 160, 120
GAUGE: The flow at *Rodgers Crossing on the Main Kings* is roughly twice what you'll see on the South Fork (flow phone).
BOATING SEASON: Summer
WATER SOURCE: Natural
USFS and *TOPO MAPS*: Sierra NF; *Tehipite Dome* (15 series)

Warning: If you suffer from claustrophobia, do not attempt this run. Once you enter the canyon, you're committed to either running an unscoutable class VI drop (Fear and Loathing) or making the semi-desperate climb out of the canyon. A small rock bar just upstream of Fear and Loathing allows an insufficient glimpse of the drop. Here the right shore is a 500-foot vertical wall, while the left shore rises 50 feet. The runout below this is a class V+ double waterfall (Porter Falls). It's a do or die situation. Fear and Loathing rapid is a jumbled-up mess of rocks with a multitude of pinning opportunities. It's been run, but it's not pretty. To abort the descent requires portaging upstream in the water—if the river is too high you're stuck! A quarter of a mile downstream is another mandatory class V (Little Crux).

During the winter of '85/'86 a major flood rearranged the upper rapid, Fear and Loathing. Before the flood the rapid was a clean 5-foot ledge. After the flood, the rapid was an evil jumble of pin rocks. The first time we confronted this mess we had about 800 cfs—just enough water to cover the rocks. All four members of the party ran the rapid without incident, but none of us liked it. The second time there was around 500 cfs—after an hour of deliberation, we elected to scale the canyon wall to get to the road. There is no way to portage Fear and Loathing!

With this dire warning out of the way, I'll go on to say that Horseshoe Bend is an unforgettable experience. The road halfway up the rugged canyon doesn't intrude on the overpowering feeling of solitude. Other than the two mandatory drops, all of the major rapids can be scouted and portaged at river level. When you consider the extreme gradient, it's amazing that all of the rapids on this section have been run!

Before committing yourself to the run, carefully scout the drops in the main canyon from the road. Binoculars are very helpful. About a mile downstream from Boyden Caves is a large roadside turnout that offers a good view. Below the turnout is the first must-run rapid, Fear and Loathing. The other mandatory rapid, Little Crux, is a quarter-mile downstream. To scout both drops, you must hike out on the large rock outcropping 0.3 miles downstream of the turnout. From the outcropping, look upstream to get a clear view of both trouble spots.

Below the put-in at Boyden Caves the river starts out class III but, within half a mile, the difficulty increases to class V. The closer you get to Fear and Loathing the harder it gets. One of the major drops in this section is Not ConVinced, named for Vince Hayes' uninspiring run of this 12-foot falls—the rest of us portaged. The last opportunity to hike out of the canyon is just before the river bends to the left above Fear and Loathing. Below the main canyon, the rapids let up somewhat, but there are still several major class IV and V rapids. The last drop of the main canyon is known as Home Free, while the rapid on the right hand turn has been dubbed Redwood Corner. The ten-foot drop found in the lower section is Bob's Choice—named for Bob Porter's wise decision to avoid the falls by running the left-hand channel. The final half mile above the Yucca Point Trail is fast class III.

The take-out is the Yucca Point Trail, which meets the river at the confluence of the South and Middle Forks of the Kings River. The best plan is to leave your boat at the river, and hike up the 2-mile trail to the road to camp. The next day, walk back down and run the Kings Canyon section. Kings Canyon Lodge, a rustic bar and restaurant, is a nice place to eat and relax after the trip. The food and service are marginal, but the beer is cold. It's a mile from the Yucca Point trailhead.

To get to the take-out, drive east on Hwy. 180 from Fresno toward Kings Canyon National Park. After driving through Sequoia National Park, you'll come to the Kings Canyon Lodge. Drive about a mile further to the unmarked Yucca Point trailhead, a small dirt turnout on the left. The put-in is 4 miles upstream at the Boyden Caves parking lot.

—CS

ONE OF THOSE DAYS

Richard Montgomery and I were running the South Fork of the Kings River from Sequoia National Park down to Boyden Caves on a lovely summer day. We were there because the Kings Canyon run was too high, and this was better than nothing. A mile or two below the park boundary, we carefully approached the first class V drop.

Richard led as we cautiously eddy-hopped our way down the class III approach to the rapid. From the next-to-last eddy, we could see that the river dropped over an 8-foot river-wide ledge. We couldn't see what lay below. I stayed put while Richard ran a small 3-foot drop just above the last eddy, which he caught easily. I was totally relaxed as I shot the small drop that lay only 40 feet before the river-wide ledge. Richard had just made it, and this was only a wimpy class III move anyway.

My relaxed state of mind quickly changed to dismay as I saw blue sky on my way over. What a time to execute a perfect backender. As I went over, my paddle was twisted in my control hand, which delayed my roll for several crucial seconds. I rolled up as my boat dropped over the ledge. Just to my left, the water landed on a boulder, I pulled my elbow out of harm's way in the nick of time. As I disappeared in the hole at the bottom, I felt my sprayskirt pop. After I surfaced I had time to look downstream to see that the hole I was about to drop into was backed up by a massive boulder. The hole chewed on me for a while before I was spit out and shot to the shore where I grabbed a rock and held on for dear life.

It wasn't a fun ride.

—*CS*

KINGS RIVER (Kings Canyon Run)

DIFFICULTY	FLOW	OPTIMUM	MILES	PORTAGES
V	800-2500	1500	14.5	0

PUT IN: Yucca Point Trail (2,240 ft.)
TAKE OUT: Mill Flat Campground (1,050 ft.)
SHUTTLE: 50 miles (16 miles OK dirt)
RAFTS: NO
AVERAGE GRADIENT: 82 fpm; mi/mi: 80, 80, 90, 160, 160, 120, 90, 100, 60

GAUGE:	**The *Flow at Rodgers Crossing* is 2.5 miles below the take-out (flow phone).**
BOATING SEASON:	**Summer**
WATER SOURCE:	**Natural**
AAA, USFS, and *TOPO MAPS*:	**Sequoia; Sierra NF; *Tehipite Dome, Patterson Mtn.* (15 series)**

I experienced a 4-hour adrenaline rush the first time I ran Kings Canyon. This was my first class V descent. Fearless Dick Sunderland managed to pull my brother Bill and me through the experience in one piece. I have not had an adrenaline rush on a river or in a slalom race since; that day consumed my lifetime supply.

When I shoot the canyon nowadays, I wonder what the big deal was. Today we run all but one of the rapids; on our first run, we portaged 9 times while declaring the rapids nuts. Have I become a better paddler or just insane?

The run begins with a pleasant 2-mile carry down a well-marked trail to the river; once on the trail, you can't get lost because it intersects the river just downstream of the confluence of the Middle and South Forks. Once on the water, you can look forward to about 3 miles of class III and IV before the good rapids begin. The next 3 miles have many big drops separated by pools. The typical rapid has a class III or IV entrance and ends in a class V drop; it's advisable to avoid bombing drops blind. Raging whitewater will be found at mile 4—this is the Garlic Falls section. Here you'll find a nearly continuous section of big class V. It has all been run (Lars Holbek ran everything at 2,500 cfs), but the entire section can be portaged with moderate effort.

Garlic Falls is one of the all-time classic rapids. Vertical cliffs form both shores. On the right, Rough Creek and Garlic Creek cascade into the river; between the walls lies a half mile of class V whitewater. No one will ever forget this rapid.

Below Garlic Falls, the river mellows out a bit, but there are still some big drops ahead. After the big drop, about 2 miles above Garnet Dike, the river is class II and III all the way to the take-out. The last big drop is named "The Hand of God" due to Chuck Koteen's miraculous survival during an upside-down run of the rapid; Chuck attributes his survival to the assistance of an "unseen hand."

Time is a precious commodity when running the Kings River. My most recent descent, accompanied by a group of moderate strength, required 8.5 hours to reach the take-out. We started hiking at 7:45 a.m. and were paddling by 8:30. I know the river quite well; we had no disasters, and we took only a 20-minute lunch. We got off the river at 5:00 that afternoon. It's a long day if everything goes well—it will be a very long night if it doesn't. So get an early start and be prepared for a bivouac in the event that it's one of those days.

Kings Canyon has one of the all-time killer shuttles! Don't be fooled by the

Garreth Peddie lowbracing on Kings Canyon, 1983.
Chuck Stanley

Jerry Kauffman about to be launched, Kings Canyon, 1983.
Chuck Stanley

◀ **Richard Montgomery at the start of the Garlic Falls Canyon on the Kings River (Rough Creek Falls entering on the right), 1980.**
Lars Holbek

50-mile distance; it requires 2.5 dusty hours of driving. Taking out at Mill Creek Campground, 4 miles downstream of Garnet Dike, cuts out 9 slow miles of dirt road driving. If you can swing it, get someone to drive the shuttle.

To get to the put-in, drive up Hwy. 180 through Sequoia National Park and continue towards Kings Canyon National Park. If the rangers at the gate inform you that kayaking isn't allowed in the national park, tell them you're going to paddle in the national forest, outside the park boundaries.

The Yucca Point trail is on the left side of the road. About a mile past Kings Canyon Resort, there is a small turn-out on the left. The sign that used to mark the trail has disappeared. To get to the take-out from the put-in, drive back to Sequoia on Hwy. 180, drive through the park, and continue west toward Fresno on Hwy. 180. About 6.5 miles past the park entrance, turn right on Mill Flat Road, across the road from Black Oak Flat Road. Drive 16 miles on a dirt road to the campground where the road meets the river. A couple of unmarked turns on the dirt road make the USFS map very helpful.

To get to the take-out from Fresno, follow the signs to Pine Flat Reservoir; follow the road along the lake until you reach the river. A few miles above the reservoir, you'll find Rogers Crossing, a one-lane bridge across the river. Continue on the river left past the bridge 4 miles (on the now dirt road) to Mill Flat Campground. To get to the put-in from this point, continue driving on the dirt road until you reach Hwy. 180, then turn left and follow your nose.

— *CS*

KINGS RIVER (Banzai Run)

DIFFICULTY	FLOW	OPTIMUM	MILES	PORTAGES
III	1000-3000	2500	10	0
III+	3000-5000			
IV	>5000			

PUT IN:	**Garnet Dike Campground (1,240 ft.)**
TAKE OUT:	**Kirch Flat Campground (930 ft.)**
SHUTTLE:	**10 miles (7 miles slow dirt)**
RAFTS:	**YES (commercial run)**
AVERAGE GRADIENT:	**30 fpm**
GAUGE:	**The *Flow at Rodgers Crossing* is 3 miles above the take-out (flow phone).**
BOATING SEASON:	**Spring Summer**
WATER SOURCE:	**Natural Natural**
USFS and *TOPO MAPS*:	**Sierra NF; *Patterson Mtn.* (15 series)**

The Banzai section of the Kings River is a great class III run. The rapids are spread evenly along the length of the river; in general, they're just big riffles with an occasional rock or hole in the way. Banzai, the first rapid on the run, is an easy class IV that got its name from all the suicidal attacks by beginning paddlers over the years. The entire run can be scouted from the shuttle road.

The Kings River is one of the larger rivers in the Sierras. During the spring run-off, the river commonly flows 10,000 cfs or more. At higher flows, it's a continuous fun class IV. Please be forewarned: the U.S. Forest Service has been known to kick boaters off the river at high flows.

The scenery in the area is very pleasant. The large hills that form the canyon are covered by oak and digger pine forests. There are several decent campgrounds in the area. One drawback, or perhaps an advantage, is the lack of stores or gas stations in the area. Be prepared for the "wilderness."

To get to the take-out, drive east on Hwy. 180 out of Fresno towards Pine Flat Reservoir. About 15 miles from the freeway, turn left on Trimmer Springs Road and drive until you reach Kirch Flat Campground. To get to the put-in, continue up the road about 2 miles, where you'll find the Rogers Crossing bridge. Cross it and continue upstream on the dirt road until it ends at a small campground. There are several rough spots on the dirt road, so don't drive your Jaguar.

—CS

NORTH FORK KAWEAH RIVER

DIFFICULTY	FLOW	OPTIMUM	MILES	PORTAGES
IV-V–	800-1500	1200	6.4	2

PUT IN: Yucca Creek (1,720 ft.)
TAKE OUT: Kaweah bridge (950 ft.)
SHUTTLE: 7 miles (dirt)
RAFTS: NO
AVERAGE GRADIENT: 120 fpm
GAUGE: Runnable when the *Inflow to Terminus* (Lake Kaweah), 6 miles below the take-out, is 2,000 to 3,000 cfs (flow phone).
BOATING SEASON: Winter Spring
WATER SOURCE: Natural Natural
USFS and *TOPO MAPS*: Sequoia NF; *Giant Forest, Kaweah* (15 series)

This surprisingly good run is steep and continuous. Most of the rapids are created by the underlying bedrock; hence many drops are in the form of ledges. Trees growing in the river are a problem, though the most dangerous and annoying section is in the last few miles, well below the most difficult area. When driving upriver from the take-out bridge, the road stays nearly level with the river for a few miles, but then climbs several hundred feet. The road winds to the put-in over the next 4 to 5 miles. The hardest rapids cannot be seen from the road. Eventually the road forks. The right branch is private, the left is public and leads to the river in less than a mile.

The put-in is on the Sequoia National Park Boundary, at the confluence of Yucca Creek. Shortly below is a steep rapid that is quickly followed by one of the biggest drops on the run. Many good rapids ensue, and several need to be scouted. Below is a thundering 15-foot falls. The portage here tests one's scrambling ability. I portaged the rapid just below this, though it is probably runnable. Directly below here is a 6-foot dam, conveniently anchored to large boulders in the river. This I found runnable by ski-jumping in a spot where a "foundation" boulder sloped into the pool below. Much more action follows to the point where the shuttle road is near river level. This is 4.3 miles from the put-in, and the average gradient to this point is 138 fpm. One can take out here, to avoid the worst of the brush, or continue on to unique "intuition" rapids (choosing the correct fork when the river splits). Inflow to Lake Kaweah was 2,000 cfs when I made this run. An inflow of 3,000 cfs would be better.

To reach the put-in, drive 30 miles east on Route 198 from Visalia (at Route 99) to the town of Three Rivers. On the west side of town, turn left on North Fork Road and cross the main Kaweah River. The take-out is in 3 miles at the bridge across the North Fork in the tiny community of Kaweah. The put-in is 7 miles farther.

—LH

MIDDLE FORK KAWEAH RIVER (Hospital Rock)

DIFFICULTY	FLOW	OPTIMUM	MILES	PORTAGES
V	400–800	800	4.8	8
V+	>800			

PUT IN: Hospital Rock (2,630 ft.)
TAKE OUT: Roadside 4.8 miles below put-in (1,660 ft.)
SHUTTLE: 5 miles
RAFTS: NO
AVERAGE GRADIENT: 202 fpm: mi/mi: 250, 210, 195, 215, 165

GAUGE:	**The *Inflow to Terminus* (Lake Kaweah), you'll have about two-thirds of the inflow (flow phone).**
BOATING SEASON:	**Spring**
WATER SOURCE:	**Natural, however there is a 100–200 cfs diversion 2 miles below put-in.**
AAA and *TOPO MAPS*:	**Sequoia National Park; *Giant Forest, Kaweah* (15 series)**

Warning: This section of the Kaweah is in Sequoia National Park—it is against park rules to kayak or raft on the river.

With that out of the way, let me get on with the description. This section of the Kaweah isn't a classic, but it's well worth running if you enjoy very steep, boulder-strewn rivers and don't mind portaging around some very scenic, unrunnable rapids. The river bed is classic Sierra granite pool and drop. With an average gradient of 202 fpm, you know that the drops are big! I recall many good class V rapids with clean 4- to 6-foot vertical drops—big fun in the air. About a mile below the put-in there is a narrow granite gorge. The gorge, and much of the run, is visible from the road, which follows the entire length of the run. The road is close enough to allow a bird's-eye scout, yet far enough away that it isn't noticed once you're on the water.

In general, the river is runnable; however, I recall portaging 8 times. The first portage, just below the put-in at Hospital Rock, is typical—not too long, at river level, and entailed schlepping around big boulders. Overall, not too bad. The portaging action really picks up upon entering the granite gorge (about one mile below the put-in). At the head of the gorge there is a gnarly 15-foot waterfall which we elected to portage. The choices were: either carry up the canyon wall on the right and hike a ways, or else do a 20-foot seal launch off a giant mid-stream boulder into the pool below. We chose to go airborne. Both the launch and the landing weren't bad. However, at flows higher than 500–600 cfs, getting onto the launch boulder will be desperate. The next portage of note is in the heart of the gorge, a short distance downstream of the entrance falls. Here we made a short portage on the right at river level; the route entailed carefully walking on a smooth, sloping granite slab. One slip and you fall into the class VI maelstrom below! Don't wear a pair of slimy, Tabata wet suit booties on this run—put on some real shoes.

On the first descent in June of '84, Lars, John Armstrong and I had a flow of about 500–600 cfs. This flow was adequate until we reached the diversion dam about two miles below the put-in. Here 100–200 cfs are diverted into a canal—it was bye-bye river. Below this point, we were left with around 400 cfs. This was OK for the next couple of miles, as the river bed is constricted. I remember several great 6-foot ski jumps and a few more portages. Around two miles below the diversion, the river bed spreads out and the going gets tough. After a couple of kayak jam-ups and portages due to lack of fluid, the not-so-tough decided to quit! Our original goal was to continue 2 more miles to the confluence with the East Fork of the Kaweah. These last two miles drop 185 and 175 fpm. Although the gradient is below the magic 200 feet per mile, I'm confident there'll be some big rapids. Lars and I are planning a second attempt at a higher flow.

To get to the take-out, drive east on Hwy. 198 towards Lake Kaweah, continue past the town of Three Rivers to Sequoia National Park. Upon entering the park, drive about two miles (past Ash Mountain National Park Headquarters) to where the road is close to the river—this is the take-out. To get to the put-in, continue upstream five miles to Hospital Rock. There you'll find a parking lot and some nice Indian petroglyphs. Remember, it is illegal to boat in the park. Don't come crying to me if you get a ticket or are arrested by some Dudley Do-Right ranger. I recommend a commando put-in and take-out. Play dumb and apologetic if busted. Whatever you do, don't show the ranger this book!

—*CS*

MIDDLE FORK KAWEAH RIVER (Gateway Bridge to Three Rivers)

DIFFICULTY	FLOW	OPTIMUM	MILES	PORTAGES
IV	500-1000	1000	6	0
IV+	>1000			

PUT IN: Gateway Bridge (1,260 ft.)

TAKE OUT: Three Rivers (760 ft.)

SHUTTLE: 6 miles

RAFTS: YES

AVERAGE GRADIENT: 85 fpm

GAUGE: Runnable when the *Inflow to Terminus* (Lake Kaweah), 4 miles below the take-out, is 1,500 to 2,500 cfs (flow phone).

BOATING SEASON: Winter Spring

WATER SOURCE: Natural Natural

USFS and *TOPO MAPS*: Sequoia NF; *Kaweah* (15 series)

In the first edition of this book, Chuck described this run from the fogged recollection of a past slalom race in Three Rivers. He wrote, "all or some of the information contained herein may deviate from reality." I kayaked the run in 1986 with Beth Rypins, so this firsthand account supersedes the original.

The river at Gateway Bridge is essentially a continuation of the run above. It's a tough place for the intermediate boater to start, as the river is fast class IV. The gradient lessens shortly below, but the rapids maintain a class-III-IV character. Throughout the run, which is fast-flowing in the upper half and of pool-drop character in the lower half, are several challenging drops. Shortly above the take-out bridge is a series of large drops, formed by underlying granite. These rapids deserve a scout, as one has a nearly river-wide reversal in it.

To get to the put-in, refer to take-out directions for the previous Kaweah run (Hospital Rock). The take-out is either behind the gas station in Three Rivers, or a little farther downstream at the main bridge across the Kaweah on the western edge of town.

—LH

KAWEAH RIVER (Three Rivers to the Reservoir)

DIFFICULTY	FLOW	OPTIMUM	MILES	PORTAGES
II-III	500-2500	1500	4	0

PUT IN:	**Three Rivers Bridge (760 ft.)**
TAKE OUT:	**Lake Kaweah (694 ft., spillway)**
SHUTTLE:	**4 miles**
RAFTS:	**YES**
AVERAGE GRADIENT:	**20 fpm**
GAUGE:	**The *Inflow to Terminus* (Lake Kaweah) is what you'll be on (flow phone).**
BOATING SEASON:	**Spring**
WATER SOURCE:	**Natural**
USFS and *TOPO MAPS*:	**Sequoia NF; *Kaweah* (15 series)**

This section of the Kaweah is a good run for budding paddlers out for a big thrill. Overall, the rapids are class II with a couple of III's tossed in. The only "tough" rapid is 3.5 miles below the put-in. When the reservoir is high, this rapid runs out into the lake.

To get to the take-out, drive east from Visalia on Hwy. 178 to Lake Kaweah. Follow the road along the reservoir, park where the river enters.

To get to the put-in, continue east a few miles to Three Rivers, and turn left onto North Fork Road. Put in a short distance downstream of the bridge.

—CS

KAWEAHN LAWLESSNESS

May, 1984. It was close to the end of an era. Few, very few, first descents were to be found in the mountains of California. Most everything left was of the type where kayaking skill had little to do with a successful descent. Stamina and boat-carrying ability were more important. Navigating Sierra streams from their headwaters was pretty much the game now. More an adventure with a 12-foot plastic backpack than a kayak trip, it was under these circumstances that we kept a lid on one of the last unnavigated rivers in the Sierra that both ran along a road, and appeared to be mostly runnable.

Chuck Stanley, John Armstrong and I pulled onto a dirt road near Hospital Rock in Sequoia Park well past 2 a.m. We flopped in the dust at road's edge, too tired to care about legal camping.

Dawn came agonizingly early. By 6 a.m. it was too hot to sleep any longer. We tossed and thrashed, trying to rest a little bit more before the arduous day began.

While Chuck and I bemoaned our substantial sleep deficit, John ambled off down the road in search of toilet facilities.

We'd only begun to clear our groggy minds when the ranger drove up. He chastised us for illegal camping, but after hearing our pre-recorded plea of ignorance, chose not to cite us. This surprised us, for he was fairly irate over having caught John relieving himself third-world style on the edge of the road.

We silently thanked the stars that these infractions weren't going to cost us, and hoped the tree fuzz would end his tirade soon so we could get on the river. Then we noticed his gaze shifting from our boats to the tumultuous river below.

"You boys aren't going down the river in those are you?" he asked. We stared at him in disbelief. We knew that we were now treading the thin line between a day of kayaking and a premature bust.

"Down there?" we pointed, "No way!" I forced myself to exclaim. "That would be crazy. You'd die in a second down there."

Chuck took over, "We're going paddling down on the lake. We're only beginners."

The ranger smiled to himself, thinking "These guys might be illegal campers, and crude in their toilet habits, but they're not dumb." Apparently satisfied that we had no intentions of illegally kayaking the river within the park, he bid us good day.

Our minds raced to cover the options. To get caught now would be doubly severe. We had lied, and no self-righteous ranger would let that one slip. We decided on a plan.

We loosened the tie-down straps on the boats and drove slowly back toward Hospital Rock Ranger Station. Where the dirt road joined the pavement, just out of view of the station, we nonchalantly—but very quickly—launched the boats down the embankment toward the raging river. We then parked the car in visitor parking next to the station and skulked away, praying that the ranger we'd just met wouldn't notice us or the now boatless car.

Our voices camouflaged by the roar of the river and our movements by the tree cover (the road only 300 feet above), we could relax a bit as we set about the task of portaging the first quarter mile of rapids. Soon the river eased up and we began kayaking. The water level was quite low, making the river very technical.

We scouted a difficult rapid that would require 90-degree direction changes at the correct instant in order to safely navigate it. Chuck went first, sprinting through and making the essential moves nicely. Then John started down, in a rubbery Taurus he'd borrowed from Chuck. He had a bit of a reputation for being a boat bender, and was quite sensitive about it. He was determined to quell it on this trip. He negotiated the first 90-degree turn well. On the second sharp bend the trick was to ride up on the crest of a surge of water that folded viciously on itself, thereby keeping the ends of the boat out of the water and maneuverable. John undershot it, the nose of the boat spearing through the ridge of folding water. Before the boat's buoyancy could raise the nose, it slammed into part of the rock that created the upsurge.

Almost instantly the force of the water proved greater than the strength of the boat. Before it sprang free, I was able to snap a photo of the boat bent under water. John eddied out, irritation on his face. Noting that Chuck was too far downstream to be able to see the bent boat clearly, he jokingly urged me to keep this new development to myself. Chuck's eyes rolled only slightly when he found out, and the tweaked Taurus quickly resumed its original shape. Easy bend, easy return.

Onward we moseyed, lack of sleep rapidly draining us. After running a beautiful, smooth-walled granite gorge we arrived at a small hydro diversion. A flume stole about 200 cfs of the estimated 500 cfs. The kayaking quality dropped drastically. We were now crashing and bashing our way downstream, any joy being rapidly consumed by exhausted minds and bodies.

Still a mile or two above our planned take-out, we decided to quit. Chuck retrieved the car while we slept by the river. When he returned we hauled our boats up to the roadside turnout where the car was parked, stripped off our wet boating gear, and got into comfortable clothes.

Just then a ranger pulled up, luckily not the same one we'd met that morning. Our wet boats and gear were strewn about, making it obvious that we'd just come from the river.

The ranger stepped out of his patrol car. I don't recall his exact features, but I remember that he impressed me as the junior nerdley type, if you will. The kind of guy who probably lived life by the rules.

"You guys aren't going down there, are you?" he said motioning to the river. We looked at each other, somewhat surprised by his question.

I piped up, "No sir, it's much too dangerous down there. We were getting ready to go—that's why our gear is unloaded—but we've just thought better of it."

"Good," he said. "'Cause you guys wouldn't last 5 minutes down there. It's mighty treacherous water and most people who try to run it die, or at least need to be rescued. Besides, it's against park regulations."

"Yes sir, we wouldn't dare chance it down there, nor break the law," I lied. He continued to babble about the dangerous river and the park regulations prohibiting boating on it. We three kayakers glanced at each other, amazed that he didn't realize we were fibbing.

He seemed harmless and besides, he hadn't caught us on the river.

So I turned to him and said, "you look like a cool guy." He looked at me in bewilderment. His face warmed faintly. "We just came down the river from Hospital Rock," I spilled.

"NO!" he shouted in disbelief. We nodded yes. A smile warmed his face further. "Nah . . . really?"

"Yeah, we just got done," we hooted in chorus.

"Oh my God," he said in spastic amazement, barely able to contain his excitement. "You've *got* to let us know when you're down there," he said sternly. "We've got to be able to come rescue you."

He finally calmed down, and suddenly seemed eager to go share the news with his peers. After he left we hurriedly loaded the boats and exited the park, mildly worried that the first ranger would track us down for a reprimanding lecture.

—*LH*

The authors demonstrating marginal C-2 technique at the Trinity River Rodeo (note bow paddler's hand position). ***Pinky Collamer***

KERN RIVER (Upper Run)

DIFFICULTY	FLOW	OPTIMUM	MILES	PORTAGES
V	500-2500	1500	37	12

PUT IN: Junction Meadow (8,000 ft.)
TAKE OUT: Forks of the Kern (4,660 ft.)
SHUTTLE: 162 miles (21-mile hike over Mt. Whitney!)
RAFTS: NO
AVERAGE GRADIENT: 90 fpm
GAUGE: The *Flow at Kernville* is, more or less, what you'll be on AFTER spring run-off. During spring run-off, you'll have a fair bit more than that (flow phone).
BOATING SEASON: Spring
WATER SOURCE: Natural
AAA and *TOPO MAPS*: State of California; *Mt. Whitney, Kern Peak, Hockett Peak* (15 series)

This run was pioneered by Reg Lake, Doug Tompkins, and Royal Robbins in 1981. The approach is the crux of the journey, as it involves a 21-mile hike over a 13,777-foot pass to reach the put-in. As one of the first high-Sierra river descents, it has been regarded as somewhat crazy. Since the first descent, however, there have been at least four more descents including: two groups of kayakers; a 6-person, 2-raft descent; and, reportedly, an open-canoe descent! The original party hired porters to assist on the 2-day put-in hike. Later, one 2-man kayak team allegedly hiked in with homemade wooden packframes, which they burned at the put-in. The rafting group hiked up from "The Forks" put-in with mules.

Twelve portages were reported by the first team in '81, however, later groups report as few as four portages. Everyone warns of several logjam portages. The logistics of this trip are overwhelming, and anyone capable of undertaking it doesn't need any advice on how to organize. All parties report incredible scenery, and say that the trip merits the effort involved. The Kern differs from all other Sierra rivers, which drain west, in that, from its origin at Junction Meadows, it flows south, paralleling the Kern Canyon Fault to Lake Isabella. There it begins its descent west.

The hike over Mt. Whitney begins near Lone Pine on the eastern side of the Sierra, and every group to date has continued through "The Forks" Run to Johnsondale Bridge. Neither Chuck nor I have done this run yet, but it looms in the future.

—LH

KERN RIVER (Forks of the Kern)

DIFFICULTY	FLOW	OPTIMUM	MILES	PORTAGES
IV–V–	600–1500	1500	14.3	0
IV+–V–	1500–3000			
V	>3000			

PUT IN: Forks of the Kern (4,660 ft.)
TAKE OUT: Johnsondale Bridge (3,740 ft.)
SHUTTLE: 30 miles (hike 2 miles)
RAFTS: YES (commercial trip; note hike in)
AVERAGE GRADIENT: 65 fpm
GAUGE: The *Flow at Kernville* is what you'll have (flow phone).
BOATING SEASON: Spring
WATER SOURCE: Natural
USFS and *TOPO MAPS*: Sequoia NF; *Hocket Peak, Kernville* (15 series)

Warning: A USFS permit is required to run this section of the Kern River. Call or write (see appendix) for the current permit procedure.

Since the first edition of this book I was able to work up the courage to shoot this section of the Kern. The toughest part was driving my car 7 hours from the SF Bay Area to get there. But hey, it was worth it. All the reports of an excellent run are true. Even the trail to the put-in was shorter than I had heard. In the first edition it's listed as 3.75 miles; it's really only a couple of miles on a good trail.

This river has some whitewater! There are tons of good rapids throughout the length of the run. When I shot the shoals at around 1,500 cfs I called it a solid class IV with a few easy V's. Many of the rapids are fairly long, but not too steep. There is plenty of time and space to maneuver around the many rocks. At flows above 2,500 cfs the rapids become very fast and long—the rocks metamorphose into holes! The first six miles of river has many class IV and IV+ drops, which are followed by four miles of relaxing class II. The biggest and baddest rapids are evenly spaced throughout the final seven miles of river. The lineup of easy class V's are: Big Bean, Vortex (mile 11.5), Westwall, and Carson Falls (.5 miles above the take-out). In between the biggies, you'll find many class IV rapids and a few calm sections to catch your breath.

The two biggest rapids on the run are Vortex and Carson Falls. Vortex is 11.5 miles downstream of the put-in, and Carson Falls provides thrills half a mile upstream of the take-out. Vortex's crux is a wicked, 6-foot-high ledge hole at the top of the rapid. When the river is above 1,300 cfs, the gut of the ledge hole can be cheated by sliding down an easy ramp which opens up on the right. Below this level, it's either ski-jump the hole or portage—don't go in the hole! There are lots of stories of everything from turkey kayakers to Avon Pro Rafts being eaten alive in the Vortex. To add to the thrill, the run-out is a long, class IV rapid. Please use your good judgement and skill to avoid a sad story. Carson Falls, on the other hand, named after that river pioneer Doug Carson, is simply a cheap thrill.

Now, I enjoy whitewater thrills as much as the next guy, but I hate to get my face wet. To my horror, I discovered that there is no way to avoid a thorough dunking when shooting Carson Falls. My buddy, Matt Gaynes (from Hollywood), was showing us Northern California types the ropes. There we were, Matt, Richard Montgomery, Mike Schlax, and I, all scouting Carson Falls while the rest of the crew did the portage shuffle. Matt told us to simply paddle off the five-foot drop into the boiling maelstrom below. He said, "Don't worry, you'll disappear for a few seconds and then surface about 20 feet downstream. It's easy." Richard, Mike, and I looked at each other and said, "Sure, you go first." Well, he was right! Matt ran it down the gut and was gone, only to surface upright exactly where he said he would! We all said no way! For the next ten minutes we plotted our route. By group consensus, we decided the best shot at not getting wet was to ski-jump off the left side of the drop. Richard volunteered to give it a try, confident of showing these Southern California types some finesse. Richard's approach looked great, good speed, proper angle. Totally in control, he shot over edge and, to our dismay, disappeared into the maelstrom. He reappeared exactly where Matt said he would! Like I said, cheap thrills.

In addition to the great whitewater, the Forks has wonderful wilderness scenery with a high Sierra feel to it. From the pine tree-studded shores to the stunning granite needles high above the river, all is beauty. After 15 miles of paddling, the grandeur of Dry Meadow Creek's cascading waterfalls will provide inspiration for the tired river traveler. Scenery doesn't get any better, it just gets different.

The commercial rafters typically run three-day trips, while kayakers often blitz the run in one day. If you plan a one-day trip, be sure to get an early start. It's both a long trail and long paddle on the river. Depending on your skill level, lots of time can be consumed scouting and portaging the many class IV and V rapids. Please be prepared: carry a first aid kit, food, spare paddle, throw ropes, and matches.

To get to the take-out, drive east (upstream) from Kernville on the highway towards the Johnsondale Bridge. The bridge is about a mile upstream of the Limestone Campground. There is a big, paved parking lot on the river right, just upstream of the bridge.

To get to the put-in, continue east on the highway, towards Johnsondale. A short distance past Johnsondale, turn right on a paved road toward Lloyds Meadow. Drive until you see a sign to Forks of the Kern (about 15 miles). Turn right onto this dirt road and drive 2 miles to the trail head.

—CS

Kathy Eisemann demonstrating "enthusiastic" playing technique on Chili Bar. ***Chuck Stanley***

KERN RIVER (Limestone)

DIFFICULTY	FLOW	OPTIMUM	MILES	PORTAGES
III	500–1500	1000	2.5	0
IV	1500–2500			
IV+	>2500			

PUT IN: Johnsondale Bridge (3,740 ft.)
TAKE OUT: Fairview Dam (3,632 ft.)
SHUTTLE: 2.5 miles
RAFTS: YES (commercial run)
AVERAGE GRADIENT: 45 fpm
GAUGE: The *Flow at Kernville* is what you'll have (flow phone).
BOATING SEASON: Spring
WATER SOURCE: Natural
USFS and *TOPO MAPS*: Sequoia NF; *Kernville* (15 series)

Warning: A USFS permit is required to run this section of the Kern River. Call or write (see appendix) for the current permit procedure.

Limestone is a short-but-sweet run. The reliable natural spring flow, nice scenery, and good rapids all combine to explain why this is one of the more popular Kern runs. While the rest of the Kern Canyon is formed from granite, this section cuts through limestone to form a scenic gorge. About a mile below the put-in is Limestone Rapid. About a quarter mile below Limestone is Joe's Diner, the other big rapid on the run. Both of these shoals are of medium length and require a bit of maneuvering. The difficulty of the two major rapids depends on the water level—the higher the water, the wilder the action. At 500 to 1,500 cfs, I'd call them class III. The rest of the run is mostly class II with a couple of easy III's tossed in. However, note that the difficulty of the entire run goes up with the flow!

As a final safety note, please don't run Fairview Dam.

To get to the take-out, drive east (upstream) from Kernville about 17 miles to Fairview Dam. There is a roadside turnout a few hundred yards upstream of the Dam. To get to the put-in, continue upstream 2.5 miles to the Johnsondale Bridge. Cross the bridge and turn right into the parking lot. It's a short walk to the water.

—*CS*

KERN RIVER
(Fairview Dam to Gold Ledge Campground)

DIFFICULTY	FLOW	OPTIMUM	MILES	PORTAGES
IV–V–	600–2500	1200	6.5	0
V	>2500			

PUT IN: .4 miles below Fairview Dam (3,600 ft.)
TAKE OUT: Gold Ledge Campground (3,200 ft.)
SHUTTLE: 6.5 miles
RAFTS: YES (note the class V rapids)
AVERAGE GRADIENT: 62 fpm
GAUGE: Subtract 500 cfs from the *Flow at Kernville* to determine the flow (flow phone).
BOATING SEASON: Spring
WATER SOURCE: Natural (with a 500 cfs diversion)
USFS and *TOPO MAPS*: Sequoia NF; *Kernville* (15 series)

Warning: A USFS permit is required to run this section of the Kern River. Call or write (see appendix) for the current permit procedure.

The Kern River, from Fairview Dam down to Gold Ledge Campground, is a mixed bag of tricks. There are a couple of short sections of class II–III separated by sections of class IV and V rapids. The section starts out with a bang if you opt to put in just below Fairview Dam and run Bombs Away (class V–). Some folks of the intermediate boater persuasion might enjoy the class II–III section that begins .4 miles below Fairview Dam and ends 3 miles downstream at Calkins Flat. Below Calkins Flat the river turns away from the road and enters Chamise Gorge. Here the white water action picks up. In the depths of the gorge there are a couple of good class IV's (or V's at flows higher than 2,500 cfs). Below the gorge, the road returns to the river and the action really picks up. Salmon Falls is the brand-name, class V drop that will be encountered about 5 miles below the put-in. Many paddlers will opt for the portage route up on the highway. There are also a couple of major class V rapids between Salmon Falls and Gold Ledge Campground. If you're not psyched for all this action, take out above Salmon Falls and call it a day.

To get to the take-out, drive east (upstream) from Kernville to Gold Ledge Campground. To get to the put-in, continue driving east on Hwy. 190 about 6.5 miles. Put in .4 miles below Fairview Dam. Thrill seekers will want to put in just downstream of Fairview Dam and run Bombs Away (class V–).

—*CS*

KERN RIVER (Gold Ledge Run)

DIFFICULTY	FLOW	OPTIMUM	MILES	PORTAGES
IV+	500–2500	1200	8.5	0
IV–V–	>2500			

PUT IN:	**Gold Ledge Campground (3,200 ft.)**
TAKE OUT:	**Powerhouse #3 (2,690 ft.)**
SHUTTLE:	**8.5 miles**
RAFTS:	**YES (note difficulty)**
AVERAGE GRADIENT:	**60 fpm**
GAUGE:	**Subtract 500 cfs from the *Flow at Kernville* for the flow (flow phone).**
BOATING SEASON:	**Spring**
WATER SOURCE:	**Natural (with a 500 cfs diversion)**
USFS and *TOPO MAPS*:	**Sequoia NF; *Kernville* (15 series)**

Warning: A USFS permit is required to run this section of the Kern River. Call or write (see appendix) for the current permit procedure.

This section of the Kern is primarily class II–III with several major class IV+ rapids. If the water is up, we're talking easy class V action. The first test arrives around 2.5 miles down from the put-in: a pair of stiff class IV's (the second one is called Sock-em-Dog). Below here you'll encounter several big shoals on your way to the take-out. Fender Bender, at mile 5, is one of the rougher ones. Cable Rapid, another rad shoal, is about 6 miles below the put-in (near Camp #3 Campground). From here on, the river is no harder than class IV–. Many boaters put in above or below Cable and paddle down to Kernville. The road follows the entire length of the run, greatly facilitating a prerun scout or a midrun bailout, if need be. Be forewarned that you can't see all the big rapids from the road.

To get to the take-out, drive through Kernville and cross the bridge. At the stop sign, turn left and drive about 1.5 miles to the turnoff at the powerhouse (it's on the left). To get to the put-in, continue upstream until you reach Gold Ledge Campground.

—*CS*

KERN RIVER (Kernville Run)

DIFFICULTY	FLOW	OPTIMUM	MILES	PORTAGES
II+ (one III)	500-1500	1200	2	0
III (one IV)	>1500			

PUT IN:	**Powerhouse #3 (2,750 ft.)**		
TAKE OUT:	**Riverside Park, Kernville (2,690 ft.)**		
SHUTTLE:	**2 miles**		
RAFTS:	**YES**		
AVERAGE GRADIENT:	**30 fpm**		
GAUGE:	**The *Flow at Kernville*, the take-out, is more or less what you'll be on (flow phone).**		
BOATING SEASON:	**Winter**	**Spring**	**Summer**
WATER SOURCE:	**Power**	**Power/Release**	**Power**
USFS and *TOPO MAPS*:	**Sequoia NF; *Kernville* (15 series)**		

Anti-Warning: This section of the Kern River does NOT require a permit; however, the U.S. Forest Service should have flow information and helpful hints for inexperienced paddlers.

This is an excellent beginner run. The only rapid that might put the fear of God into the novice paddler is Ewings rapid, which is just upstream of the bridge in town. Ewings can be portaged on the right by those so inclined. The other rapid of note is Big Daddy, the first shoals below the powerhouse. Here is a fast little chute which will thrill the socks off any newcomer to the sport. Most of the rapids are simple rock-strewn riffles which require little boat maneuvering. The run is capped by running the slalom course rapid, which is in beautiful downtown Kernville.

To get to the take-out, drive east from Bakersfield on Hwy. 178 towards Kernville. Just as you enter town, turn right on the first street you see; the Riverside Park will be to your right. To get to the put-in, drive across the bridge just upstream of the park and turn left at the stop sign. Drive about 1.5 miles to the left turn to the powerhouse.

—CS

KERN RIVER (Miracle to Democrat)

DIFFICULTY	FLOW	OPTIMUM	MILES	PORTAGES
IV– (one V)	600-1200	1200	11.5	0
IV	1200-3000			
IV+	>3000			

PUT IN: Hobo Hot Springs Campground (2,260 ft.)
TAKE OUT: Democrat Hot Springs (1,900 ft.)
SHUTTLE: 12.5 miles
RAFTS: YES (commercial run)
AVERAGE GRADIENT: 30 fpm
GAUGE: The ***Release from Lake Isabella***, a few miles above the put-in, is what you'll have (flow phone).
BOATING SEASON: Spring Summer
WATER SOURCE: Spill/Power Power
AAA and *TOPO MAPS*: Sequoia; ***Glenville*** (15 series)

Warning: A U.S. Forest Service permit is required to run this section of the Kern River. Call or write (see appendix) for the current permit procedure.

This is "The River" for Los Angeles-based paddlers. It is the closest whitewater available and it's a very good run. The reliable release of irrigation water from Lake Isabella provides the lifeblood river enthusiasts crave. On a given summer weekend, you'll find tons of rafters, a gaggle or two of kayakers, and some low-life bikers swimming in the various hot springs. It has an L.A. feel. But don't get me wrong, I've always enjoyed myself on the Kern.

Once on the water, you can look forward to some excellent class III and IV water. The river is pool and drop. The rapids are formed by bedrock outcroppings, which tend to form steep drops. The result is some good holes and blind drops. I can recall some tense moments, in a midstream micro-eddy, peering over my shoulder at a blind drop. All of them, though, turn out to have a clean run.

The Miracle to Democrat run has what all popular class III-IV runs should have: an awesome class V rapid. Here the wimps, punks, and showboaters get theirs; only a real expert or macho L.A. river dude could ever hope to survive the Royal Flush. The crux of the rapid is a killer ledge that runs out into an undercut wall on the left. But it's no big deal. I've personally conquered this shoals twice on the extreme river right. I credit my success to my choice of footwear—NIKE waffle trainers. They give excellent footing on the slippery granite rocks.

My route is no big deal for experienced expedition kayakers. However, those with less boat hiking experience will probably label the 50-yard carry horrendous. The main problem is the 15-foot boulder at the start, after which the going is better. The put-in is a bit rough. I recommend an "atomic launch" off the rock with the little bridge leading to it. For rafts there is an overhead cable; don't ask me how to use it. Below the Flush, you can look forward to some good rapids and a lot of flatwater.

To get to the take-out, drive east from Bakersfield on Hwy. 178. After driving past miles of terrifying class VI whitewater, keep your eyes peeled for the Democrat Hot Springs turn-off on the left. Follow this dirt road to an official take-out parking lot, with stinky porta-potties, overflowing garbage cans, and cars. Be sure to scout the take-out, as you can't see the cars from the water. If you go over a 30-foot dam, you've gone too far.

To get to the put-in, continue east on Hwy. 178 until you cross the second bridge. Within 0.5 mile, there will be a road to the right—take it. Drive a short way to the old highway and turn right. It's about 1.5 miles to Hobo Hot Springs Campground.

—CS

KERN RIVER (Cataracts of the Kern)

DIFFICULTY	FLOW	OPTIMUM	MILES	PORTAGES
IV–V	700–2500	1800	4.7	1

PUT IN: 2.6 miles up river from Call Box #2 (1,600 ft.)

TAKE OUT: 2.1 miles down river from Call Box # 2 (1,240 ft.)

SHUTTLE: 4.7 miles

RAFTS: YES, difficult rapids, thick brush

AVERAGE GRADIENT: 77 fpm

GAUGE: You'll have the same flow as ***Release from Lake Isabella*** 20+ miles upstream

BOATING SEASON: Spring/Summer

WATER SOURCE: Spill

USFS and *TOPO MAPS*: Sequoia NF; ***Democrat Hot Springs, Mt. Adelaide, Rio Bravo Ranch*** (7.5 series)

This run encompasses the most benign stretch of the Kern between Democrat and the canyon mouth. I made the run with some Kernville locals who knew the put-in and take-out, but by gauging one's mileage from Call Box #2, these points are easy to find. The whole stretch is visible from the road and it is apparent that much of the river above and below this run is characterized by big, marginally runnable drops.

We put in below "Toilet Bowl," a big, nasty rapid that drops 15 feet in a hard right turn. The mandatory portage on this run is 1.4 miles below the put-in. I'd advise road-scouting it beforehand, as brush obscures it.

One of the biggest rapids on the run is shortly below the put-in. There are some nasty fang rocks in the main channel. About 3 miles down the run is a fantastic nosestand hole. This is the right kind of hole (especially at 1,800 cfs) for multiple enders and wild pirouettes.

Due to the warming effects of shallow Lake Isabella, the lower Kern water temperature is moderate in spring and nearly tepid in late summer. The brush and trees detract somewhat from the quality of this run, but the classic granite character and dependable flows make it worthwhile.

To arrive at the take-out drive east on route 178 from Bakersfield. In 7 or 8 miles you'll enter the canyon. In 1.6 miles you'll pass emergency Call Box #1. The take-out is 3.2 miles upstream from here. Continue 4.7 miles to find the put-in.

—LH

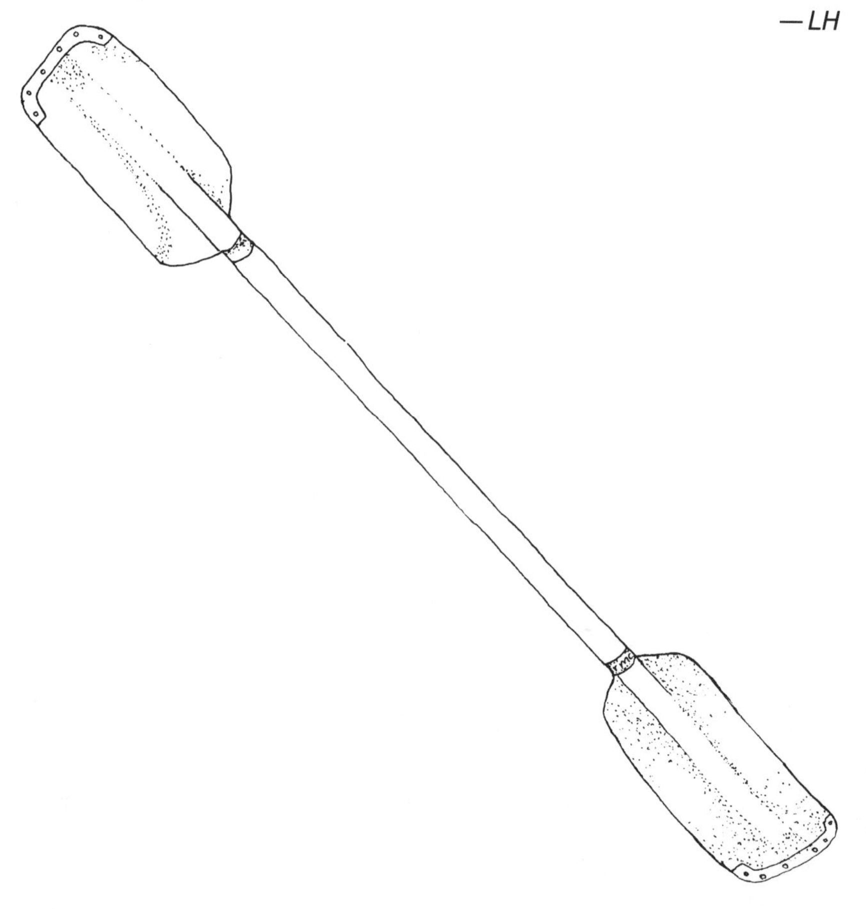

Sierra Nevada Rivers

East Slope

WEST WALKER RIVER (Upper Run)

DIFFICULTY	FLOW	OPTIMUM	MILES	PORTAGES
IV–V	300–450	375	2.3	4

PUT IN:	Leavitt Station Trailhead (7,120 ft.)
TAKE OUT:	Pickle Meadow (6,800 ft.)
SHUTTLE:	2 miles
RAFTS:	NO
AVERAGE GRADIENT:	142 fpm; mi/mi: 240, 80, . . .
GAUGE:	No gauge, but runnable during the peak of a normal year. Don't run this section if the water is too high!
BOATING SEASON:	Spring
WATER SOURCE:	Natural
AAA MAP:	Lake Tahoe

The following description was written by Eric Magneson, who did the first descent of this section August 28, 1982 with his brother John and Steve Arrowsmith. As Eric will describe, this section of the West Walker is very steep and very continuous—don't attempt this section if flow is too high! This section of the West Walker is dangerous and unforgiving.

Between Leavitt and Pickle Meadows, the meandering peaceful flow of the Upper West Walker river becomes momentarily interrupted as it abruptly enters into a small-scale but dramatically steep canyon. Here, in this tightly twisted gorge, the West Walker plunges over 300 feet during its course through the two-mile passage. Because of the blind turns, severe drops, and crumbly, sheer walls characteristic of parts of this canyon, extreme discretion is advised before allowing oneself to become committed to the canyon's descent.

My brother John, Steve Arrowsmith and I put in above this intriguing gorge at the Leavitt Station trailhead parking lot. This put-in can be reached by either descending east from Sonora Pass on Hwy. 108, or by turning west off of Hwy. 395 at the Hwy. 108 intersection. Once in the stream-sized river, the short half-mile float leading up to the Leavitt Campground footbridge is uneventful class II and III, but it is here that the gorge begins and the river begins its dramatic transformation.

Shortly below this footbridge, we portaged around a horn-obstructed drop. At this point, it is seriously recom-

mended to boaters to take the extra time to climb up and out of the now steeply-enclosing gorge walls in order to scout the upcoming blind corners created by a sharp zigzag in the gorge. This is a somewhat perilous scout on loose, heavily decomposed cliffs, but it is necessary in order to plan routes and to determine the successive runability of this extremely blind, continuous, and steep section.

Back in the boats we ran a class IV drop which then led into a jet-propulsion, 90-degree right-turn drop—Diagonal Death. From here we continued down several more intense drops and then portaged around a rocky boat smasher. Here, the river makes a sharp left turn. At the base of this turn is a small swirling pool that provides a minute break in the action. The speed and steepness of the river below Diagonal Death were quite breathtaking and left us all feeling quite fortunate there were no casualties among us.

But, here the canyon begins to drop even steeper. During the next half-mile the gradient is over 150 fpm. This final turn of the zigzag marks the beginning of Gasmic Staircase—an exhilarating roller coaster ride with a 6-foot drop finale that submerges a kayak deeply in front of a giant end-on appearing boulder.

After Gasmic Staircase, there are numerous more class IV and V drops, including two or more short portages. In this narrow and steep part of the gorge we saw several fishermen who seemed a little surprised, and even slightly disdainful of our sudden appearance in their ruggedly isolated fishing spot.

After this steep section, the severity of West Walker's gradient begins to greatly lessen, and the canyon walls begin to noticeably open apart. During this remaining mile until the take-out, the steep rock cliffs gradually turn into soft earth and conglomerate rock and the rapids soon become easygoing class II and III gravel bar riffles interrupted by occasional logjams (one of which we had to portage). The take-out is best made where Hwy. 108 can first be seen on the left, within 30 feet of the shore. If this opportunity is missed, there is another chance to take-out just downstream onto a side road that connects back with Hwy. 108. If this is missed, however, then one must endure the scenic flatwater doldrums of Pickle Meadow.

Eric's naming of the rapid Diagonal Death was prophetic. A year after his run, a kayaker, Rick Sanders, drowned when he missed the last eddy above the gorge and swam the entire section. His body was recovered in a logjam at the bottom of the canyon.

—CS

WEST FORK WALKER RIVER
(Hwy. 395 Bridge to Walker)

DIFFICULTY	FLOW	OPTIMUM	MILES	PORTAGES
IV	600-1000	1000	11	0
V	>1000			

PUT IN:	**Hwy. 395 Bridge (6,570 ft.)**
TAKE OUT:	**Walker (5,440 ft.)**
SHUTTLE:	**11 miles**
RAFTS:	**NO**
AVERAGE GRADIENT:	**105 fpm**
GAUGE:	**No gauge, but runnable during the peak of a normal year.**
BOATING SEASON:	**Spring**
WATER SOURCE:	**Natural**
AAA and *TOPO MAPS*:	**Lake Tahoe Region; *Chris Flat* (7.5 series)**

Are you stuck in the classic Sierra pool-and-drop rut? Here's your chance to bust loose and shoot an 11-mile-long rapid. The West Walker gets started with a bang and doesn't come to a halt until the take-out. The difficulty of the rapids varies from class II to V (above 1,000 cfs). Almost all of the rapids, except the hardest one, can be scouted from the road that follows the entire length of the run.

This 11-mile rapid starts with a roar that few will forget. After a gentle warm-up for the first mile or so, the bottom drops out from the last pool. The rapid is a rude awakening for the unprepared. From the road, this section looks like fun class III; when you're in it, the action is ever so fast. The blinding waves make it difficult to spot and react to the many rocks that lie just under the surface of the water. It's a thrill you won't soon forget. The action tapers off around the corner, but the break is short lived. The river continues on, building up to another class IV section and then tapers off only to build again. The most difficult section is the Miracle Mile, which is located near Shingle Mill Campground. Here, the gradient of the river picks up and the rapid really takes off. This mile-long section is super fast continuous class IV, which adds up to a class V rapid. The last few miles, the river mellows out to continuous class II and III. The take-out bridge is a welcome sight after so much action.

To get to the take-out, drive to the small town of Walker on Hwy. 395. The take-out is the bridge on Eastside Road, which is off Hwy. 395 on the "upstream end" of Walker. The put-in is the Hwy. 395 bridge, 11 miles upstream of Walker.

—CS

EAST FORK CARSON RIVER
(Markleeville to Route 395)

DIFFICULTY	FLOW	OPTIMUM	MILES	PORTAGES
II	500-1000			
II+	>1000	1500	20	0

PUT IN:	**Hangman's Bridge (5,500 ft.)**
TAKE OUT:	**Route 395 (4,980 ft.)**
SHUTTLE:	**25 miles**
RAFTS:	**YES (commercial run)**
AVERAGE GRADIENT:	**25 fpm**
GAUGE:	**The *Flow at Gardnerville*, 5 miles below the take-out, is what you'll have (flow phone).**
BOATING SEASON:	**Spring**
WATER SOURCE:	**Natural**
AAA and *TOPO MAPS*:	**Lake Tahoe Region; *Markleeville, Topaz Lake, Mt. Siegel* (15 series)**

In order to avoid a lawsuit, I'll make the first words of this description a dire warning: **Take out just above an abandoned dam. Before your run, study the final approach.** This cautionary note is primarily aimed at benumbed rafters that have imbibed a few too many beers. I've heard tell, such a crew inadvertently shot the 15-foot-vertical drop with tragic results. Any kayaker worth his salt could easily paddle to shore in the flat pool above the obvious breached dam. There are also warning signs on the shore well above the dam.

The Carson River is a wonderful run for budding paddlers. The scenery is beautiful, juniper-covered hills, the camping is excellent, and the plentiful whitewater will thrill the up-and-coming. Although the rapids aren't particularly difficult, their continuous nature makes them unforgiving. Some sections are nonstop class II for miles. This is not a run for the first-time paddler by any means. The typical rapid is a riffle around a bend; on the outside of the turn, the river hits an exposed rock cliff which creates wicked boils and eddies. All this can be avoided by hugging the inside of the turn—it's no big deal.

A major feature on the Carson is the camping site with the hot springs—deluxe. While sitting in the hot water, one can view the river and the surrounding hills. Another feature of the camping scene is the lack of potable water; the river is a bit silty and there are many cows and mines in the drainage area. On our trip, the problem was so bad we were forced to rations of beer and champagne.

Vince Hayes, a hot-springs party casualty, East Fork Carson River, 1983. ***Chuck Stanley***

While on the subject of the Carson, I'll mention the upper section of the river. The run starts up at the confluence with Wolf Creek. Nine miles of continuous class III and you're at Hangman's Bridge, the put-in for the normal run. There are often some nasty logs on this run. Please be extremely careful. One kayaker has been claimed by a logjam on this section! The average gradient is about 60 fpm, more than twice the lower run.

To get to the put-in, drive on Hwy. 89/4 to Markleeville; continue about a mile past town to Hangman's Bridge. There is a parking area and an outhouse on your left. To get to the take-out, drive to Nevada on Hwy. 88 to Route 395. Go south on Route 395 out of Gardnerville, about 5 miles, to a dirt road that follows the river where Route 395 leaves it. Drive about a mile upstream to a parking area. The take-out is 400 yards upstream of the broken dam.

—CS

TRUCKEE RIVER (River Ranch Run)

DIFFICULTY	FLOW	OPTIMUM	MILES	PORTAGES
III	500-1000	800	11	0
VI (low bridges)	>1000			

PUT IN:	**River Ranch (6,200 ft.)**
TAKE OUT:	**Truckee (5,860 ft.)**
SHUTTLE:	**11 miles**
RAFTS:	**YES**
AVERAGE GRADIENT:	**30 fpm**
GAUGE:	***Tahoe Pass at Fanny Bridge*** **is what you'll have (flow phone).**
BOATING SEASON:	**Spring Summer**
WATER SOURCE:	**Spill/Power Power**
AAA and *TOPO MAPS*:	**Lake Tahoe Region; *Tahoe City, Truckee* (7.5 series)**

The River Ranch was once the sight of the glorious Truckee River Slalom and Wildwater races. What made the race special was the patio bar that overlooked the river. Between runs, I always had a cocktail or two. As usual, progress pushed us out of the picture; they built tennis courts up to the edge of the river. Although the races are gone, the river remains unchanged.

The first 3 miles below the River Ranch are semi-continuous class II and III. The only major hazards are the low-clearance bridges. At water levels higher than 1,000 cfs, the situation could become desperate in a few spots. The final 8 miles down to Truckee are class II. There are many alternative access points along the entire length of the run.

To get to the put-in, drive from Truckee towards Lake Tahoe on Hwy. 89 until you reach the River Ranch Restaurant. Drive a short distance past the restaurant until you find a good put-in alongside the road. The take-out is the Hwy. 267 bridge just out of Truckee. There are many other potential take-outs and put-ins for this section of the river.

—CS

TRUCKEE RIVER (Floriston Run)

DIFFICULTY	FLOW	OPTIMUM	MILES	PORTAGES
II (one IV)	500-1000	800	6	0
III	>1000			

PUT IN:	Boca (5,570 ft.)
TAKE OUT:	Floriston (5,410 ft.)
SHUTTLE:	5 miles
RAFTS:	YES (note last rapid)
AVERAGE GRADIENT:	25 fpm; last half mile is 100 fpm
GAUGE:	*Tahoe Pass at Fanny Bridge* plus *Release from Boca Reservoir* is what you'll have (flow phone).
BOATING SEASON:	Spring Summer
WATER SOURCE:	Natural/Power Power
AAA and *TOPO MAPS*:	Lake Tahoe Region; *Boca, Martis Peak* (7.5 series)

Floriston isn't an all-time great run, but it has about the only class IV rapid on the Truckee. The first 5.5 miles of the run are class II, the last half-mile is a good class IV rapid. There is a railroad track (often used) that facilitates portaging.

To get to the put-in, take the Boca exit off I-80, 7 miles east of Truckee, and drive north to the river. To get to the take-out, continue east on I-80 to the Floriston exit. Drive to the bridge over the river.

—*CS*

Bob Porter racing on the Truckee River. ***Chuck Stanley***

A Memorial

Whitewater kayaking is a great sport. It offers the challenge of the rapids, the breathtaking beauty of river canyons, and the special bond formed when individuals work together as a team meeting the challenge of river running.

On a personal level, running a challenging rapid demands the total focus of one's physical and mental abilities, followed by the exhilaration of success. Our civilized world offers few such opportunities.

The challenge of running rapids is to go near, but not be touched by the danger. To take the calculated risk of pitting one's mental and physical skills against the demands of the rapid may seem foolhardy to some. But to me, running rapids is one of the few times in my life when I'm completely focused. All other thoughts are banished, my mind is clear. Without the danger there would be no risk; without the risk there would be no demand, no focus, no thrill.

Inherently, when risks are taken, some must fail and pay the price. Most often the price is little more than a swim, a bump on the head, or a scraped knuckle. But some must pay the ultimate price. All paddlers, from the novice to expert, must recognize and accept these risks. I feel that the individuals who pay the ultimate price for passage down the whitewater make an investment for all of us. Let's not forget our fellow river travelers.

The following are the names of California paddlers who have perished. Some were close friends, some I never met; to all I pay my deepest respects:

Andrew Palmer, April 4, 1987; SF American, Golden Gate.

Bob Porter, July 8, 1986; Kings River, Kings Canyon Run.

Al McManus, April 20, 1986; MF Feather, Sloat to Nelson Point.

Dave Decot, May 20, 1985; Merced River, The Motels Run.

Mark Allen, May 2, 1985; NF American River, Giant Gap.

Sean Smith, November, 1984; Eel River, Pillsbury.

Rick Sanders, June 26, 1983; West Walker River, Upper, near Sonora Pass.

Harold Greischaber, 1982; Salmon River, Bloomers Falls.

Kenneth Hunter, 1980; East Fork Carson River, Upper Run.

Stephen Umberger, May 31, 1974; Truckee River, in Nevada near Reno.

John Chromy, May 26, 1956; Merced River, 6 miles upstream of Briceburg.

—*CS*

Additional Runs

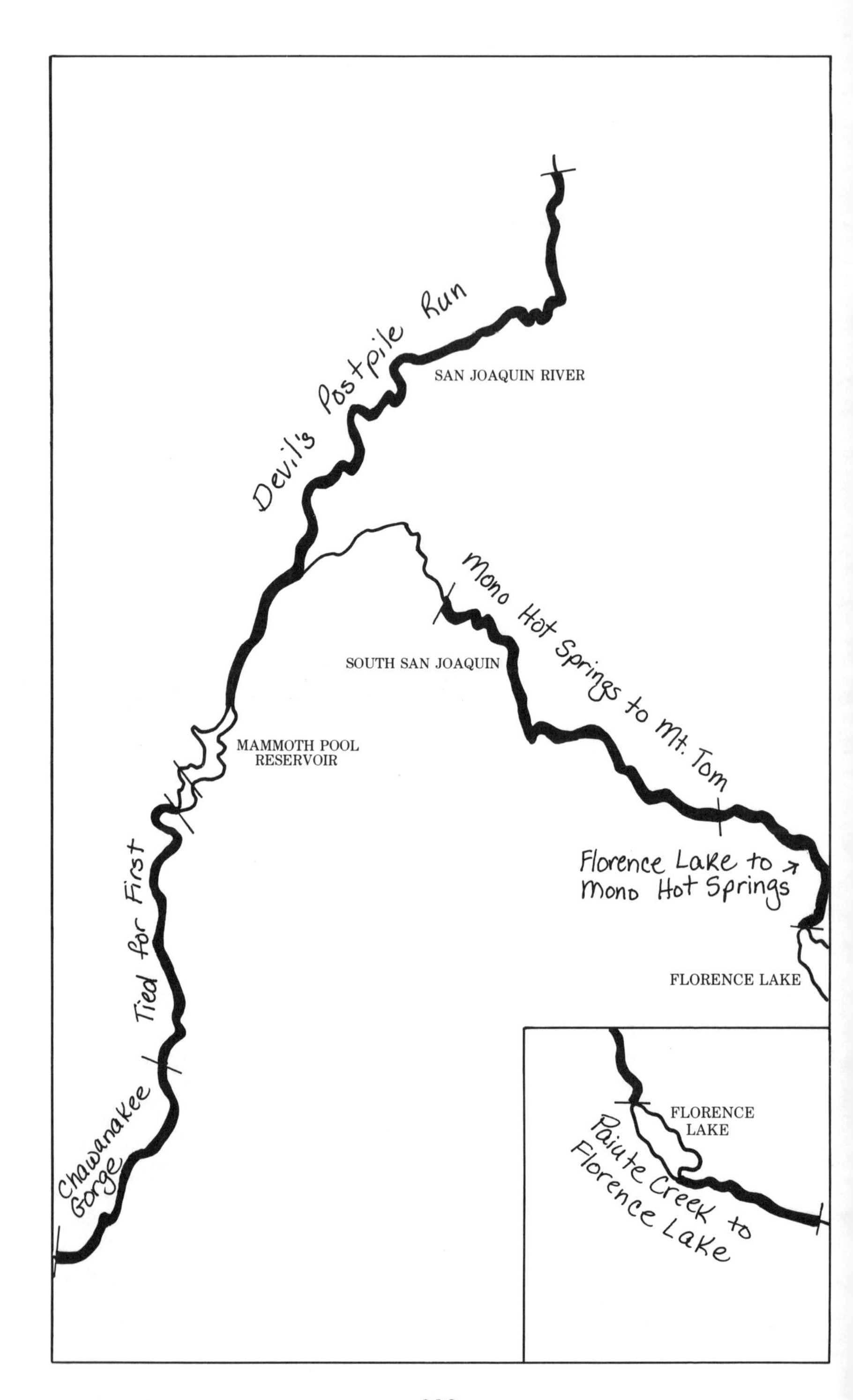
Devil's Postpile Run
SAN JOAQUIN RIVER
Mono Hot Springs to Mt. Tom
SOUTH SAN JOAQUIN
MAMMOTH POOL
RESERVOIR
Tied for First
Florence Lake to
Mono Hot Springs
FLORENCE LAKE
Chawanakee
Gorge
FLORENCE
LAKE
Paiute Creek to
Florence Lake

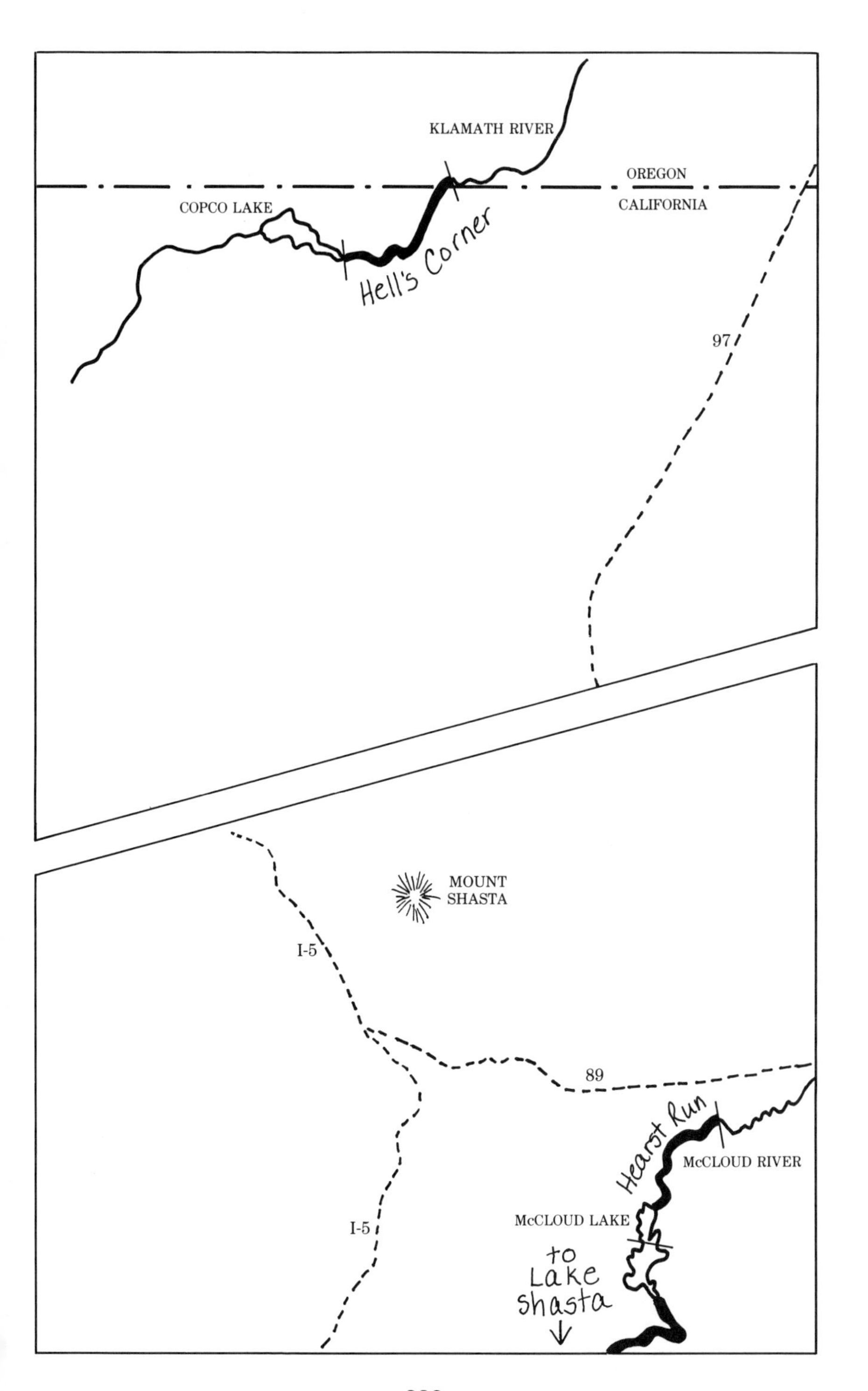
KLAMATH RIVER
OREGON
CALIFORNIA
COPCO LAKE
Hell's Corner
97
MOUNT SHASTA
I-5
89
Hearst Run
McCLOUD RIVER
McCLOUD LAKE
I-5
to Lake Shasta

FORDYCE CREEK
(Fordyce Lake to Lake Spaulding)

DIFFICULTY	FLOW	OPTIMUM	MILES	PORTAGES
IV–V	350–600	500	12 (2 miles across Lake Spaulding)	12

PUT IN:	**Fordyce Lake (6,240 ft.)**
TAKE OUT:	**Lake Spaulding (5,010 ft.)**
SHUTTLE:	**16 miles (5 dirt, 2 almost 4WD)**
RAFTS:	**NO**
AVERAGE GRADIENT:	**123 fpm; mi/mi: 150, 210, 120, 80, 50, 80, 110, 90, 120, 220**
GAUGE:	**None, but runs 400 cfs June through August in normal years**
BOATING SEASON:	**Summer**
WATER SOURCE:	**Power**
USFS and *TOPO MAPS*:	**Tahoe NF; *Webber Peak, English Mtn., Cisco Grove* (7.5 series)**

Imagine the South Yuba along I-80 without the freeway, without bridges, powerlines or any human habitation. Imagine it in this relatively natural state. This is Fordyce Creek.

Fordyce Creek flows through a wild sub-alpine canyon for 10 miles before it is captured by Lake Spaulding. In normal years Fordyce Lake releases 400 cfs from June 1 into late September. In June there may still be snow on the 7,000 ft. shuttle road, and the river will be cold. In late August the lake is warm, as is the weather. The result is warm outflow on a scenic class IV–V creek in late summer when few other rivers are flowing.

This run was first done in '83 by Walt Garms, Mike Fentress and Tim Stringari. They reported it a good run except in the last mile or two where it turns into a portage-fest of sorts.

I made two runs on the creek in September, '86 and found it enjoyable. The run starts out great, with evenly spaced portages, and continues at a high-quality clip until a few miles above Lake Spaulding. At this point (on both trips) I noticed that a combination of fatigue and increasing difficulty led to an impatient state of mind. A two-day descent or a long lunch rest above this final section might help alleviate this condition.

There are two portages in the first half mile, but don't get discouraged. Our third portage was around a long, explosive falls/ramp. Just below this is a wonderful 8 ft. ledge drop that we ran without incident. We named the next major drop "Bishop's Balcony." The only runnable route we could find involved jetting down a kayak-wide, 30-foot-long "balcony" with a 4-foot drop inches to the left. A major 20-foot falls/ramp constituted our fourth portage. This drop looks very runnable, but we admitted we were plain "chicken". Several great drops in mini-gorges lead to a 3-foot-wide slot. This too looks runnable, but we let prudence reign. Below here the river flattens out for a long stretch before a portage around a nasty 25-foot waterfall. Shortly below a footbridge (a potential foot-trail escape route) is a long, complicated rapid that ends in a sharp drop. Below here, portages are more frequent and there is a fun, runnable waterfall over a wide 20-foot-high granite shelf. When the river disappears into an endless boulder field (only ¼ mile from the lake), and your patience is sapped, look for a trail on river left in the woods. I've found this to provide a nice escape from the final stretch of irrigated boulders.

If you aspire to running one of the multi-day High Sierra runs, I'd advise a warm-up run on Fordyce Creek. It'll give you a good feel of what to expect, without committing to several days. If Fordyce seems like too much work and strain, you may as well set your High Sierra dreams free, for those runs are much more demanding.

To get to the take-out, drive approximately 70 miles east on I-80 from Sacramento to the Route 20 exit and go 2.3 miles west on Route 20 to a right turn for Lake Spaulding. One mile down this road is a parking area overlooking the lake.

To get to the put-in, drive back to I-80 and go 5 miles east to the Cisco Grove exit. Cross the freeway and the South Yuba and turn left at the stop sign. In a few hundred yards, turn right (just before the entrance booth to a private park) onto Fordyce Lake Rd. Drive 5 miles uphill on reasonable dirt to the summit. The remaining 2 miles down to the lake are very rocky, and negotiable only in higher-clearance rigs. Garms reports it was impassable without 4WD on their '83 run. The road has been improved, as I did fine in my small pickup.

—LH

INDIAN CREEK

DIFFICULTY	FLOW	OPTIMUM	MILES	PORTAGES
V+	800–1500	1200	5.5	3

PUT IN:	Near Crescent Mills (3,440 ft.)
TAKE OUT:	Spanish Creek (2,880 ft.)
SHUTTLE:	5 miles
RAFTS:	YES (below Indian Falls)
AVERAGE GRADIENT:	102 fpm; mi/mi: 90, 240, 100, 50, 80
GAUGE:	Runnable during normal runoff
BOATING SEASON:	Winter/Spring
WATER SOURCE:	Natural
USFS and *TOPO MAPS*:	Plumas NF; *Greenville* (15 series)

Indian Creek meanders down from 7,000-foot peaks east and north of Quincy. It then flows through a wide valley past Crescent Mills on its way to join Spanish Creek. There the two creeks form the East Branch of the North Fork Feather River.

About 2 miles downstream of Crescent Mills, the placid waters of Indian Creek give way to one of the most chaotic, frightening stretches of runnable whitewater imaginable. The river changes from class I to class IV in an instant, and quickly increases to class V–VI until the whole river charges over Indian Falls 1.5 miles downstream. Below here the run takes on a more benevolent character.

The initial mile and a half, which plummets about 300 feet, defies "rock-by-drop-by-eddy" description. The entire stretch is visible from the road, 200 feet above, and should be laboriously scouted beforehand. It is relatively easy to escape to the road at any point on this run.

In the spring of '84, after a miserably cold, low-water run of upper Mill Creek, a contingent of the spring Sierra pro-leisure kayaking tour and I stumbled upon Indian Creek quite by accident.

"Miraculous," we thought. "Why, right here 'long side this big 'ol paved road! 'Magine that!" We'd never heard of Indian Creek. Without further ado we put in and spent the next 3 hours navigating 2 miles of river. We executed 3 short portages with Indian Falls the last. We judged the flow 1,200–1,500 cfs.

In the spring of '85 Dweeter King and I pulled over next to Indian Creek to inspect what we planned to run that day. The flow was 10–20% higher than we'd run it in '84, and after only moments we were both seized by irretractable fear. Inexplicably, we began to experience lower intestinal rumblings and an uncanny sympathy for the billions of frightened rodents that inhabit the earth. We leapt into the car and sped off before any semblance of optimism could return.

The remaining 4 miles below Indian Falls contain good playing and several impressive class IV drops. One in particular is a river-wide ledge which could become quite dangerous at higher flows.

This 4-mile stretch makes a good run by itself, and avoids the horror show above Indian Falls. A reasonable put-in exists shortly below Indian Falls, where the river swings away from the road—look for a dirt road that leads toward the river. Access is blocked by a locked gate, but it's a short walk down this road to an old bridge that spans the river.

The take-out for this run is 11 miles north of Quincy where Highways 89 and 70 meet. The put-in is 5 miles up Hwy. 89 toward Greenville. If you're having trouble, find Lake Almanor on a map and look south on Hwy. 89 for Greenville and Crescent Mills.

—LH

KLAMATH RIVER (Hell's Corner)

DIFFICULTY	FLOW	OPTIMUM	MILES	PORTAGES
IV–IV+	600–3000	3000	16	0
IV++	>3000			

PUT IN: **John C. Boyle Powerhouse (3,300 ft.)**
TAKE OUT: **Fishing Access #1 (2,620 ft.)**
SHUTTLE: **39 miles, 1.5 hours**
RAFTS: **YES (commercial run)**
AVERAGE GRADIENT: **43 fpm; mi/mi: 70, 30, 30, 20, 20, 40, 65, 110, 60, 65, 50, 20, 30, 20, 30, 20**
GAUGE: ***Release from J. C. Boyle Powerhouse* (flow phone).**

BOATING SEASON:	**Spring**	**Summer**	**Fall**
WATER SOURCE:	**Spill/Power**	**Power**	**Power**

AAA and *TOPO MAPS*: **Northeastern California; *Copco, Secret Spring Mtn., Mule Hill* (7.5 series)**

This description is included primarily to warn the unwary. The Upper Klamath, fittingly dubbed "Hell's Corner" by rafters, definitely has some drawbacks. What you'll encounter is funkhauser foamy brown water, wicked sharp volcanic rock, and a long shuttle. However, on the plus side is very pleasant semiwilderness scenery, reliable dam-released summer flows, and an ample supply of beer and chips at the take-out store.

During the spring of '86, Lars and I set out to make our personal first descents of Hell's Corner. The sole purpose of the trip was to get the information for this writeup—we had already heard that this section was marginal. Armed with a AAA map and a 6-pack of Meister Brau, Lars, his brother Suren and I headed out on our quest for knowledge. The first thing we learned was to bring more beer. Hell's Corner is in the middle of nowhere and it takes forever to get there. The next lesson, don't drive to the put-in by following the dirt road upstream along the river. We just barely made it in my whimpy little car. A high clearance 4 × 4 is the ticket for this section of road. If you don't have a macho rig (and don't enjoy abusing a normal vehicle), you'll have to drive around the long way. See the put-in instructions for the gory details.

Upon our arrival at Frain Ranch (5.5 miles below the normal put-in) it began to snow. At this time Lars unselfishly volunteered to forgo the run and drive the shuttle. Boating in the snow isn't fun, but somebody's got to do it.

With the snow blowing in our faces, Suren and I set off paddling towards Caldera, the first big class IV+ rapid located just downstream of Frain Ranch. The 5-mile stretch from J. C. Boyle Powerhouse to Frain Ranch, which Suren and I deftly avoided, is reported to be class II. Although Caldera is a bit steeper than average, it's a typical Hell's Corner rapid. You'll find a very long, low-angle rapid littered with gnarly black rocks and chaotic waves. At 1,700 cfs (one turbine at the dam) the major obstacles are the half-covered sharp black rocks. As an added feature, about every tenth wave has a sharp black horn hidden within dark brown water. I found boat-scouting this drop a bit nerve-wracking. A prerun scout is recommended. The three other class IV rapids on the run aren't as steep, but follow the same pattern. The rapids are wide, very long, and continuous with plenty of angry rocks strewn throughout. Suren contracted a case of facial road rash when he tipped over and smacked his face on an abrasive rock. Unfriendly rocks! The whitewater peters out four miles below Frain Ranch. The final 7 miles are class II interrupted by an occasional broken-down diversion dam.

Although there is plenty of action, due to the continuous nature of the rapids, there are very few fun play spots for kayakers. Due to the sharp rock and hidden horns, I found the run to be a bit tedious. However, if you knew where the hidden horns were, it could be fun. Also, if the water was up to 3,000 cfs (two turbines at the dam) most of the horns would go away and the waves would be more fun. However, at any level, please don't swim or you'll be lacerated on the rocks.

To get to the take-out, drive 12 miles north of Yreka on I-5 to Henly. From Henly follow Ager road (as marked on AAA) about 10 miles east to Ager-Beswick Road and turn east (left). Continue on the Ager-Beswick road about 16 miles until you reach the take-out, Fishing Access #1 (just upstream of Copco Reservoir). Much of the way is dirt road and there are some ambiguous turns. Be sure to have a AAA map handy, as it's very easy to get lost!

There are three options for getting to the put-in. The first option is to simply continue upstream on the dirt road along the river. The road is rough, but we made it in my Nissan Sentra. If you have a high-clearance vehicle and just want to run the best rapids, driving up to Frain Ranch is a viable option. To get to Frain Ranch continue driving upstream from Fishing Access #1 to Fishing Access #6 (a good take-out). From Fishing Access #6, drive 7 rough and rocky miles to a left turn at an old abandoned house. Follow this good dirt road down to the river. All of the good stuff (rapids) starts just downstream of Frain Ranch.

The second put-in option is to drive downstream on the north side of Copco Reservoir to Copco. At Copco turn right (north) onto a dirt road, follow this road 11 miles to Hwy. 66 (in Oregon) where you turn right (east). Drive until you reach the Klamath and a dirt road to J. C. Boyle Powerhouse (it's on the river right). The marked put-in is just downstream of the powerhouse. This route takes about 1.5 hours.

The third option is drive back to I-5. This is a last resort when the Copco dirt road is too muddy. This is the long way!

—CS

KLAMATH RIVER
(Happy Camp to Dillon Creek Campground)

DIFFICULTY	FLOW	OPTIMUM	MILES	PORTAGES
II–III	1000–3000	3000	21.5	0
II–III+	3000–5000			
III–IV–	>5000			

PUT IN: Happy Camp, Curley Jack Campground (1,057 ft.)

TAKE OUT: Dillon Creek Campground (710 ft.)

SHUTTLE: 23 miles

RAFTS: YES (commercial run)

AVERAGE GRADIENT: 16 fpm; mi/mi: 18, 20, 15, 25, 15, 20, 15, 13, 13, 5, 20, 12, 18, 17, 13, 22, 7, 26, 12, 14, 16, 10

GAUGE: The flow at the take-out is the *Flow at Orleans* (flow phone) minus the flow of the Salmon River (the Salmon is dry during the summer).

	Winter Spring	Summer
BOATING SEASON:	Winter Spring	Summer
WATER SOURCE:	Natural/Spill	Spill

AAA and *TOPO MAPS*: Northwestern California; *Happy Camp Ukonom and Dillon Mtn.* (15 series)

In the first edition of this guidebook, Lars wrote off this section of the Klamath with "There are many good class II–III runs on the Klamath above the Ikes run, but they . . . have been described in great detail in Dick Schwind's *West Coast River Touring.*" Well, that's great for people that started boating in 1974 and have a copy of Schwind's book. For the rest of you, I'll get you pointed in the right direction and leave the adventure of discovering the details to you. However, please note that Ishi Pishi Falls (class VI) is located 17.5 miles below the Dillon Creek take-out. Don't run Ishi Pishi Falls.

I ran this section in the spring of '74 with that celebrity boater Don Banducci and some friends. We had a flow of 4,000 cfs for our great two-day raft-supported trip. There was plenty of food and beer! As you might imagine, years of hard living have dimmed my recall of the trip. However, that won't stop me from saying that the river is primarily class II with a few fun class III rapids tossed in. In general, the class III drops are found when the mile-by-mile gradient exceeds 20 fpm. Several of the brand-name rapids are Kanaka Creek (mile 3), Devil's Toenail (mile 3.7) and Dragons Tooth (mile 15.4). On our trip we camped on a lovely beach somewhere on the side of the river. The scenery was nice; the presence of the road (Hwy. 96) was noticed, but there isn't a lot of traffic. The road presents many opportunities to access the river. Most convenient if you don't want to camp out of your boat, or prefer to cut your trip short. It is also possible to put in 36 miles upstream of Happy Camp at Sarah Totten Campground. Above Happy Camp the river is a bit easier (popular with open canoes at flows below 2,000 cfs), but watch out for a few class III rapids. It's also possible to run an additional 14 miles of class II below Dillon Creek. Take out about a quarter of a mile upstream of Reynolds Creek, where you'll find a dirt road down to the river. Again, watch out for Ishi Pishi Falls which is about 4 miles downstream.

There are two ways to get to the Klamath. You can drive from I-5; turn off I-5 4.89 miles north of Yreka, and follow Hwy. 96 downstream until you reach Happy Camp. Once at Happy Camp, cross the river and follow the signs to Curley Jack Campground (it's on the river left). The other option is to go through Eureka. Take Hwy. 299 until you hit Hwy. 96; follow Hwy. 96 up the river until you reach Dillon Creek Campground (one of many potential take-outs). Continue about 25 miles upstream on Hwy. 96 to reach Happy Camp, where you cross the river to reach Curley Jack Campground (the put-in).

—CS

McCLOUD RIVER (Hearst Run)

DIFFICULTY	FLOW	OPTIMUM	MILES	PORTAGES
II to −III	200	200 (at put-in)	11 (3 miles on lake)	0
III to IV	>200			

PUT IN: Fowler's Campground (3,210 ft.)
TAKE OUT: McCloud Reservoir (2,660 ft.)
SHUTTLE: 17 miles
RAFTS: YES (note low flow upstream of Big Springs)
AVERAGE GRADIENT: 69 fpm; mi/mi: 135, 80, 80, 85, 60, 40, 35, 35 . . .
GAUGE: No gauge, normally runnable throughout the year.
BOATING SEASON: Spring Summer
WATER SOURCE: Natural Natural (spring-fed)
AAA and *TOPO MAPS*: Northeastern California; *Shoeinhorse Mtn.* (15 series)

This section of the McCloud has something for everyone: a runnable waterfall for daredevils, a continuous class II+ to easy III run for neophytes (at summer flows), spectacular springs and scenery for nature lovers, and finally the Hearst summer retreat, Wyntoon, for all you architecture buffs out there. The McCloud is spring-fed, thus the river runs at a nearly constant flow all year. At the put-in you'll find a paltry 200 cfs. However, two miles downstream, Big Springs gushes in with a most welcome 500 to 1,000 cfs. If the flow at Fowler's Campground is greater than 200 cfs, watch out for the first steep mile of river (135 fpm). At 200 cfs it's easy, but at 1,000 cfs it will probably be class IV. Thus, if upon your arrival at the put-in you see a raging river, send your neophyte friends around to the take-out with the wine coolers.

Let's talk about the whitewater first. As advertised, there is a runnable 10-foot waterfall, Lower McCloud Falls, located at the put-in. I watched Lars unsuccessfully probe for the bottom of this drop—don't worry, it's plenty deep. I also watched a couple of other yahoos totally botch the drop. I'm talking running the falls upside down and backwards, and still rolling up smiling. However, please note that the wall on the river right is severely undercut and could cause some big trouble (i.e., death). Please don't swim into the undercut! At flows higher than 200 cfs use your own good judgement whether or not to run the falls. For you super-nut-case-type daredevils, Middle McCloud Falls is located approximately one mile upstream of Fowler's Campground. This is the 48-foot waterfall that Lars

Holbek ran in an effort to attain glory. A photo of Lars shooting this shoals was featured in *Outside Magazine.* I don't recommend it to you kids at home!

After the thrill of the waterfall or the sense of relief at having decided to put in below the falls, you can look forward to some miniature golf-style rapids while paddling through Pine Tree Hollow. Although the gradient for the first mile is 135 fpm with a flow of only 200 cfs, you can't expect too much. There are some fun, narrow sections which require some deft rock-dodging, but with slow flow it isn't too tough. What's tough are the few wide sections where you'll have to scrabble over the shoals or else portage due to the low flow. Rafters will not have much fun on this section. Please be forewarned that if the river at Fowler's Campground is much higher than 200 cfs, be prepared for some class IV action for the first mile.

On arriving at Big Springs, 2.2 miles below Fowler's Campground, the whitewater picks up. In general, the rapids are wide, shallow and long. There are several sections where the rapids seem to go on for miles! The average rapid is a big riffle with an occasional exposed rock. There are several sections that are easy class III; here the rapids are a bit steeper (faster) and there are a few more rocks. The rocks are black volcanic, but they aren't too gnarly. The water is super clear and cold! If you make it to an old log bridge (4.5 miles below the put-in) you've made it through all the rough stuff. Below the Hearst spread (Wyntoon), 6 miles below the put-in, the river mellows out to class II. The end of the run is signaled by The Bend where you'll find a second grandiose mansion. This unit is used as a fishing lodge. Brace yourself, for just around the corner is the lovely McCloud Reservoir and a 3-mile paddle to the Tarantula Gulch boat ramp.

Please note that below Big Springs both sides of the river are private property owned by the Hearst Corporation. They'll be disappointed if they find you trespassing—please don't stop to eat lunch, make a pit stop, or drop in at Wyntoon to talk to Patty about the bourgeois exploitation of the proletariat masses. Due to the continuous nature of the rapids, cold water and the lack of public access, this isn't a run for non-rollers (kayakers) or leaky rubber duck rafters.

The natural scenery on the McCloud is great. The beautiful river canyon is forested with pine trees. Big Springs gushes from high on the hillside in an explosion of whitewater onto moss-covered rocks. The super clear spring-fed water is a dazzling electric blue. The wilderness character of some sections of the upper part of the run are only slightly marred by the presence of an untraveled dirt road. This section of the McCloud has a unique combination of natural beauty found nowhere else in California.

The Hearst family summer retreat, Wyntoon, will interest the floating architecture fans. There you'll see an eclectic collection of structures built on the river's edge. The collection includes a couple of Swiss cottages decorated with fairytale murals, a three-story medieval castle keep (built with composite shingles) and a lovely Cape Cod cottage. A few hundred yards downstream of Wyntoon is a smaller castle keep built from granite—it looks authentic. Floating by Wyntoon allows a glimpse into the backyard of yesteryear's ultra-rich. Money doesn't buy good taste.

To get to the take-out, drive 6 miles north of Dunsmuir on I-5 to Hwy. 89. Follow the signs to the town of McCloud (about 10 miles off I-5). Once in town, turn right on Squaw Valley Road (there is a sign pointing toward Lake McCloud). Follow this road 9 miles until it dead-ends at the Tarantula Gulch boat ramp on the reservoir. To get to the put-in from McCloud, continue driving 5.5 miles east on Hwy. 89 to the dirt road (there may be a sign to Fowler's Campground) and turn right. Once on the dirt road, drive half a mile to a four-way intersection, go straight and them immediately take the right fork at a sign for Lower Falls. Follow this road half a mile to the parking lot at Fowler's Campground which overlooks Lower Falls.

—CS

WOOLEY CREEK

DIFFICULTY	FLOW	OPTIMUM	MILES	PORTAGES
IV–V	500–1500	1200	13	0

PUT IN: North Fork Confluence (1,900 ft.)

TAKE OUT: Cal Salmon Confluence (560 ft.)

SHUTTLE: 14 miles (hiking on a trail)

RAFTS: YES (commercial run) note hike in on trail.

AVERAGE GRADIENT: 103 fpm; mi/mi: 90, 120, 120, 120, 80, 90, 130, 80, 80, 110, 100, 110, 110

GAUGE: The flow will be approximately 10 to 20% of the *Flow at Somes Bar* (flow phone) on the Cal Salmon. Somes Bar is five miles downstream of the Wooley Creek confluence.

BOATING SEASON: Spring

WATER SOURCE: Natural

AAA and *TOPO MAPS*: Northwestern CA; *Medicine, Orleans, Somes Bar* (7.5 series)

Here's yet another second-hand river description. Rather than relying on some garbled second-hand story, I have a *San Francisco Chronicle* article describing the first commercial raft descent. In addition, I also have the raft company's brochure! The brochure gives the details of the 5-day/13-mile commercial river trip. In addition, I chitchatted with a couple of the folks who kayaked along with the first commercial run. The true first descent was done in 1985 by the same rafting company (Munroe's Wilderness Adventures).

The logistics and low gradient of Wooley Creek explain why the rafters managed to beat the hardcore kayaker types to the first. Lars' comment upon hearing that some rafters had done the first descent was, "Why bother to hike your boat 14 miles upstream for a lowly 100-fpm run!" As usual, the rafters applied siege tactics—they hired a fleet of donkeys to haul their stuff upstream. Well, enough of the kayakers' sour grapes, let's talk about the river.

As mentioned, the "shuttle" entails hiking 14 miles upstream along the river. The trail (as marked on the topo map) starts out with an uphill section about half a mile long with 600 feet of elevation gain. This is followed by two miles of downhill which leads to a 1.5-mile-long hill with a 900-foot elevation gain. From the summit of this hill it's another two miles to Wooley Camp which is the first possible put-in after a total of 6 miles of boat hiking. There is one more small 250-foot hill, after which the trail basically follows the river.

The raft trip packed 13 miles upstream to Bear Skull Creek. It's another mile of upstream trekking to get to the confluence with the North Fork. From the confluence it's 13 miles to the take-out on the Salmon River. However, if your boat is getting heavy, you could put in at Haypress Creek (near Buck's Cabin), after only 7 miles of toil, and catch all the good class IV and V sections. The 7 miles of river above Buck's Cabin is primarily class III with a couple of IV's. The raft company's brochure reports that the section from Haypress Creek down to the confluence with the Salmon River has seven class V (and one class V+) and many class IV rapids. They have bestowed the rapids with names such as Whoa! Mule! and The Fat Lady Sings. However, my conversation with the pair of kayakers (Don Banducci and Donna Casey) and one of the raft guides (Julie Munger), that were part of the commercial first descent, led me to rate it class IV with three class V's. Commercial rafters usually rate rapids one-half to a full class higher than western kayakers. However, the newspaper article describes some wild action—so watch out!

A final boat hiking note: the U.S. Forest Service map (Marble Mountain Wilderness) shows a 3-mile downhill trail from Camp Three Camp to Wooley Camp. I have no idea what the trail or dirt road to Camp Three Camp is like—the adventure of discovery is yours if you want to try this shortcut.

To get to the trailhead from Eureka (Hwy. 101), drive east on Hwy. 299 (40 miles) towards Willow Creek. At Willow Creek, turn left (north) on Hwy. 96 and drive north (47 miles) to Somes Bar. Turn right onto Salmon River Rd. and drive 2 to 3 miles upstream to the marked trailhead (it's on the left). There is a pleasant paved parking lot. If you cross a bridge over the Cal Salmon you've driven too far! The parking lot is a few hundred yards before the first bridge. It would be prudent to drive about a mile upstream to inspect the flow on Wooley Creek before embarking on your upstream trek. The area can also be accessed from the east (I-5), it's a long, twisted ride over a mountain pass on the Cecilville Road. Get out your AAA map and figure it out!

—CS

BOUND FOR GLORY

The first edition of this guide book contained a story about a group of kayakers who spent an unplanned night camping on the SF of the Eel. Rashad and Donna found that story entertaining reading while driving north on Hwy. 101 towards the South Fork Eel put-in. Upon arrival at Ten Mile Creek (the S.F. Eel put-in), the pair experienced a bit of literary deja vu, for ". . . on this particular day, it was raining and the river was rising." The flow was a hefty 8,000 cfs.

The duo was a bit apprehensive at the put-in, but they were determined to make the run. Donna is an experienced kayaker and felt up for the trip. Although Rashad is a strong paddler, he was unfamiliar with the handing characteristics of his new Sabre squirt boat. The first few miles of Ten Mile Creek are easy, and with the high flow, the pair made good time. Upon entering the final two miles of Ten Mile Creek, the tone of their journey changed for the worse. To Rashad's chagrin, he was involuntarily squirted by the big class IV water. After a couple of unplanned backenders and a mystery move, he decided to quit while he was ahead. Donna agreed, and they decided to hike out on the river right.

Rather than hike four miles upstream back to the put-in, Rashad led the way to the summit of Brush Mountain in search of a short direct route to Hwy. 101. The kayaks were left behind after 200 yards of uphill toil. The route up the mountain was steep and brushy. At times they found themselves crawling up through the brush on their hands and knees. Upon reaching the summit, they saw nothing but more hills. Hwy. 101 was nowhere to be seen. Now lost in the wilderness with only a small Tekna knife, they prepared a pine bough shelter for a night of camping in the rain. They had no matches to build a fire. Fortunately, they both were wearing dry suits.

The next day the bushwhacking resumed. Their disoriented search for Hwy. 101 took them to the canyonside above the rapid named "The Hole That Ate Chicago," approximately five miles downstream from the confluence of Ten Mile Creek and the South Fork. In the afternoon they could hear the calls of the rescue party kayaking down the river, but they were too far away for their cries for help to be heard. Once again, they prepared for a long, wet, cold night by building a shelter with that little Tekna knife.

The next morning they hiked to the river and waited for the rescue crew to arrive. They were exhausted and looked foward to the helicopter ride out.

The moral of the story: IF YOU BAIL OUT ON THIS RUN, WALK UPSTREAM ALONG TEN MILE CREEK IF POSSIBLE. IF YOU'RE TOO FAR DOWNSTREAM, EITHER WAIT FOR HELP OR PLAN ON SWIMMING TO THE TAKE-OUT!!!

—CS

YIPPIE I YO KY YEAH!

Every summer weekend, Class-V cowboys ride their kayaks down Cherry Creek. One of the meanest sections is Rockpile, in the middle of fearsome Flat Rock Falls. Here, the mighty Tuolumne snakes through a jumble of granite boulders, then drops right away over a six-foot falls onto and under a giant boulder. It's not a pretty sight.

To ride Rockpile, a kayaker has to head toward one of two possible boulder-choked chutes. Any error in angle or speed results in a pinned buckeroo. Half the river below goes over the falls, while the other half trickles to the big roundup eddy, which must be caught. Many a river dude has seen the error of his ways when bulldogged by Rockpile.

During the summer of '84, I was leading a big Cherry Creek trip. The boys were doing fine at Rockpile. Half had already come down, the rest waited their turn above. A fella named Tom's turn came up. I could see by the look in his eyes that he wasn't sure he could make it, but he had the guts to head toward the left-hand chute. He had the right speed as he went down, but his kayak caromed off a boulder and stuck nose first into a bull-sized rock. He was stuck mid-chute with his stern pointing skyward at a 45-degree angle.

The rest of us wasted no time in getting out our ropes. Chip Kaufman, a Texan, jumped out to the boulder nearest Tom. He was a paddle-length away, but couldn't reach him. The obvious way to free Tom was to lasso the stern of his kayak and pull it free, so I yelled at Chip to rope that kayak. Well, it turns out that my grandmother could throw a lariat better than that dang Texan. He missed time and time again. Meanwhile, Tom was getting a big worried looking at Flat Rock Falls, which awaited just below.

Some of the other boys decided to try their hand at lassoing Tom's kayak from shore. They tied tight bow line knots into their ropes and commenced throwing. By now, it had been about 10 minutes since Tom first got stuck, and he was getting a bit concerned about all this lassoing going on; but, the boys on shore had strong arms and were getting close. On the fourth throw, one of them lassoed Tom around the neck. He was not pleased. With a quick flick of the wrist, Tom got that darn lariat off his neck and told those boys to ride off into the sunset.

With this kind of help, Tom decided he'd better save himself. He started bucking and rocking his kayak, and after a few minutes, it busted free and bolted down the chute. With a cheer from the boys, Tom caught the big roundup eddy at the lip of Flat Rock Falls. Yahoo!

—CS

AND IT WAS RED!

After a very successful Cherry Creek run (and a spontaneous post-trip Lumsden Falls party), Lars and my brother Bill helped Richard Montgomery tie their kayaks onto his car. As on a ship, the captain of the car has final authority in all tie-down matters. Lars started to tie a bow line (a rope from the front bumper to the grab loops on the kayaks), but Richard told him not to bother with one. With the boats "securely tied," the trio motored towards the San Francisco Bay Area.

It was a dark and moonless night as they headed up the always-windy Altamont Pass section of Hwy. 580, where the freeway is four lanes wide. Lars had just finished off the last of the tortilla chips when Bill noticed that the guy in the car alongside them was waving frantically and rolling down his window. Lars commented that the guy was probably some turkey kayaker who wanted to swap river stories. However, the guy pointed out that they had just lost one of the kayaks off their roof! In disbelief, they looked out the rear window, only to see Bill's kayak on the trunk. Lars' brand-new red T Slalom was gone! With a screech of tires, they pulled over. Lars jumped out of the car and ran to retrieve his new red T Slalom. Bill and Richard stayed with the car.

Lars found his boat about half a mile down the road. The red T Slalom, pitoned nose-first into the center guardrail, was hanging out into the fast lane of traffic. Due to the darkness, car after car ran over the trapped boat. After several minutes, Lars made a desperate dash across four lanes of traffic and freed his boat. This was followed by an equally desperate dash carrying his severely tweaked boat back to safety.

Meanwhile, back at the car, Richard and Bill were busy getting the remaining kayaks back onto the roof rack. Out of the darkness, a passing car swerved to the roadside in front of them and skidded to a halt. The bug-eyed driver jumped out of his car and exclaimed, "I just ran over a BODY, and it was RED!"

The moral of the story: ALWAYS USE A BOW LINE!

—CS

BURNT RANCH GORGE

Burnt Ranch Gorge presents a mysterious challenge to river runners traveling the highway on the rim of the Trinity River Canyon. Below the road one can only catch glimpses of the river. What awaits in the canyon is unseen and unknown. The towering walls, which obscure a clear view, stand to warn the river runner to stay clear. A glance at a topographical map reveals a steep gradient. The river drops over 100 feet per mile in the heart of the gorge. Only the most intrepid souls would consider venturing into such a place.

Mel Schneller was the first to accept the challenge of Burnt Ranch Gorge. Mel, a pioneer of the kayaking sport in the 60's, was not known as a fearless river explorer, but rather as a boat designer, instructor and organizer of a sport then in its beginnings. After his first look at the gorge he must have known that he would return to run it one day.

That day came during the summer of 1971. It was a good day for a first descent. The river flowed a reasonable 350 cfs. The weather was clear and warm. The party consisted of Mel, his son Mike, and Dick Schwind. Although they traveled light, carrying no bivouac gear, the men were prepared for the canyon, coming equipped with ropes and pitons.

The rock-climbing equipment must have offered them little comfort as they entered the mouth of the gorge, where the smooth water-polished vertical walls seem to tower into the sky. Peering downstream into the canyon, they could see only the horizon line of Auto-End-On, a steep six-foot drop. The men then realized that the river would be run only with the canyon and river's permission—a brute force attack would fail.

The group, paddling fiberglass kayaks, made slow-but-steady progress down the river. Mike, the best kayaker, took the lead, running several difficult drops which Mel and Dick elected to portage. The entire group walked the Burnt Ranch Falls Trilogy. After the final portage around Gray's Fall, they knew that they had made it through the canyon. Mel had realized his dream.

Shortly after emerging from the gorge, Mel told Dick, "You know, this is going to be the high-water mark of my boating career. I don't really expect to explore another river. I'll leave that to you younger guys. This is the one I wanted to do." Mel Schneller, age 56, died of a heart attack at the take-out.

The awesome beauty, mystery, and ruggedness that compelled Mel to challenge the Gorge has the same effect on paddlers today. All who run Burnt Ranch Gorge know it isn't just a great river trip, it's an experience remembered a lifetime.

—CS

Appendices

APPENDIX I

FIRST DESCENTS

The following is a necessarily incomplete logging of California river first descents. Apologies are hereby lodged for any errors. Our hope is that, with reader input, subsequent printings will be more comprehensive and accurate. In the meantime, and to the best of our knowledge . . .

North Fork American River

Chamberlain Falls to Ponderosa Way: Carl Trost, Noel DeBord, and Monty Rowell; May 8, 1965.

Generation Gap: Chuck Stanley, Lars Holbek, Mike Schlax and Richard Montgomery; June 13, 1980.

Giant Gap: John Ramirez; July 4, 1971.

Ponderosa Way (to Lake Clementine): Carl Trost, Glen Gaumer, Bob Hawley (raft) and Bob Cutter (raft); 1958 or 1959.

South Fork American River

Lovers Leap: Lars Holbek, Richard Montgomery, and Mike Schlax; June 1978.

Kyburz to Riverton: Walt Harvest and Noel DeBord; 1965.

Riverton to Peavine: Tom Allen, Barbara Campbell, Norm Glickman, John Googins, Dave Kelsey, Gerald Meral, Ron Smith, Bill Stanley, Chuck Stanley, and Bert Welti; May 28, 1973.

Golden Gate: Richard Montgomery, Lars Holbek, and Chuck Stanley; March 29, 1980.

Slab Creek: Louis Debret and Tom Anderson; April 20, 1982.

Rock Creek to Chili Bar (pre-Chili Bar Dam): Carl Trost and Fen Salter; mid 1960's.

Chili Bar to the Gorge: There are several firsts here depending on how long your memory is.

1. Livermore used to run logs down the river, he hired Swedes that ran wooden dorys down the river.

2. Various sections were run by the Sacramento White Water Kayak Klub, of which John Jastraub and Bill Cameron were members, in the early to mid 1950's.

3. Bill Webber made a complete descent in a raft (rubber) in the late 1950's.

4. Maynard Munger and Bryce Whitmore ran the Gorge in kayaks in 1959.

East Fork Carson River

Dixon Mine to Silver Creek, Silver Creek to Markleeville: Carl Trost, Monte Rowell, Fran Cutter, Dave Kelsey, John Ramirez, John Googins, Jerry Meral, Jim Sindelar, Steve Shimek, Bill Kruse, Jim Morehouse; July 4, 1969.

Markleeville to Rt. 395: Carl Trost, Monte Rowell, Helmut Donner, Fran Cutter, Steve Shimek, Bill Kruse; July 5, 1969.

Clavey River

Upper: Dennis Johnson and Rob Kirby; around 1980.

Lower: Dennis Johnson and Rob Kirby: around 1980.

Cosumnes River

Upper Run: Chuck Koteen and Bob Holland; 1973.

Lower Run: Carl Trost, Fen Salter, and Helmut Donner; May 18, 1963.

Middle Fork Cosumnes River

Slub Gulch to Hwy 16: Gerry Meral, Chuck Koteen, and Carl Trost; April 12, 1963.

Deer Creek

Upper Run, Potato Patch to Ponderosa Way: Bill Stanley, Mike Schlax, John Googins, Dave Kelsey, Tom Allen, Bert Welti, Ron Pardee, Dan Pardee, Dick Roberts, and Gunter Hemmersbach; 1974.

Lower Run, Ponderosa Way to Rt 99: John Googins, Gunter Hemmersbach, Dick Sunderland, Jim Morehouse, Bill Hewlett, and Dick Roberts; March 25–26, 1972.

Main Eel

Hearst to Tutu: Maynard Munger and Bryce Whitmore; 1963. Upper Main Eel: Lars Holbek (solo); April 30, 1978. Pilsbury: active Sierra Club RTS run by mid 60's. Dos Rios to Alderpoint: Peter Whitney, Carl Trost, Elsa Bailey, Bryce Whitmore, Maynard Munger, et al.; May 1960.

Middle Fork Eel

Black Butte to Dos Rios: Bob Ehrman, solo; 1952.

South Fork Eel

Branscomb put-in: Maynard Munger and Bryce Whitmore; February 1, 1959.

Ten Mile Creek: run prior to 1963.

Middle Fork Feather

Devils Canyon: Bert Welti et al.; mid 70's.

Bald Rock Canyon: Richard Montgomery, Chuck Stanley, and Lars Holbek; March 31, 1980.

Fordyce Creek

Walt Garms, Mike Fentress and Tim Stringari; September 1983.

Hayfork Creek

Lower Gorge: Carl Trost; May 24 and 25, 1969.

Kaweah

Three Rivers to Lake: Maynard Munger and Bryce Whitmore; 1960.

Middle Fork Kaweah

Hospital Rock: Lars Holbek, John Armstrong, and Chuck Stanley; June 1984.

Kern River

Upper Run: Reg Lake, Royal Robbins, and Doug Tompkins; 1981.

Forks of the Kern: Doug Carson and Dennis Johnson.

Kern Canyon: Doug Carson et al.; 70's.

South Fork Kern

Reg Lake, Royal Robbins, Jeff Jones, and Doug Tompkins; May 1985.

Kings River

Kings Canyon: Maynard Munger, Bryce Whitmore, and Roger Paris; July 3 and 4, 1960.

Middle Fork Kings River

Triple Crown: Reg Lake, Newsome Holmes, Royal Robbins, and Doug Tompkins; summer 1982.

South Fork Kings River

Horseshoe Bend: Dennis Johnson, Richard Montgomery, and Chuck Stanley; July 1980.

Klamath River

Happy Camp to Salmon River: Bryce Whitmore, Roger Paris, and Maynard Munger; July 4, 1961.

Ikes Falls: Carl Trost, Quentin Johnson, Helmut Donner; July 6, 1963.

Mad River

Swinging Bridge Run: Dick Schwind et al.

Mark West Creek

Mark West Lodge Run: Mike Schlax; early 70's.

McCloud River

McCloud Springs to Lake Shasta (before McCloud Reservoir): Noel DeBord, solo; May 1965.

Merced River

Merced Gorge: Dieter King, Eric Magneson, Chuck Stanley, Lars Holbek; July 1986.

Bridge to Briceburg: Lower sections were run by Sierra Club RTS in 1959.

Briceburg to Bagby: Maynard Munger and Bryce Whitmore; June 6, 1966.

South Fork Merced

Upper run: Ron Thompson; 1979.

Mill Creek

Upper: Dennis Johnson and Rob Kirby; 1980.

Lower: Tom Allen, John Googins, Chuck Koteen, Charles Martin, John Ramirez, Carl Trost, and Bert Welti; April 7–9, 1973.

Mokelumne River

Electra Run: Sierra Club RTS scheduled trip in 1958.

North Fork Mokelumne

Fantasy Falls: Chuck Stanley, Don Banducci, Richard Montgomery, Rick Fernald, and Lars Holbek; June 1981.

Bear River to Devil's Nose: Dan Gaut, Bert Welti, and Charles Martin; May 20, 1973.

Devil's Nose to Tiger Creek Dam: Dan Gaut, John Googins, Dick Sunderland, Dave Kelsey, Chuck Koteen, and Bert Welti; June 10, 1973.

New River

Gorge: Mike Schlax, Richard Montgomery, and Lars Holbek; spring 1979.

Redwood Creek

Lacks Creek to Orick: Maynard Munger and Bryce Whitmore; February, 1964. They named the "Emerald Mile."

Rubicon River

Hell Hole Dam to Ellicott Bridge: Richard Montgomery, Lars Holbek, and Chuck Stanley; June 1982.

Lower Run: Richard Montgomery, Lars Holbek, and Chuck Stanley; June 1982.

Russian River

Squaw Rock: Old time run, first prior to 1958.

Sacramento River

Box Canyon: Carl Trost and Noel DeBord; May 31, 1965.

Dunsmuir to Castle Crag: Maynard Munger (solo); May 31, 1963.

Castle Crag to Sims Road: Maynard Munger; May 31, 1963.

Sims Flat to Gibson: Carl Trost, Walt Harvest, John Googins, Harry Neal, Charlie Grant, Scott Fleming, and India Fleming; July 1, 1967.

Gibson to Dog Creek Road (Lake Shasta): Monte Rowell and Helmut Donner; May 31, 1965.

Salmon River

Cal Salmon: run prior to 1963.

North Fork Salmon River

Upper, White Gulch to Sawyers Bar: Carl Trost, Dick Sunderland, Bert Welti, Joel DeYoung, and Mart Rigney; May 31, 1976.

South Fork Salmon River

Limestone Bluffs to Matthews Creek Campground: Gunter Hemmersbach; 1970's.

San Joaquin River

Tied for First: Richard Montgomery, Bob Porter, Jerry Kauffmann, Chuck Stanley, Reg Lake, Royal Robbins, Doug Tompkins, and Newsome Holmes; spring 1982.

Horseshoe Bend: Dick Sunderland, Jerry Meral and Cliff Cordy; May 31, 1969.

Middle Fork San Joaquin River

Devil's Postpile: Reg Lake, Royal Robbins, and Doug Tompkins; summer 1980.

South Fork San Joaquin River

Paiute Creek to Florence Lake: John Armstrong, Lars Holbek, and Chuck Stanley; spring 1984.

Florence Lake to Mono Hot Springs: Reg Lake, Mark Adams, and Christy Bretani; 1982.

Mt. Tom Run: Reg Lake, Bob Porter, Royal Robbins, Jeff Jones, Brian Clark, et al.; June 1982.

San Lorenzo River

Henry Cowell State Park Bridge to Santa Cruz: Maynard Munger and Bryce Whitmore; February, 1961.

Scott River

Kelsey Creek to Scott Bar: Noel DeBord, Carl Trost (DNF, wrecked boat), Helmut Donner, and Monte Rowell; May 29, 1965.

Stanislaus River

Camp Nine (now history): run prior to 1958.

Goodwin Dam: Charles Martin, et al.; spring 1972.

Middle Fork Stanislaus River

Dardanelles Run: Steve Arrowsmith, Eric Magneson, and John Magneson; August 28, 1982.

Donnells Run: Mike Schlax and Rick Fernald; early 80's.

Sand Bar Flat Run: Mike Schlax and Rick Fernald; early 80's.

Mt. Knight Run: Bob Porter, Walt Garms, Dave Blau, Chuck Stanley, Richard Montgomery, and Lars Holbek; June 12, 1979.

South Fork Stanislaus

Strawberry: Mike Stemmler et al.; early 80's.

Little Sulphur Creek

Healdsburg-Geyserville Road to confluence: Louis Debret, Eric Magneson, and John Magneson; January 30–31, 1981.

Sulphur Creek

Upper: Lars Holbek and Mike Schlax; January 1979.

Lower: Lars Holbek, Mike Schlax, and Richard Montgomery; January 1979. Gunter Hemmersbach et al., had a previous DNF.

Trinity River

Burnt Ranch: Mel Schneller, Mike Schneller, and Dick Schwind; summer 1971.

North Fork Trinity River

Hobo Gulch to Bridge: Lars Holbek and Gunter Hemmersbach; June 1979.

South Fork Trinity River

Klondike Mine Run: Maynard Munger, Bryce Whitmore, and Ted Fostiak; May 10, 1967.

Lower: Carl Trost and Monte Rowell; June 18, 1967.

Truckee River

River Ranch: Maynard Munger and Bryce Whitmore; June 1961.

Tuolumne River

Grand Canyon: Lars Holbek, Chuck Stanley, Richard Montgomery, John Armstrong, Reg Lake and Royal Robbins; August 27–28, 1983.

Cherry Creek: Dick Sunderland and Jerry Meral; November 16–17, 1968.

Lower: Another popular first descent!

1. Melvin Belli (the big time attorney) and Harry Cobden, to the Clavey on a log raft; 1927.

2. Helmut Donner, Henry Millard, and Rod Kiel in rubber rafts; October 1962.

3. Noel DeBord, solo; 1965.

North Fork Tuolumne River

Dieter King, Walt Garms, Richard Montgomery, Lars Holbek, and Chuck Stanley; 1985.

West Fork Walker River

Hwy. 395 to Walker: John Googins, Dave Kelsey, and John Ramirez; July 6, 1969.

Yuba River

Englebright Dam to Hwy. 20: Mel Schneller et al.; 60's?

Middle Fork Yuba River

Hwy. 49 to Englebright: Mike Fentress, Lars Holbek, Richard Montgomery, and Chuck Stanley; April 30, 1982.

North Fork Yuba River

Sierra City to Downieville: Dick Sunderland, Jerry Meral, Ben Parks, and Cliff Cordy; June 1, 1968.

Bullards Bar Dam to Middle Fork: Vince Hayes, Gordon Patchin, and Chuck Stanley; July 3, 1983.

South Fork Yuba River

Indian Springs to Lake Spaulding: Reg Lake, Mike Snead, John Googins; early 80's.

Washington to Edwards: Fen Salter and Carl Trost; 1964.

Edwards to Purdons: Charles Martin, Dick Sunderland, John Googins, Carl Trost, and Gunter Hemmersbach; 1973.

Hwy. 49 to Bridgeport: Reg Lake, Dick Sunderland, John Googins, and Tim Yarish; early 80's.

—CS

Donna Casey at First Threat, Chili Bar. ***Chuck Stanley***

APPENDIX II

SAN FRANCISCO BAY AREA KAYAK SURFING

Kayak surfing on the California coast can be big fun or a big bummer. The deciding factors are: the waves, your thrill threshold, and the board surfers. Finding good waves is a matter of knowing where to look and good luck. Occasionally, you'll find more wave than you might want. Kayak surf lore is full of stories that start with: ". . . there we were, sitting outside the break, when this giant 10 ft. wave appeared out of nowhere; the wave hit me with the force of a Mack truck and sent the kayak cartwheeling . . ." This type of action is big fun if you like it, or terrifying if you don't. Finding good waves that aren't packed with board surfers is tough. Typically, the better the surf, the more surfers you'll find. In general, surfers don't want to share. For some reason, they resent being speared in the back by out-of-control kayaks.

Ocean kayak surfers can be divided into two classes: real kayak surfers and river yahoos. The real kayak surfer rides either a surf shoe or a wave-ski. These are specialized craft built for one purpose, riding ocean waves. With skill, you can consistently maintain control and blend in with the surfer hierarchy. On the other hand, the typical river boater is totally out of control in the surf. An average ride: catch the wave, ride it straight at the pack of surfers, get closed out (i.e., the wave breaks), get caught sideways in the wave and run over the surfers! It's big fun!

Safety first! Wear your lifevest and helmet when ocean surfing. Some people, no doubt reckless daredevils, elect not to wear these essential items. In their defense they point out that surfers don't wear helmets and that lifevests make it impossible to swim under the waves. Personally, I feel much safer with my "armour" on when battling surfers or fellow kayakers. One surfboard (or kayak) to the head can ruin your entire day. Further, most kayakers aren't up to swimming around in the surf. After a few flailing strokes against a rip current they'll be crying to the surfers they just ran over for help—good luck! Don't be stupid, wear your helmet and lifejacket.

The ideal kayak surfing spot has: a point break or a deep channel where the waves don't break, mushy waves (i.e., waves that crumble from the top) and no surfers. With these factors in mind, I'll describe some of the better SF Bay Area kayak surf spots.

—CS

STEAMER'S LANE

LOCATION: Santa Cruz, 65 miles south of San Francisco.

TYPE OF BREAK: Point break, depending on the tide and wave size there are 3 to 4 breaks. It's easy to paddle out.

WAVE SHAPE: The waves tend to be on the mushy side, with well-defined shape. Great waves for kayak surfing! The rides are long to very long.

TIDE: At low to medium tide the waves are best and the cliff hazard is minimized.

SURFERS: There are lots of surfers—the better the day, the more there are. A major hassle—verbal insults common.

THE BEACH: There is none. The surf crashes into a 30-foot cliff. There is sidewalk along the edge of the cliff and several parking lots overlooking the waves. Not a bad spot to watch the action.

SPECIAL HAZARDS: The major hazard is the cliff. When the tide is high and the waves are big, the surf crashes into the cliff! At low tide, a shelf appears and the waves don't quite reach the cliff. Another fun feature is kelp beds in the surf. I've had some great times rolling with the kelp twisted around my paddle, boat, and neck! Steamer's Lane is not the place to learn how!

Steamer's Lane has the best surfing in Northern California. The bigger the waves the better it gets. Naturally, the place is infested with surfers. The area is also popular with river kayak surfers due to the well-formed mushy waves. Thus, the board surfers have seen the kayaks and the damage is done! Good luck.

On a typical good day there will be around 100 surfers on the water. If you dare to paddle your river kayak out there, you'll soon be informed that you're unwelcome. If you venture out to the main break where the best waves and hot surfers are, brace yourself. You'll immediately be told to get out of there. If you insist on riding their waves, you'll get a surfboard in the head! I'm not kidding. The best strategy is to ride the second- or third-rate waves; these break to the south a bit. Here you'll compete with the little kid surfers. They won't tell you off until you hit them a couple of times.

Steamer's Lane isn't a place to learn how to surf! When the surf is up, the combination of the kelp, cliff and homicidal surfers add up to a class V situation. However, on small and medium days a good time can be had without too much hassle.

To find Steamer's Lane, take Hwy. 17 from the San Jose area to Santa Cruz. Follow signs to the Boardwalk (an amusement park) and the city pier. You can park and put in by the pier; paddle north around the point to reach the waves. Another option is to turn left onto West Cliff Drive (this area is like a maze!) and continue north to the lighthouse. From here you can check out the waves. About halfway between the pier and the lighthouse there is a small parking lot and a stairway down to the water. This is also a good put-in.

—CS

PLEASURE POINT

LOCATION: Santa Cruz, 65 miles south of San Francisco.

TYPE OF BREAK: Point with several breaks, easy to paddle out.

WAVE SHAPE: The waves tend to be on the mushy side with well-defined shape. The rides are medium to long.

TIDE: At low tide, a few rocks appear—no big deal.

SURFERS: There are lots of surfers—the better the day, the more there are. A hassle, but not as bad as Steamer's Lane.

THE BEACH: Not much of a beach, but there is one. Several good spots to watch the action.

SPECIAL HAZARDS: At low tide a few rocks and a shelf appear near the shore, but they aren't too dangerous. The northern part of the break lands on a cliff—watch out on big days. There are also a few kelp beds in the surf zone.

Pleasure Point has the next best surfing in Northern California. As with Steamer's Lane, the surfers are plentiful and a bummer. However, the surfers at Pleasure Point aren't as vocal or violent as those shark-bait surfers at Steamer's.

The waves at Pleasure Point are formed by a shallow shelf off a point, very similar to Steamer's Lane without the cliff. However, on the northern end of the break, the waves do crash into some rocks and a small cliff. If you're cliff shy, just stick to the waves to the south a bit. It's easy to paddle out in the deep water just south of the waves.

To get to Pleasure Point, drive south on Hwy. 17 from San Jose. When you get near Santa Cruz, take Hwy. 101 south (toward Monterey). Drive 3 miles and take the 41st Ave. exit and turn right. Follow 41st Ave. 1.5 miles until it hits the Pacific; follow the road when it bears to the right. Drive a few hundred yards further and park where the road is leaving the cliff. You can see the point and the waves from the road. There is a good place to walk down to the water here.

—CS

DAVENPORT

LOCATION: Davenport is 12 miles north of central Santa Cruz, 55 miles south of San Francisco.

TYPE OF BREAK: Point break, a shallow shelf to the north and a deep channel to the south where the waves don't break.

WAVE SHAPE: I've only been once at high tide, then the waves were mushy.

TIDE: At high tide the waves are mushy.

SURFERS: When the waves are good, there are up to 30 surfers; on an average day you'll run into 2 to 10 of them.

THE BEACH: This is an OK beach with nice scenery and fairly close to the action.

SPECIAL HAZARDS: Launching and taking out on the steep beach can be exciting when the waves are big. Also, there are some exposed rocks on the north side of the beach.

The trick at Davenport is to hit a mediocre day. On such days the waves are OK, and there aren't too many surfers. I've been out here once and had a great time riding giant mushy waves. Surfers don't like mushy waves. Several other times I've checked out the area only to find the place packed with surfers.

To find Davenport (surf area), drive north from Santa Cruz on Hwy. 1 to the town of Davenport. From there, continue about a mile to Cement Plant Rd. (it's on the east side of Hwy. 1). Turn left (west) onto the unmarked Davenport Landing road and drive a few hundred yards to the beach. Park alongside the road; it's a short walk to the beach. The road continues and rejoins Hwy. 1 within another few hundred yards (i.e., the road is a cut-off loop of old Hwy. 1).

—CS

GREYHOUND ROCK

LOCATION: Greyhound Rock is 6 miles north of Davenport, 18 miles north of central Santa Cruz, and 49 miles south of San Francisco.

TYPE OF BREAK: Deep channel (where the waves don't break) with breaks on either side. Easy to paddle out if the waves aren't too big (i.e., over 4 to 5 feet). When the waves are up (above 5 feet) the situation gets desperate!

WAVE SHAPE: Fairly steep waves with good form. Ride toward the deep channel. The rides are medium to short.

TIDE: At low tide there are many shallow areas and exposed rocks in the surf. It's best at high tide.

SURFERS: Very few surfers, maybe a couple. No problem.

THE BEACH: Great beach: AAA scenery, good for picnics and long walks. Close to the surfing action.

SPECIAL HAZARDS: Greyhound Rock is a big rock sticking out of the ocean. Although not too bad, caution and skill must be exercised to avoid hitting it. At low tide, there are also shallow areas (i.e., rocks under water) and small rocks exposed in the surfing area. Wear a helmet!

I've been to Greyhound Rock three times: the first two times it was good, the third time was a bust (the waves were too big). The combination of great scenery, good surf and no surfers is hard to beat. I'm planning on going back for another try.

Greyhound Rock is 6 miles north of Davenport. To get there either drive north on Hwy. 1 from central Santa Cruz 12 miles to Davenport. From there continue 5 miles until you see an unmarked developed parking lot on the west side of the road. One could also drive south on Hwy. 1 from San Francisco. It's a short walk down a steep trail to the beach.

—CS

PACIFICA

LOCATION: Pacifica, about 10 miles south of San Francisco, on Hwy. 1.

TYPE OF BREAK: Beach break, waves typically break all at once with a thump! On big days it's difficult to get out past the break.

WAVE SHAPE: The waves break sharply, sometimes tubing. The rides are short. On occasion, the waves have good form (i.e., break from one side or the other). Wave size varies greatly—don't go here on a big day!

TIDE: I never could figure out what was best. Just go look.

SURFERS: There are usually a few surfers around. There are plenty of places to surf, so it's easy to avoid them. No major hassles.

THE BEACH: There is an OK beach, with a parking lot, toilet, A&W hamburger stand, and assorted low-lifes. It's easy to watch surf action from the beach.

SPECIAL HAZARDS: None. However, the waves can be very big and vicious. On big days watch out for rip currents. Don't go out if the waves are too big.

Pacifica isn't a very good surfing area, but it's popular with river kayak ocean surfers. The primary reason is the lack of surfers. Another feature is easy access. Every time I've surfed here (around 10 times) the waves broke sharply (crunch) and with bad form (i.e., no left or right shoulder). Although not great, surfing at Pacifica beats watching football games!

To get the Pacifica, drive south on Hwy. 1 from San Francisco and follow the signs to Pacifica. Before entering the main section of town (it's only a few hundred yards long) there is a public beach access area on the right (next to the A&W hamburger joint). The AAA map has the beach marked as Pedro Valley Beach, which is about 2 miles south of Rockaway Beach.

—CS

BOLINAS BAY

LOCATION: Bolinas Bay, 7 miles north of Stinson Beach, 24 miles north of SF.

TYPE OF BREAK: A bay mouth (like a river) with a beach break on either side. Easy to paddle out.

WAVE SHAPE: The typical Bolinas wave is mushy and small (2 to 4 feet). Long rides.

TIDE: An outgoing tide is best. This is when the discharge from Bolinas Bay provides a free ride back out.

SURFERS: There are usually a dozen or so surfers around; in general they aren't in the way. No major hassle.

THE BEACH: There is a nice beach for building sandcastles and watching the action. The scenery is also nice.

SPECIAL HAZARDS: Overall, Bolinas is a safe and forgiving break. However, the discharge from Bolinas Bay is like a river to Japan. The current is very strong; swimmers and equipment caught by the flow are swept out. Also, two hundred yards north of the bay outlet, there are some broken-down pier pilings sticking out of the beach. Further north is a concrete sea wall.

Bolinas is a great place for a first-time ocean surfer. On a typical day the waves are mushy cream puffs 2 to 4 feet tall. There is no problem punching right through them. When the waves are happening, you'll get some great long rides. Also, when the tide is going out, there is the added feature of a free ride out on the discharge from Bolinas Bay. Overall, I'd say Bolinas is the best place to give river kayak ocean surfing a try.

To get to Bolinas, drive to Mill Valley on Hwy. 101, and follow the signs to Stinson Beach. In addition to being very scenic, this section of Hwy. 1 is very slow due to the many tortuous curves. Once you get to Stinson Beach, continue north on Hwy. 1 about 5 miles, and turn left on the UNMARKED road to Bolinas. Follow this road 2 miles to "downtown." Continue through town on the main drag (200 yards) and follow the road another 200 yards to where it dead-ends at the beach. There is plenty of parking along the road. The North Bay Counties AAA map will facilitate your search for Bolinas.

—CS

LARS HOLBEK: SEA KAYAKER SANS LUNCH

With a strong sense of adventure, Lars embarked from Eureka on his first major sea kayaking journey. His destination was San Francisco, some 280 miles south. He had his sea kayak loaded for his one-week journey. He also had on his gum boots to keep his toes dry. Although the ocean was a bit rough, the twelve-foot swell didn't intimidate Lars, an experienced whitewater kayaker.

Lars' plan was to simply paddle south down the coast, just outside of the surf, using a distant headland as a guiding beacon. Unfortunately for him, he embarked just north of the Humboldt Bay mouth. When the tide is incoming, which it was when Lars was there, strong currents develop along the beach to the north and south. Thus, when paddling towards the bay mouth, he was getting a free ride south. However, once across the bay mouth he was fighting a strong current.

Paddling against the current and the twelve-foot swell, Lars was making slow-but-steady progress. With the peak of each wave, he could see the distant headland, only to lose sight upon falling into the trough of the swell. Thus with each wave, Lars would lose his sense of direction and veer off course. All this zig-zagging and up and down started to have an unusual effect. With each swell, he felt just a bit worse. Bad feelings soon escalated into bad action—barfing, barfing, and more barfing. After half an hour of dry heaves, Lars was looking for the Coast Guard!

The only option was to attempt to land on the beach through the twelve-foot surf. The beach Lars selected is typical for Northern California. It had a steep beach break with wicked ripcurrents and undertows. Lars wasn't too worried, he knew how to ride waves!

Lars, most pleased that he'd elected to wear a lifevest, sat outside the break and watched the sets of twelve-foot waves come through, After the last big wave of the set went by, Lars floored it toward the beach. His plan was to catch a "small" six-foot wave and ride it in. Once committed, Lars looked over his shoulder only to see the biggest wave yet storming his way! With time only for a couple of desperate strokes, he braced for the onslaught. The impact of the giant wave sent the sixteen-foot sea kayak cartwheeling. After a couple of rotations Lars felt the cold rush of water hit his bare legs. His spraycover was blown! With a bit more pummeling, the waterlogged boat washed free of the wave. Lars successfully rolled the half-sunken kayak only to find himself in the middle of the surf zone. His instinct was to sprint toward shore, but unfortunately the bow of the kayak was under water. He now wished he had put in some float bags! His last resort was to backpaddle towards shore. It didn't take long for the next wave to catch up!

This wave wasn't as big, but in his submarined condition, it didn't need to be. The wave hammered the sea kayak stern-first to the bottom. With a slamming jolt, Lars and his gum boots were ejected into the ripcurrent-strewn surf. After a couple of waves, he discovered that swimming in an undertow with gum boots on wasn't good fun. He threw his paddle aside and swam for his life. After a prolonged battle against the undertow, Lars managed to lift his feet to the surface and catch a ride to the beach. Like the legendary half-drowned rat, he crawled up the beach to safety, ever so happy to be alive!

After a brief rest, Lars' concern turned to his equipment! Racing up and down the beach he managed to collect everything but his sponge!

Plan "B" was to portage over the dunes to the calm and safe Eel River mouth and paddle ten miles upstream to a friend's house. Lars figured he'd leave the boat with his buddy and come back when the weather calmed down and continue the journey.

As of this writing, it's been two years and the weather still hasn't settled down!

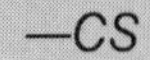

—CS

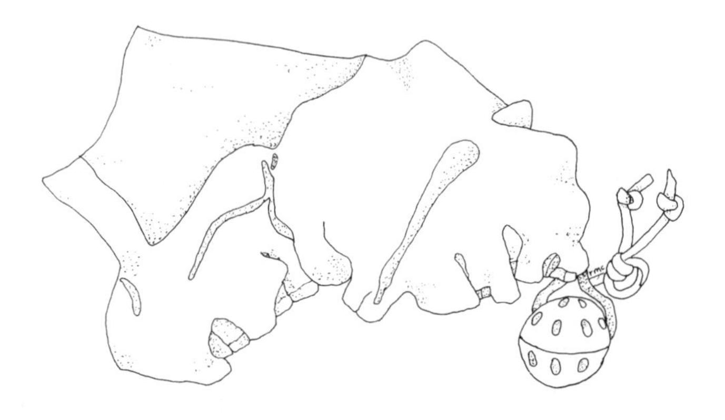

TAKE THAT

Ocean surf kayaking lore is chock full of stories about confrontations between fun-loving kayakers and board surfers. The best surf story I've heard was told to me by my kayak racing friend Matt Gaynes.

One day Matt decided to go kayak surfing at Rincon Beach in Southern California. For you landlubbers I'll explain: Rincon is a great surfing area infested with the most aggressive and territorial surfers in California. It's definitely a "Locals Only" beach. Well, Matt is not a little whimp. He's a tall beefy type who is good with martial arts weapons. It's quite a sight to watch him whip his Num Chuckas through their paces. He is not easily intimidated.

As could be expected, Matt was being hassled by a few surfers throughout the day. After a while, a particular surfer got really ticked and decided to get Matt. A typical surfer trick is to shoot the surfboard into the kayaker's face. This isn't nice. After the surfer missed a couple of shots, Matt began to get a little mad. Rather than run away, he stood his ground and continued surfing, ignoring the verbal and physical threats.

With all the practice, Matt figured his "surfer buddy" would be improving his aim. Thus, when he took off on a nice wave and noticed he also had his friend along, he was ready for action. After making the steep drop and cutting a rad bottom turn, Matt glanced up only to see a thunder bolt-emblazoned surfboard hurtling straight toward his forehead! With lightning quick Ninja Warrior reflexes, Matt speared the surfboard with his paddle and cut out of the wave. The surfer, who was attached to his board by a bungie cord leash, looked at Matt and his skewered board in disbelief. "Is this yours? I found it on the wave," Matt said, as he shook the paddle free of the surfboard and stroked on out for another ride.

He didn't have any more trouble with surfers.

—CS

APPENDIX III

RIVER DIFFICULTY CLASSIFICATION

The following is the International Canoe Federation class I through VI whitewater rating system, used throughout the world to provide some reasonably standard measures of a river's difficulty.

Class I. Moving water with a few riffles and small waves. Few or no obstructions.

Class II. Small-scale rapids: waves up to 3 feet; wide, clear channels that are obvious with some maneuvering required.

Class III. Rapids with high, irregular waves, narrow passages often requiring complex maneuvering.

Class IV. Long, difficult rapids with constricted passages often requiring precise maneuvering in very turbulent water. Scouting from shore often necessary. Conditions make rescue difficult. Decked boaters should be able to eskimo roll.

Class V. Extremely long, difficult, very violent rapids with highly congested routes. Rescue conditions are difficult, and a mishap means considerable hazard to life. Ability to eskimo roll essential.

Class VI. Difficulties of class V carried to extreme. Nearly impossible and very dangerous. For teams of experts only, at favorable water levels and with all precautions.

Over the past ten years, as the standards "in the field" have been climbing, the written standards as quoted above have remained the same. The result has been a crowding, particularly in the class IV category, which now serves as a very large catch-all for everything that's challenging but not downright scary for the experts.

In this book, we've followed a convention among western boaters regarding class VI: we use it almost exclusively for unrun rapids. If a rapid is pushing the envelope of class VI, but has been run repeatedly, we might refer to it as class V+. In general, our feeling is that difficulty is such a subjective matter, dependent among other things on variables such as water level and temperature, that hair-splitting is futile.

The only concrete amendment we might make to the ICF standards, besides that already mentioned regarding class VI, is that an extremely reliable roll is essential in anything we call class III or better.

APPENDIX IV

RIVER PERMITS

KERN RIVER

Permits are required for private trips on several sections of the Kern River from May 15–Sept. 15. Contact:

U.S. Forest Service, Sequoia National Forest
P.O. Box 6
Kernville, CA 93238
Phone: (619) 376-3781

TUOLUMNE RIVER

The U.S. Forest Service requires permits to run the Cherry Creek run and the Lower Tuolumne. Call or write the Groveland Ranger Station for the current permit system.

U.S. Forest Service, Groveland Ranger Station
P.O. Box 709
Groveland, CA 95321
Phone: (209) 962-7825

APPENDIX V

U.S. FOREST SERVICE MAPS

The USFS publishes maps of all the Forest Service lands in the state of California. The maps are updated regularly and for the most part are complete and reliable. They can be purchased through the mail at the state office or at area ranger stations. Most of the maps cost $1 as of this writing.

For USFS maps, write or call:

U.S. Forest Service
Pacific Southwest Region
630 Sansome Street
San Francisco, CA 94111
Phone: (415) 556-0122

U.S. GEOLOGICAL SURVEY TOPOGRAPHICAL MAPS

Topo maps can often be purchased at the better backpacking stores for about $2. Another option is to use the map collection of public or university libraries. The USGS office in Menlo Park, California, sells all their maps at their office or by mail. Their address and phone number are:

U.S. Geological Survey
Western Region Headquarters
Maps and Publications
345 Middlefield Road
Menlo Park,CA 94025
Phone: (415) 323-8111

AMERICAN AUTOMOBILE ASSOCIATION (AAA) MAPS

AAA regional maps are great! They clearly show nearly all rivers and creeks and the roads to them. We use AAA maps as our basic road navigation tool. When they lack detail, we use the USFS or topo maps to fill in the blank. Always carry these maps. They publish regional maps of the entire state of California. To find an AAA office, look in the phone book for the office near you.

There are two ways to obtain AAA maps:

1. Find a friend that has an AAA membership. Take their card down to the AAA office (located in every major city in California) and smile when they hand over the free maps.
2. Join the AAA for $42.

APPENDIX VI

RIVER FLOW INFORMATION RESOURCES

The following phone numbers are listed to assist boaters in obtaining current river flow information; the whitewater recording (updated each Tuesday, Thursday and Friday) can answer 90 percent of your questions, so please use this whenever possible. If you cannot get the desired information from the recording, and must call one of the office numbers, please have your questions ready (e.g., inflow or release from which reservoir). And please, don't call them for flows that are on the recording! If these office numbers are abused, and the staff becomes irritated by nonsensical requests, we may lose this valuable resource.

1. Department of Water Resources, Flood Operations whitewater recording, **(916) 322-3327.** ***The Flow Phone—our primary resource.***

2. Department of Water Resource, Flood Operations, **(916) 445-3555.**

3. Department of Water Resources, Eureka Recording, **(707) 443-9305** (specifically ***Mad River*** and ***Redwood Creek***).

4. Department of Water Resources, Eureka office, **(707) 443-8467** (for additional information on ***Klamath, Mad, Redwood Creek, Smith, Trinity, Van Duzen***).

RIVERS ON THE WHITEWATER RECORDING

Smith
at Jedediah Smith State Park

Trinity
release from Lewiston
flow at Hoopa

Salmon
flow at Somes Bar

Klamath
flow at J C Boyle Plant
release from Iron Gate
flow at Orleans
flow at Klamath Glen

Eel
release from Lake Pilsbury to Van Arsdale
release from Van Arsdale to Russian River
release from Van Arsdale to Eel River
flow at Fort Seward
South Eel; flow at Leggett

Russian
flow at Hopland
flow at Healdsburg
flow at Hacienda bridge

Sacramento
release from Lake Siskiyou
flow below Keswick Dam

Feather
release from the Oroville complex

Yuba
release from Englebright Dam
inflow to New Bullards Bar Reservoir (North Fork)

South American
flow at Kyburz
stream inflow to Slab Creek
release from Chili Bar powerhouse

Middle American
release from Oxbow powerhouse

North American
inflow to Lake Clementine

Cache Creek
flow at Rumsey bridge

Cosumnes
flow at Michigan Bar

Mokelumne
inflow to Pardee Reservoir

Stanislaus
flow at Orange Blossom

Tuolumne
release from Holm powerhouse
flow at Meral's Pool
inflow to Don Pedro Reservoir

Merced
inflow to Lake McClure

Kings
flow at Rodgers Crossing
inflow to Pine Flat Reservoir

Kaweah
inflow to Terminus (Lake Kaweah)

Kern
flow at Kernville
inflow to Lake Isabella
release from Lake Isabella

East Carson
flow at Gardnerville

Truckee
release from Tahoe Pass at Fanny Bridge
release from Boca Reservoir to Truckee River

Index

ABOUT THE AUTHORS

CHUCK STANLEY, the 1980 U.S. National Champion in K-1 slalom, was introduced to whitewater kayaking in 1964 by his father. Over the course of 15 years of competition, Chuck has won more than his fair share of races. He was a member of the U.S. National Team in 1975, 1977, and 1980, and raced in Yugoslavia, Austria, and Wales. He has also boated a fair percentage of the moving water in the state of California, and has considered boating the rest. He may well be the only man to have conquered (in a C-1) both the Wilderness Whitewater Ride at Six Flags Over Georgia in Atlanta, as well as the Umkomas River, South Africa's premier class V run.

Between boating trips, Chuck is a rocket propellant chemist in Sacramento, California.

LARS HOLBEK grew up in Santa Rosa, California and became a serious kayaker in 1974. Since then, he has: been a member of the first team to descend the Grand Canyon of the Stikine River in British Columbia; been one-third of the first team to descend the 240 miles of the Paucartambo/Yavero River, a tributary of the Upper Amazon in Peru; pioneered many of the new class V runs in California; spent 5 years in a rent-controlled VW bus; personally destroyed 4 indestructible plastic boats.

Between boating trips, Lars is a serious mountaineer and rock climber. He was 17 when he successfully climbed El Capitan in Yosemite. Since then he has climbed extensively both in the Sierras and Rockies as well as in South America and Alaska.